Structuralism

Edited with an Introduction by

JACQUES EHRMANN

ANCHOR BOOKS

DOUBLEDAY & COMPANY, INC.

GARDEN CITY, NEW YORK

1970

The Anchor Books edition is the first
publication in book form of *Structuralism*

Anchor Books edition: 1970

STRUCTURALISM

Jacques Ehrmann is with the Yale French Department. He has written *Un Paradis désespéré, l'amour et l'illusion dans l'Astrée,* and with Michel Beaujour, *France Contemporaine.* He is presently doing a study of utopias and social structures in the eighteenth century.

CONTENTS

Introduction   vii
  The Editor

LINGUISTICS

Structure and language   1
  André Martinet

Merleau-Ponty and the phenomenology of
language   9
  Philip E. Lewis

ANTHROPOLOGY

Overture to *le Cru et le cuit*   31
  Claude Lévi-Strauss

Structuralism in anthropology   56
  Harold W. Scheffler

ART

Structural analysis in art and anthropology   79
  Sheldon Nodelman

PSYCHIATRY

Jacques Lacan and the structure of the unconscious   94
  Jan Miel

The insistence of the letter in the unconscious   101
   Jacques Lacan

LITERATURE

Structuralism: the Anglo-American adventure   137
   Geoffrey Hartman

Structures of exchange in *Cinna*   158
   Jacques Ehrmann

Describing poetic structures: Two
approaches to Baudelaire's *les Chats*   188
   Michael Riffaterre

Towards an anthropology of literature   230
   Victoria L. Rippere

BIBLIOGRAPHIES

Linguistics   239
   Elizabeth Barber

Anthropology   244
   Allen R. Maxwell

Jacques Lacan   253
   Anthony G. Wilden

Structuralism and literary criticism   260
   T. Todorov

Selected general bibliography   262
   The Editor

Introduction

The Editor

> Man is made in such a way that he continually has to de-
> fine himself and continually escape his own definitions.
> Reality is not about to let itself be completely enclosed in
> form. Form for its part does not agree with the essence
> of life. Yet all thought that tries to define the inadequacy
> of form becomes form in its turn and thus only confirms
> our tendency towards form.
>
> —Witold Gombrowicz

Some remarks are probably necessary as an introduction to
the subject of this volume. We may begin by asking to what
extent structuralism is a French cultural phenomenon. Even
the most rapid glance at the bibliographies printed at the end
of this collection will show that the world did not have to
wait for the French before discovering structuralism. In the
area of linguistics, for example, the great centers of influence
have been—and in some cases remain—Geneva, Prague,
Copenhagen, New York, and Cambridge, Mass.—as well as
Paris. If we look only at the United States, we find that it has
made vital contributions to structuralism which has been
practiced with brilliance by linguists as well as anthropologists.
Among the more recent trends, one thinks, in linguistics, of
the work of Naom Chomsky and his theory of generative
grammar; and in anthropology, of W. H. Goodenough and
F. G. Lounsbury for their method of componential analysis.
By contrast, American psychoanalysis has shown hardly any
interest in structural methods, while in France the difficult
works of Dr. Jacques Lacan offer a major contribution. The
first article of his to be translated and published in English is
printed in this volume.

Though it is limited to certain of the disciplines in the social sciences, structuralism is none the less quite alive in this country. It has its own tradition behind it. As a result, we cannot say that the French are the pioneers in this domain. But it is evident to anyone who observes the French intellectual scene with some care that structuralism has been playing a key role in France for several years. More specifically, around 1962 structuralism, from a working method known to and practiced by specialists, became a fashionable philosophy discussed in as many circles as Sartre's existentialism had been after World War II; that year saw the publication of Claude Lévi-Strauss' *La Pensée sauvage* which contained a chapter-length refutation of the importance given to history by Jean-Paul Sartre in his *Critique de la raison dialectique* (1960). We shall not speculate at any length on the reasons behind the French enthusiasm for this new "ism." It may result from a combination of various factors such as the centralization of French intellectual life in Paris, the tendency of French intellectual milieux to think in terms of schools of thought and follow in the steps of eminent figures, the fairly homogeneous tradition of hegeliano-marxist theory around which issues crystallize, the end of the French colonial wars which, given the semi-failure of engagement theories, allowed this new kind of formalism to gain ground.

Whatever the combination of factors, we should be aware of the fashionable aspect of this trend and not accept it uncritically, but rather attempt to present as informative an analysis as possible.

If we should keep a critical distance from structuralism as fashion or panacea, we should not reject it automatically because it goes against our habitual patterns of thinking; rather, we should appraise it dispassionately, with attention to its value as method of investigation and analysis, we should test it through reflexion and practice, appreciate its valuable qualities, pass judgments on its weaknesses, possibly improve its efficiency as a tool, and only after careful examination reject it if we feel it is no longer suitable to our needs.

But who constitutes this "we?" First of all the readers of this volume who have been attracted to it either because of previous familiarity with structuralism or curiosity to know more about it. It is also all those who, as amateurs or specialists, are interested in the sciences of man. Finally and perhaps especially, it is those who are concerned with the study of literature where structuralism has as yet made little impression. As a result, we have given an important place to the literary aspects of structuralism.

What is structuralism? Before being a philosophy, as some tend to see it, it is a method of analysis. Even as such its many facets and different uses make it a subject of various interpretations, debate, even polemics. No simple or single definition applies to it except in very general terms. One could say a structure is a combination and relation of formal elements which reveal their logical coherence within given objects of analysis. Although structuralism can hardly be subsumed in some overall formula, or be given any label which will identify it for public consumption, we can say it is first of all, when applied to the sciences of man, a certain way of studying language problems and the problems of languages. Initially it was concerned with the structure of languages (*langues*), an area first explored by linguists whose interest developed the methods under study. It was then applied to anthropological inquiries, and in particular to the study of myths which are of the nature of a language (*langage*). The structural method also extends to the structures of the unconscious, as they are apprehended in psychoanalytical discourse, to the structures of the plastic arts with their language of forms, to musical structures where Lévi-Strauss believes he finds the very type of structural activity, and to the structures of literature since literary language, drawing upon ordinary language, transforms it into *langage* par excellence (from the point of view of the literary critic, at least!).

Thus, structuralism attempts to uncover the internal relationships which give different languages (*langages*) their form and function. On a broader point of view, scholars are now trying to lay the bases for a science of signs—semiotics—which would include not only these languages but also any system of signs. Without pursuing this tangent, we can simply say that since languages have in common their function as communication, it is impossible to overestimate the degree to which each discipline—the social sciences especially, but the natural sciences as well—can profit from the methods of neighboring disciplines.

Of course it is not a question of blindly applying the methods of one discipline to others. Since the nature of literary language cannot be confused with that of myth or ordinary language, the concern of literary criticism will be above all with what is particular to poetic discourse. Literary texts, however, can also reveal their structural relationship contemporaneous with political, economic, social realities. The different human languages in question have enough in common for us to seek what unites them without losing sight of their singularity. Such an undertaking presupposes that our curiosity will always be alert to the methods used by other disciplines and that from them we will enrich our thinking. If literary critics have much to learn from linguists, anthropologists, psychoanalysts, we may hope that the reverse will also be true.

Still, we must be cautious. Whatever the efficacy of the structural method—or, better, of structural methods—in giving form to languages and human relations (or in finding _their_ form), they will doubtless always elude man's grasp. It is for this reason that we have taken our epigraph from the words of the great Polish writer, Witold Gombrowicz, who proposed "to show man . . . stretched out on the procrustean bed of Form."

If we have cautioned, we must also exhort in order to provide a transition to the following texts. What the reader will find here is a group of studies which are as serious, openminded, and equitable as possible. Necessarily, they do not cover the whole range of the field. While seeking to avoid all dogmatism, we have tried to show structuralism as a _living_ question—contradictory sometimes, polemical at other times. We have tried to show structuralism's openness to several disciplines; we have also tried to show its roots in the traditions of Anglo-Saxon and European thought; finally, we have tried to indicate how it is expressed in the texts of eminent thinkers, as well as in the texts of distinguished scholars who are now creating instruments of a personal system of thought; we have also tried to give space to younger thinkers, some of them students, whose intellectual dynamism seems incontestable. In other words, our hope has been to show the vitality of a tradition as it is expressed and contested by different generations, different families of thought, and different disciplines. Our wish is that structuralism should be seen, not as a readymade answer, enclosed within itself, but as a series of interrogations which question structuralism itself and of course also the reader.

September 1966

J. E.

NOTE

The present volume appeared in 1966 as a special issue of *Yale French Studies*. Since that date the debate around structuralism has continued in France, spreading elsewhere in Europe, and evidently also in the United States. But a few years do not represent a significant gap for a movement that tries to come to grips with some of the most fundamental epistemological issues of a given period. And we believe that the material and perspectives presented here have not lost any of their actuality, or been invalidated by subsequent research. The titles we have added to the General Bibliography will suffice to indicate to the reader the major and most recent developments in the structuralist trend.

May 1968

J. E.

STRUCTURALISM

Structure and language

André Martinet

There is probaby no term which linguists of the last thirty
odd years have used more insistently than "structure." And
although "structuralists" have, in many cases, been eager to
give precise definitions of the terms they use, this effort has
seldom been extended to "structure" itself. More exactly,
even if certain linguists agree in designating certain segments
of speech as structures, those who are inclined to recognize
structure in language have been little tempted to explain what
they mean by this. In so far as conclusions may be drawn from
some scholars' statements or practices, it seems that most
linguists hesitate between a realist's point of view according
to which structure may be sought in the object under study,
and a conception which sees in structure a construct set up
by the scholar to allow a better understanding of the facts
without putting the question as to the conformity of this construct to the object itself. In fact, it remains to be proven that
a structure of the latter type might reach its goal, namely account for the facts, if it did not tally with the data afforded
by the object itself. It is easier, in these matters, to startle
one's readers or even to dazzle them by a certain virtuosity
than to convince them. Since structure is, if not always that
of the object, at least that which is established in consideration of this object, it would seem that the relations of structure to object may never be considered as unimportant.

Instead of starting, as is so often done, from a philosophical
definition of the word "structure," it may be interesting to
refer to the most basic and probably most current meaning
of the term. Structure, according to the Oxford Concise
Dictionary is the "manner in which a building or organism
or other complete whole is constructed." It is not a matter
of the building itself nor the materials of which it is com-

posed, from foundations to roof timbers, from facade orna-
mentation to the refinements of interior installations. Neither
is it even a matter of certain of these materials considered as
more essential: supporting walls and roofing trusses in old-
fashioned edifices, concrete or steel skeleton in modern buildings. It is a question of the way in which these materials are
assembled and combined to obtain an object created for
specific purposes and capable of satisfying well-defined functions. It would of course be inexact to say that the physical
properties of the materials do not enter into structure since
the latter—the way in which the building is constructed—is
closely dependent on the former. Traditional materials, valued
for their weight and resistance to the elements, imply outside
carrying walls, whereas reinforced concrete allows a central
pillar from which is hung a light, insulating outer envelope.
But these properties concern structure only in so far as they
condition it. The use, in a facade, of a heavier or lighter material naturally has repercussions on the structure of the
building, but the texture of this material, its outward appearance and its esthetic qualities, as long as they do not call for
a change in weight, are irrelevant from the point of view of
structure.

It can be seen in what sense a structural viewpoint implies
a functional viewpoint. Buildings are intended to serve as protection from the elements for man, his domestic animals and
the products of his industry. That is their first and basic
function. Of course, an edifice not seldom serves, in reality,
more to impress those who look at or visit it than to ensure
effective protection. The word itself suggests architectural
splendor rather than practical efficiency. But even when
from its very conception the edifice is never considered as anything but a display, it cannot fail to give witness in its structure to its primary function of protection. Prestige is indeed
acquired through non-productive expenses, but only in so far
as these expenses are made toward the satisfaction of real
needs. Prestige is not acquired by throwing money out of
the window, as it were, but rather by showing economic
superiority in one's living quarters, eating and dressing habits,
and in the choice of one's means of getting about.

The parallelism with linguistic facts is striking. Language's basic function is communication. This does not mean that it is not frequently used to expressive ends as a means or instrument for the individual to reach a deeper awareness of himself or of the nature of his experience. But the satisfaction of the basic needs of communication is accompanied, in literary uses of language and in several others, by a prestige-seeking activity which results in style. There is, however, no valid style which does not respect the basic conditions of communication. Just as in architectural matters there is a basic function which we might designate as protection and which determines what will be called the structure of the building, even so, in linguistic matters, there is a basic function—communication—which determines what will be called the structure of the language. In the last analysis, the relevant features of a building are those which ensure its protective rôle. In language, the relevant elements are those that take part in the establishment of communication. In other words, structure, both in buildings and languages, can be identified with what we may call the relevant features of the object.

The relevant features of the building are conceived here as effectively implanted in the concrete reality of the building itself. It is probably at this point that divergent viewpoints will make themselves heard and this partly because there is no agreement on the value to be given to the term "abstraction." A structure is necessarily an abstraction in the sense that it cannot be directly perceived by the senses as can the building itself. The term "manner" in the definition we took as a starting point seems to suggest this. One may conclude that, since an abstraction is a creation of the mind, structure is as well. This opens the way for the idea that structure is not a characteristic of the object but a model set up by the scholar in order better to understand the object. But the value of "abstraction" can be interpreted otherwise. It may be a construct of the mind which retains only certain features of the physical reality considered. It is then no longer a pure and simple creation of the mind on the part of the person seeking to understand the object but an observation based on the intelligent examination of this object. When we say that the mind retains certain features of the physical reality, we obviously do not mean that elements of the physical reality are extracted from the object. These features will necessarily be symbolized in one way or another. The set of symbols which make up the structure may very well be considered as a model and a model may of course consist of mental or graphic symbolizations or even material representations such as cardboard or papier-maché for instance. We seem therefore to come back to the "model" of the conceptions presented above. But there is quite a difference between a model which is valid only in so far as it accounts for the relevant features of a given reality in their reciprocal relations, and a model which claims to be independent of the latter. In the model that an architect can set up of a building, already existent or still to be constructed, an arrow may symbolize the pressure exerted by one element on another part of the whole. If the model is correct, the arrow will correspond exactly with a set of physical facts that humans have a hard time seizing mentally without translating them into visual terms—whence the need to symbolize them with a model—but which are none the less realities in the stone or the steel armature of the concrete. It is this set of physical facts which participates in the structure and not the arrow.

Of course, it is mainly in the Social Sciences that belief in structural models flourishes, no doubt because people shun reference to psycho-physiological facts such as habits, reflexes and various complexes of nervous reactions, all of which are at bottom very imperfectly known. In these cases, above all, we are tempted to speak of structures as bundles of latent relations, which, finally, is not to say that these relations are not real, i.e. present in the facts, but simply that they are not manifest for the observer.

To sum up, the model is not the structure, for the structure is always in the object, latent as it were but only if latent is not opposed to real. The best that can be expected of a model is that it represent the structure exactly, and it will do so if the scholar has succeeded in correctly disentangling the latencies involved and has not tried to force them into a prefabricated model founded on the set of a priori ideas currently in fashion.

Comparisons must never be forced, and if the often implicit parallel drawn above has brought out certain analogies in structures which one is hardly tempted to compare, it must not be forgotten that buildings and languages are quite different in nature. The kind of structure, conceived as real, which we look for in a building is three-dimensional. It remains to be seen what must be said in this respect about linguistic structure.

When a language is designated as an object, even if it is understood that this term does not necessarily designate a physical reality at all but rather anything that is brought under examination, one is often inclined to identify language with its manifestations in speech. These manifestations are phonic in nature. Today, they can be recorded and studied as such, or a graphic transcription of them may be prepared which, in the present state of techniques, remains more immediately usable than plain machine recording. If this identification of phonic substance with its graphic transcription were accepted, the object, the language, would be symbolized by a succession of graphic elements which nothing prevents us from calling by the traditional name "text." If this word is accepted for use not only in reference to the sound chain itself but to its graphic representation as well, we could sum up the point of view presented here by saying that a language is a set of texts: those already produced and others which one can count on being produced as long as the language preserves its identity. However, given the fact that under these circumstances the language taken as object would not be entirely known at the outset but would be conceived as the product of a particular activity, one might be tempted to seek it out in the exercise of this activity rather than in what results from it. Everything incites us to regard languages as clusters of habits, that is as human behavior. A linguistic structure, under these circumstances, presents itself as the way in which the different habits which make up these clusters condition each other. But this being said, there remains the fact that if we want to get an idea of the structure of a given language, we will hardly be able to study the nature of these habits seriously without examining the way in which they manifest themselves. Even if the sound chains and their graphic transcription are not the language, or the whole language, they probably represent the essential facts from which we must deduce its structure. On this basis the structure of the particular human behavior which is called a language, can be successfully determined if we do not forget that each of the elements which go to make up the sound chain enters into two different types of structural relations with the other units of the language: on the one hand, relations with the units which coexist with it in the segment considered as chain or, in simpler terms, its neighbors, and on the other hand, relations with those units which do not appear in the segment because at the point at which they could have appeared the needs of the particular communication required that they be set aside in favor of the unit considered. The latter and those to which it was preferred are related in that speakers are accustomed to accompanying them with the same elements.

To discover the structure of a language therefore, one starts from the concrete one-dimensional object, the linear chain of speech, which unfolds along what has been called the syntagmatic axis. But at each point another dimension will be brought into play, that of choices made by the speaker and which is generally designated as the paradigmatic axis. As to the possible choices at any one point, we will get our information by comparing various segments of speech which present different elements in identical contexts. This is the operation called "commutation" and is practiced by all structural schools. Bloomfield's followers themselves, however reticent they may be to bring paradigmatic relations into their operations, cannot get along without commutation even if they are little inclined to investigate its theoretical foundations. It is easy to understand, in any event, why they fail to find structure anywhere but in the chain and do their best to discover it only through distributional criteria, that is through the relative positions of units in speech.

To the difficulties met on the one hand, in understanding the nature of the object, language, and on the other, of establishing the way in which, taking its manifestations as the base, its structure can be determined, to these must be added another stemming from the double articulation of human language: the articulation of speech into distinctive units without meaning—phonemes—and the articulation of the same speech into meaningful units or monemes. This implies for a language two structures (or should we say a double structure?), one phonologic and the other concerned with units having meaning. It is easy to understand, given the complexity of the facts and the difficulty of separating and identifying them, that disagreement concerning the nature of these structures is as great among linguists as among other scholars, in spite of the fact that Linguistics is, today, the social science most aware of its means and ends. There is a widespread idea that linguistic structure is a model which the scholar sets up for his own use and for that of his fellow linguists to understand the nature and functioning of the object, but that he need not worry about its conformity to the object. It is the same idea which is found underlying the socalled "hocus-pocus" method as opposed to the one that implies reliance on "God's truth." Linguists in fact never observe the real object of their study, i.e. the speaker's behavior, taking the word behavior in its largest sense, that is implying not only directly observable acts but all the conscious and, above all, unconscious operations which accompany the practice of linguistic communication. They work almost constantly with the graphic symbolization of the most evident and, linguistically, the most essential aspect of this behavior. They may well consider that not only is the physical reality of speech, on the basis of which they operate, not the language itself but that what represents the language in this reality must be ordered hierarchically according to the principle of communicative relevance before being considered as a feature of the structure. They will then be likely to convince themselves that the structure is in fact in the object, even though the whole object (the speaker's behavior, including what is most manifest in it, the speech sounds) cannot be identified with its structure. But if he lets himself identify the physical reality of speech with the language or, inversely, if he excludes from the language all that is speech and includes only its internal conditioning, he will have the impression that a presentation of the language which does not coincide with physical reality is a product of his mind's activity and that the facts which present themselves to him in all their natural incoherency are in fact ordered according to principles which are not derived from the nature of the observed phenomena but from the demands of the scholar's intellect.

One of the viewpoints concerning linguistic structure which has been most explicitly exposed is Louis Hjelmslev's. According to the late Danish linguist, the only relations to enter into this structure are those existing between elements, to the exclusion of the physical nature of the elements themselves or the features of the phonic or semantic substance which distinguishes them from each other. This, of course, is not to say that structure is not represented in the object itself but rather that the object is a complex set of relations and that the physical elements mixed up in the latter are not a part of it: sounds and meanings are properly foreign to language. What distinguishes this point of view from the realists' is not a different conception of relations between object and structure but another way of encompassing the object. Experience, however, shows that such a disembodied view of language can, in practice, lead to elaborations which are just as far from structures set up on the basis of relevant substance as would be those established by linguists for whom structure is a product of their own intellectual activity.

A realistic conception of linguistic structure requires that one never forget a certain number of well-established points: the linearity of speech is not the only constituent feature of this structure; the reality of the object, the language, is to be found in the speaker; the texts with which one operates in fact can be conceived as symptomatic of this reality only through the use of a procedural artifice, commutation, which consists of comparing text fragments taken from different utterances; the physical features which one can attribute to linguistic structure are often presented in terms which reflect only that manifestation which is most accessible to observation: for example, if I say that phoneme A distinguishes itself from phoneme B by a certain articulatory feature, I note thereby a structural feature which, at one point in the speech circuit, takes the concrete form of a certain movement of the speech organs. But I could just as well have formulated this feature in acoustic terms and, less easily, in terms of hearing or of voice production at the neuro-muscular level. That is perhaps a simple enough reminder of how much more complex language structure is than the structure of a brick, stone or concrete building.

Translated by Thomas G. Penchoen

M. Martinet's essay was first published in the *Revue Internationale de Philosophie*, (Brussels) No. 73-74, (fasc. ¾, 1965) under the title "Structure et langue." The issue was devoted to *La Notion de Structure*. M. Martinet's essay is reprinted here with the kind permission of the editors of the *Revue Internationale de Philosophie*.

Merleau-Ponty and the phenomenology of language

Philip E. Lewis

The work of Wittgenstein and the ordinary language school quite naturally has made Anglo-American linguists conscious of the contributions which contemporary philosophy can offer to the theory of language, particularly where the problems of semantics are concerned. An article by Rulon Wells first published in 1954 provides a succinct statement of the Wittgensteinian's reaction to Bloomfield's conception of a mechanistic psychology and suggests a perspective easily extended to the general theoretical debate between structuralism and behaviorism which permeates current discussions in psycholinguistics. Continental philosophy, perhaps simply because it stands far removed from the analyst's open preoccupation with verbal expressions, has not drawn comparable attention to its implications in the realm of language, although the major exponents of phenomenology have not failed to treat the subject. For several reasons, an examination of Merleau-Ponty's rather extensive writings on language seems especially appropriate. First, his work is relatively recent (*Phenomenology of Perception*, 1945; *Signs*, 1960). Second, his philosophy is grounded in a profound meditation on the practices of modern psychology, on the one hand, and on the other, in the development of a notion of structure—witness the two key words of the title of his first major work, *The Structure of Behavior* (1937). Third, the general direction of all his work is toward the resolution of traditional oppositions or the liquidation of apparent dichotomies, whence the interest of the linguist attentive to possible mergings of structuralist and behaviorist insights or to the transcendence of the two positions. Moreover, Merleau-Ponty's theory of language shares the ordinary language school's concentration upon the problem of meaning, providing thereby a clear alternative to the analyst's solutions.

Merleau-Ponty first broached the subject of language in the midst of a massive meditation on the problem of the body (Part II of *The Phenomenology of Perception*); later he expanded upon his theory from a more directly linguistic viewpoint (Introduction and Essays I and II of *Signs*) while detailing his reactions to some of Saussure's celebrated distinctions. We shall attempt here to represent his position in reference to structuralism first by condensing the argument of the *Phenomenology of Perception*, then gleaning from the supplementary essays certain views not previously articulated.

In the context of his analysis of the "body proper" or "natural body" (picturing the body, in its preconscious, dialectical, non-causal relationship *with its environment or given world, as a "knot of living meanings"*—PP, p. 177[1]), the description of speech and the act of meaning provides for Merleau-Ponty the chance to transcend once and for all the traditional subject/object dichotomy. In one sense, the choice of a methodological orientation, structuralist, behaviorist, or some other, can be seen to hinge upon the nature of the subject-object relationship: what are its variables and what is the nature of their interaction? As is his custom, the phenom-

---

[1] PP = *Phenomenology of Perception;* pages references are given in parentheses throughout; we have preferred to use the French language editions and to offer our own translations (*La Phénoménologie de la perception,* Paris: Gallimard, 1945). An English edition tr. by Colin Smith has been published by Grove Press.

enologist begins by asking what occurs when we first become conscious of a given "natural" activity, in this case speech.

The etymology of the word *habit* offers a glimpse of the relationship of having ("the relation of the subject to the term into which he projects himself e.g., I have an idea, I have a craving, I have fears," *PP*, p. 203) which the realm of being (the existence of things or the predicative relationship, e.g., the table is there, the table is large) normally dissimulates. We first envisage language as a group of "verbal images" which spoken words deposit in us. What is lacking in this notion of language is the speaker, the subject—there is only a flux of words, a sort of automatic, third-person language, a mechanism of cerebral imprints which are related in the same way that psychic stimuli are coordinated by the laws of association. Within this system where language seems to be formed by diverse independent influences, "man can speak in the same way that an electric bulb can become incandescent." (*PP*, p. 204)

Already the implications of Merleau-Ponty's approach for post-Bloomfieldian linguists can be perceived. At the outset, the phenomenologist will refuse to exclude mentalistic psychology in favor of a mechanistic outlook. Nor will he posit a priori that language is a closed system wherein the speaking subject appears as no more than an intermediate term. On this latter point, there is an obvious parallel to the behaviorist's reaction to the general body of linguistic inquiry. In his *Verbal Behavior*, for example, Skinner observes that linguistics has accorded to comparisons of different languages and to historical developments a marked precedence over "the study of the individual speaker," likewise that semantics as an area of linguistics has largely consisted of studying how meanings are expressed and how they have evolved in time, rather than what they are and what they express. Yet unlike the psychologist, who forthwith focuses his attention upon the speech mechanism, the philosopher states the problem in terms of well-known classical positions, then takes recourse to specific inquiries of abnormal psychology to show why he discards them. Here Merleau-Ponty chooses an example frequently studied by linguists, aphasia. The analyst recognizes that his patient typically has not lost a certain supply of words, he has lost a certain way of using them. It is no longer a question of an automatic language, of word-images; it is a matter of attitude, of function, of relating and conceptualizing. As a speech problem, aphasia can only be understood in terms of an intentional language within which the word is an instrument of action, a means of categorization. (Intentionality, with its customary conceptualization of the relationship of "being conscious *of*," of referring to something, is supplemented in Merleau-Ponty by the so-called "intentional arc," which subtends the life of consciousness, sustaining the unity of the senses, of intelligence, sensibility, and motility.) When the aphasiac cannot arrange shades of red from dark to light, he has not lost the word-image of red, he has "fallen back from the categorical attitude to the concrete attitude" (*PP*, p. 205), he has dissociated the word from the process of conceptualization. His cure will entail recovery of the "authentic language" which is conditioned by thinking.

So we posit "authentic designation" as a phenomenon of thought, thereby eschewing not only the empiricist's equation of the word and its verbal image but also the idealist's attachment of the word to its concept. Common to these two radically opposed perspectives is the tacit recognition that the word has no meaning, a recognition underlying the linguist's preference of notions like synonymy and significance to some loosely defined entity called "meaning." For the empiricist, the word is only a psychic phenomenon comparable to a neurological stimulus; for the idealist, it is an exterior sign which is unnecessary to the interior operation of recognition, it is only an empty envelope which does not possess the meaning, held by the thought alone. In both cases, then, language is no more than an external companion of thought, a sign or messenger. Merleau-Ponty proposes to surpass both empiricism and idealism in one breath by this simple edict: *le mot a un sens,* words have meaning.

From the beginning, Merleau-Ponty thus rejects the alternative of dealing "linguistically" with the problem of stating meanings, of making definitions, seeking instead to formulate "philosophically" a notion of meaning that is consistent with the overthrow of traditional orientations toward speech. To this end, he plunges unabashedly into an analysis of *la parole originaire,* i.e., the first words of an infant, the first words of primitive man, the original understandings conveyed by authors who surpass traditions, and so forth.[2] This amounts to revitalizing a question which Bloomfield discounted on the grounds that all linguists really define meanings in the same way (in terms of the speaker's situation) and which other linguists find needless thanks to the operative success of recursive definitions. The philosopher's perspective naturally leads him back to sources and suppositions, regardless of the pragmatic value inherent in functional analysis of language as we have it here and now. Ideally, at least, a theory of language should rest upon adequate understanding of the genesis of verbal communication, of the act of speech which is an act of meaning. In the comprehension of the creative act which twentieth-century esthetics has adopted more or less definitively, Merleau-Ponty discovers a good point of access to the birth of verbalized meaning.

Authors such as Mallarmé, Proust, Joyce, and Kafka have powerfully demonstrated that their thought takes form only as they are writing, that their art is fully conceived only at that moment when it receives verbal formulation. If thought preceded the formulation, notes Merleau-Ponty, we could not understand why "thinking tends toward expression as its fulfillment" (*PP,* p. 206). The most familiar object seems curiously indeterminate until we have found its name; the thinker is not sure of his idea until he has formulated it. Without *la parole,* thought could be no more than fragmentary and fleeting. The incalculable value of *la parole* therefore becomes

---

[2] The lack of convincing equivalents in English has led us to retain a few French words, of which *la parole* is the most important. Whereas *le mot* (word) is simply the objective entity used to designate things of all sorts, *la parole* can be either a word, in a more subjective sense than *le mot,* or the faculty of speech; furthermore, *la parole* frequently seems to combine speech and the words themselves in a wider general notion that might evoke for some readers the Biblical Word. Elsewhere, we have upon occasion left untranslated the words *langue* (the language of a particular people) and *langage* (language in general), also the word *pensée* when used in conjunction with *parole.* Where the distinction between *sens* ("meaning" oriented toward direction, intention) and *signification* ("meaning" oriented toward designation, definition) seems important, we have translated the latter by its English cognate or noted the French root in parenthesis.

manifest, since we appropriate and possess our thoughts through verbal expression.

Recognizing this coincidence of *pensée* and *parole* leads to numerous accessory insights. We understand, for example, what it means to designate an object by its name: designation does not follow recognition, it is the recognition. The word carries the meaning, and by imposing it upon an object, we are conscious of capturing the object (for the infant child, the name is the very essence of the object). Moreover, a listener receives the enunciated thought from the *parole,* i.e., the listener does not give words and sentences their meaning, he does indeed apprehend new and original thoughts,—all is not known ahead of time by the receiving consciousness. Obviously, if we can only discover in language what our own consciousness has put there, language can teach us nothing and at best could provide us with new combinations of what we know already. In fact, communication presupposes a system of correspondence—presumably on the order of the phonemic, morphemic, and other "interdependent linguistic levels" espoused by Harris, Chomsky, et al—which goes beyond that of the dictionary, because "the sentence gives its meaning to each word, and due to its use in different contexts, the word gradually takes on a meaning that cannot be absolutely determined" (*PP*, p. 445). So we accede to a definition of *la parole* which takes into account this potential accumulation of meaning:

> *La parole* is then this paradoxical operation in which we attempt to rejoin, by means of words whose meaning is given, and of already available significations, an intention which in principle goes beyond and modifies, which itself determines in the last analysis the meaning of the words by which it is conveyed (*se traduit*) (*PP*, p. 445-46).

This definition is remarkable in that it embodies an integral association of psycho-philosophical and semantic concepts, the intention and meaning (*sens*). The latter appears as indispensable for the accomplishment of the former.

To indicate the direction of the succeeding developments of the argument, we may note that the definition of *la parole* is internally dynamic in that it "translates itself" by means of its words. This translation relationship is not just metaphorical, as we can see by considering what takes place in translation from one tongue to another. The original one subtends a mass of definitions and nuances which are grasped only in the day-to-day exercise of that tongue; many of these are lost in translation, while the new tongue adds others, so that a radical alteration takes place, generated by the internal structures of *la parole*. In an operative sense, the habitat of *la parole originaire* is a mode of self-translation. Yet this inner dynamism is equally evident in the act of communication. The problem of understanding a given statement must always be solved retrospectively—we can interpret the words of a Bergsonian proposition as adequate symbols of his meaning only if we understand the central motifs of his thesis and have a certain feeling for his style and a sense of the direction of his argument. It is only natural that this ability to think what Bergson thought somewhat in the way he thought it should enrich our own thinking; similarly, it is clear that the words themselves carry the Bergsonian meaning of the proposition; or rather, "their conceptual meaning (*signification*) is formed by levy (*prélèvement*) on a *gestural meaning*, which, itself, is immanent to *la parole*" (*PP*, p. 209). In short, every language teaches itself, secretes its own significations, and although the power of music or painting gradually to impose its meaning appears more overtly, we can discover this same power of *la parole* upon realizing that the meaningfulness of a literary work depends less upon the ordinary meaning of its component words than upon what it contributes to modify that ordinary meaning. This unsuspected modifying element is precisely what permits Merleau-Ponty to write of *la pensée dans la parole*, thought within "speech."

In the light of this *pensée/parole* equation, how do we reinterpret the act of speaking? Clearly the thought enunciated by a speaker can no longer be considered as a representation of prior relations: his thought is his *parole*. The listener, then, hears a *parole-pensée*, and if the speech replies adequately to his expectations, he does not conceive of the spoken words as signs, his mind is fully occupied by the flow of the thought. Within this relationship, the thought of both speaker and listener remains empty in this sense, that neither conceives the meaning of what was said *as meaning* until after the speech—the meaning was there at every instant, yet was no more posited as such than the words enunciated were represented *as words.* The acquired aspect of a word resembles, rather than its "verbal image," the Freudian Imago—we retain the word's articulatory and auditory style. To use the word without conceiving directly of it, we need only its articulatory and auditory essence as a "modulation" or possible use of the body.

> I turn to the word just as my hand moves toward the spot on my body that is pinched, the word occupies a certain place in my linguistic world, it is part of my equipment, my sole means of representing it to myself is to pronounce it, as the artist has only one way of representing for himself the work he is fashioning: he must fashion it (*PP*, p. 210).

The body, as a power of natural expression, performs a function of projection: it "converts a certain motor essence into a vociferation, it transmits the articulatory style of a word in auditory phenomena . . ." (*PP*, p. 211). Referred back to this "corporeal projection," the act of speaking appears, not as an act of transmitting meaning, but as the act of meaning itself—to speak is to "signify."

Up to this point, the various elements of the argument converge toward the same fundamental contention: "Meaning is caught up in *la parole* and *la parole* is the exterior existence of meaning" (*PP*, p. 212). *Mot* and *parole* are neither signs of an object or thought nor are they garments, they are the presence of this thought in the world, its emblem or body. Merleau-Ponty now advocates a concept of existential meaning, based upon the "fact of language" as it is *used* in the act of speaking we have just outlined. He proposes a *linguistic concept* of the word, which for him implies an accentuation of the internal power of the words themselves, implies a *verbal experience* in which the word carries a meaning that conveys a thought "as a style, as an emotional value, as an existential mimicry, rather than a conceptual statement" (*PP*, p. 212). By virtue of this existential meaning which inhabits the word, the operation of expression opens up a whole new dimension of linguistic experience, it permits the man of letters to give meaning a factual existence, to make it live like a cell in an organism of words.

Advocacy of a "linguistic concept of the word" and a notion of "verbal experience" tends toward open support of a structuralist hypothesis which would treat language as a closed system and in terms of strictly linguistic precepts. We shall see, however, that Merleau-Ponty's accentuation of the linguistic experience will allow us to speak of the *autonomy* of linguistics only in a special context. If the study of language is to be an independent discipline, its status will not be that of an arbitrarily isolated dimension, but rather of a transcendent one; if language is to be a singular structural entity, it will not be so in a static or regulatory sense, but rather in a creative, expansive manner—its structures will be conceived as functions of the omnipresent speaking subject, the verbal dimension's special autonomy will derive from its unique capacity to express expressions and to express itself.

Needless to say, the prime example of this verbal dimension is esthetic expression. Merleau-Ponty cites Proust's description of *la sonate de Vinteuil* and la Berma's Phèdre: Proust realizes that the musical sounds are not the signs of musical meaning but the very substance of the sonata descending within us; la Berma is magically no longer the actress, she is Phèdre.

> Esthetic expression confers upon what it expresses existence in itself (*en soi*), implants it in nature as something perceived and accessible to everyone, or inversely snatches the signs themselves—the person of the actor, the colors and canvas of the painter—away from their empirical existence and carries them off into another world (*PP*, p. 213).

In quite the same way, verbal expression confers this *en-soi* existence upon thought, which does not exist outside of the existential world or outside of words. We tend to think of a thought for itself (*pensée pour soi*) preceding the expression quite simply on account of the vast store of previously formulated thoughts which we can remember silently. But in fact, this inner silence is bubbling with words, our internal reflective existence is actually an *inner language*. At this point, the status of the *parole originaire*, which underlies the creative act and gives birth to a thought, can be fully appreciated only if we relate it to the *parole secondaire*, "which translates an already acquired thought" (*PP*, p. 446). Every secondary word, the simple representative of a fixed idea (*pensée univoque*), necessarily entered into the linguistic domain as a *parole originaire*, so that thought may always be considered the result of expression. Taken together, secondary words provide the resources of an established language, resources which an idea seeking formulation can mould in a prototypical fashion. This act of originary expression must be taken as an ultimate fact. Any explanation of it would simply deny it. Our experience of language proves that it transcends us, for we discover that our thoughts have never been pure thoughts, that their actuated meaning always exceeds what was meant during their genesis, that *la parole* resists the grasp of thought in the very act of appropriating it.

Having depicted *la parole* as radically inexplicable, Merleau-Ponty returns to the phenomenologist's accustomed task—he will pursue the effort to *describe* it, and the rest of his argument centers upon a rigid analogy between *la parole* and the gesture. The interest of the fairly lengthy inspection of this pattern should be kept in mind from the start. In his chapter on meaning (*Language*, p. 144), Bloomfield apparently rules out any analogy between gestural and linguistic meaning on the basis of language's incomparable capacity for specificity and complexity. In Merleau-Ponty's terms, this results from the linguist's arbitrary decision to consider only the established language, the institutionalized framework of *la parole secondaire*. When Bloomfield presupposes "the specific and stable character of language" because most meanings appear indefinable, he not only elicits a correction from the Wittgensteinians, who purport to characterize meanings according to their uses, he suggests to the phenomenologist that the way out of the dilemma—and it is glaring in all of the structuralists' efforts—which stems from meaning's conceptual unwieldiness may reside in the suspension of the constancy hypothesis. Merleau-Ponty will attempt to understand meaning by taking into account not only the stable structures of *la parole secondaire*, but also the protogenic structuring accomplished by *la parole originaire*.

Just as the body falls naturally into a certain gesture when it acquires a new habit, it accomplishes a linguistic gesture when it acquires a new word. *"La parole* is an actual gesture and it contains its own meaning, just as the gesture contains its meaning" (*PP*, p. 447). Communication cannot be explained as a re-creation of mental representations by the listener; understanding of a speaker's message takes place in the same way that we understand his gestures, i.e., there is a renewal of the speaker's expressive intention which is, for the listener as for the speaker, a "synchronic modulation of his own existence, a transformation of his being" (*PP*, p. 214). Merleau-Ponty notes that we live in a world where *la parole* is taken for granted and used effortlessly—"The intersubjective, linguistic world no longer fills us with wonder . . ." (*PP*, p. 214)—by men unconscious of all that is contingent in expression and communication. To escape the superficiality and naïveté of this view, we must go back to the origins of language and rediscover the silence beneath the sounds of words, then describe the gesture which breaks that silence, and see that *la parole* implies its own world.

The meaning of a gesture "intermingles with the structure of the world that the gesture outlines" (*PP*, p. 217). Likewise, the linguistic gesture outlines its meaning and its world. Chiding psychologists and linguists who put aside the problem of language's origin in the name of positive knowledge, Merleau-Ponty contends that it may be profitably reviewed once we recognize that the mental landscape related by verbal gesticulation does not really separate the linguistic gesture from the physical one, which relates only a man and the world that is present when he gesticulates. Culture makes this so, furnishing a world constructed by previous acts of expression to which *la parole* refers itself in the same way that the gesture refers itself to the perceptible world surrounding it. The idea of a "linguistic world," then, is far from fortuitous—"the meaning (*sens*) of *la parole* is nothing else than the way in which it manipulates this linguistic world and modulates on the keyboard of acquired meanings (*significa-*

tions)" (*PP*, p. 217). This, of course, merely relocates the problem, since the cultural base of meanings was not present when words were first uttered. The point is that the first word was not what is commonly called a "conventional sign" (conventionality supposes a prior relation), that it did not represent a conceptual or terminal meaning, but presented primordially its gestural or psychical meaning (*sens émotionnel*), a spontaneous expression of lived meaning which we can recognize in an incantatory poem. Here is the core of the conclusion, with its almost poetic notion of "singing the world":

> We would then find that words, vowels, and phonemes are all just various ways of singing the world, and that they are destined to represent objects, not as the naive theory of onomatopoeia supposed, by virtue of an objective similarity, but because they extract and, in the literal sense of the word, express its psychical essence. If we could sift out of a vocabulary what is due to mechanical laws of phonetics, to contaminations from foreign languages, to grammarians' rationalizations, and to each language's own imitation of itself, we would doubtless discover at the origin of every language a relatively compressed system of expression, yet such that, for example, it should not be too arbitrary to call daylight daylight if night is called night. The predominance of vowels in one language, of consonants in another, and the systems of form and syntax would just represent various ways for the human body to celebrate the world and ultimately to live it (*PP*, p. 218).

Thus it is that the full meaning of one tongue cannot be translated to another, that we can speak several languages but normally live in only one. Completely assimilating a language requires the speaker to assume its world. Merleau-Ponty rejects entirely the notion of conventional signs: "There are but words in which is condensed the history of a whole language, and which accomplish communication in the midst of incredible linguistic accidents" (*PP*, p. 219). When we step out of our everyday constituted language, we rediscover the obscure base upon which its clarity was formed, we glimpse the birth of *la parole* in a psychic gesticulation, the original act whereby man first superposed upon the neuter world around him the world according to man. Not that the phenomenologist, like the naturalist, would reduce language to the expression of emotions—the emotion by no means compromises the originality of language because already, far from being the mechanical result of a physiological process, the emotion manifests toward these physical factors a new way of integrating them and giving them form, of joining the body and its world. And this patterning power reaches its maximum at the level of language! Accepting Merleau-Ponty's view according to which the body-subject's potential permits man to invent various emotions and to take diverse attitudes, i.e., to transcend his biological nature, we can see what differentiates various cultures and furnishes each one its unity. Each has its own manner of receiving a given datum, each develops its own gestures—physical and linguistic—according to its own dynamic.

The concept of a linguistic gesture touches on other problems particular to language. Of all our means of expression, language alone is capable of referring to itself, and language alone posits itself in an intersubjective structure of communication. *La parole* forgets itself, leads us to accept an idea of natural truth which it encloses, gives birth, as we have seen, to the illusion of thought without words. We can speak about words, notes the author, whereas the painter cannot paint about painting—this power of self-reference suggests a privilege of Reason, grounded in the fact that thought and objective language are simply two manifestations of the one fundamental operation by which man projects himself toward a world. Merleau-Ponty analyzes this originary intentional relationship in an extension of the previous examination of aphasia, demonstrating that "categorizing activity, before being a thought or a cognition, is a certain manner of relating oneself to the world, and correlatively a style or configuration of experience" (*PP*, p. 222). The categorizing act is established within an "attitude" (*Einstellung*) upon which *la parole* is also founded and of which, rather than of a thought, it provides an expression. As the instrument of a subject inconceivable except as incarnate in his world, language "presents or rather it *is* the positioning of the subject in the world of meanings" (PP 225). One is reminded of the existentialist's commitment, which on a fundamental level seems to be accomplished by speech itself. Merleau-Ponty states quite exactly that the "phonetic gesture" achieves a certain structuring of experience; the word's meaning is not in the sound, but in the "modulation of existence" enacted by the body. *La parole* appears as a step within the movement of transcendence which defines the human body: in acquiring conducts, mute gestures of communication, and finally speech, man continually transcends and transfigures his natural powers, and the resources of language institute this transcendence within his world as a permanent possibility. Little wonder then, that at the end of his discussion of the origin of language, Merleau-Ponty speaks of it as a miracle, indeed no less miraculous than the birth of love within desire. The special status of language in the midst of human activity rests perhaps in its encompassment of all activity:

> We must then recognize as an ultimate fact this open and indefinite power to give meaning (*signifier*), i.e., simultaneously to seize and to communicate a meaning (*sens*), —a power by which man transcends himself toward a new behavior, or toward other people, or toward his own thought through his body and his *parole* (*PP*, p. 226).

La parole is then distinguished from other modes of expression by its staggering ability to constitute a whole new world, the world of culture, above and beyond the natural, primarily perceived world which lies at its base.

The end of the argument is a kind of reformulation, obviously veering toward the philosophical implications of the meditation on language. Any linguistic activity assumes that there is apprehension of some meaning, though the meaning may appear at different levels (*couches de signification*)— from visual meaning up to conceptual meaning, passing en route the verbal concept. An understanding of these levels cannot be achieved through the notions of maturity or intelligence—what is necessary is simply a new notion which can integrate the levels, a function which operates in the same way on all levels. This essence of normal language can be formal only at that point where, "in the thickness of being, zones of emptiness form and move toward the outside" (*PP*, p. 229).

In other words, the capability that is essential to *la parole* is simply the intentional relationship, the movement of self-projection, what Goldstein terms the "psychic bond which unites us to the world and our fellow men." Supposing that languages (established systems of vocabulary, syntax, and expressive instruments) may be considered as the deposition and sedimentation of the expressive acts (*actes de parole*) which translate intended meaning into acquired meaning, giving it independent existence as meaning, we may reformulate the distinction between *la parole originaire* and *la parole secondaire* as a distinction between *la parole parlante* and *la parole parlée*. The former, fundamentally creative, arises as man's existence "polarizes" in a certain direction—undetermined until that moment—expressive of his intention, existence creates *la parole* as an empirical support of its own non-being. By constituting a linguistic world and a cultural world, *la parole parlante* reincarnates this purely human element in what we view as the natural world; *la parole parlée* operates in a naturalized linguistic world wherein *la parole parlante* reappears, in the hands of writers, artists, and philosophers, as an omnipresent source of transcendence and enriched expression.

The preceding argument, based on the gestural nature of *la parole,* may be profitably related to the theoretical writings of Noam Chomsky, the inveterate structuralist whose *Syntactic Structures* (1957) offers provocative arguments for viewing languages as sets of grammatical sequences and advocates the concept of the transformational level. Chomsky contends that the grammar of a given language is essentially a theory of that language and determines that the essential criterion of grammaticality is independent of any semantic basis. Merleau-Ponty unquestionably agrees with the latter point, since meaning appears prior to grammar and can admit greatly varied grammars as its linguistic framework. Yet the locus of emphasis is reversed by the phenomenologist: whereas Chomsky avers that grammar can be defined without reference to meaning, Merleau-Ponty affirms that meaning can be defined without reference to grammar. That the two statements are compatible, and that both writers recognize the capital importance of the semantic/syntactic relationship, fail to bely a divergence in perspective. For Merleau-Ponty, the priority of meaning entails acceptance of the intention, in the technical sense of the term, as the fundamental principle of a theory of language, a structuring principle that constitutes meanings within the experience of language, that permits us to envisage language as an organism which perpetually transcends itself. Language defines itself by the world it subtends, a world including its grammar, to be sure, but primordially a world of meanings. To suppose that its grammar defines a language by accounting for all possible propositions in that language is to forget that the language, by virtue of *la parole originaire,* is at every moment transcending itself, semantically and grammatically. Structuralism seems to flounder when it confronts the problem of meaning, which it cannot, however, dissociate from a theory of language. (Chomsky speaks of "undeniable, though only imperfect correspondences" between semantic and syntactic features.) The problem is not what the structuralist does, which has an evident objective, functional validity; it is the effort to conceive of meaning in terms of a posteriori structures built up around it, whereas meaning lays claim to understanding in terms of its own genesis, indeed can only be understood as the generator of language rather than as generated by language. Insofar as language is comprised of the sedimentation of meanings, it will be inaccessible to complete phenomenological reduction. We shall now see that this is the principal lesson of Merleau-Ponty's later essays on language.

The argument of *The Phenomenology of Perception,* centered on the coincidence of *pensée* and *parole,* is characterized by an effort to look at the same basic phenomena through different perspectives which may vary only very slightly among one another. To some extent, at least, this approach exemplifies what phenomenology designates as eidetic reduction, which on a methodological level may be said to entail an attempt to understand a given phenomenon through exhaustive description rather than through causal explanation. Given this point of view, we can readily understand why the successive points of the argument seem to parallel each other instead of proceeding in logical extensions toward a final conclusion. The argument constantly turns back on itself. Likewise, we can detect in the phenomenologist's attitude a source of discontent with both structuralist and behaviorist tenets, since he at once mistrusts claims to explain a given linguistic phenomenon as *determined* by the operation of grammatical rules or by a stimulus-response relation or both, and he is similarly skeptical of any attempt to close a system of relations to external perspectives.

At any rate, it is hardly surprising that *Signs* seems to offer little more than a group of additional insights which can be attached to the analyses of *The Phenomenology of Perception* without loss of continuity. In his preface, Merleau-Ponty emphasizes the groundwork of intersubjectivity and communication which undergird the philosopher's effort to employ language. In a long essay entitled "Indirect Language and the Voices of Silence," he first re-examines the sign. As we have seen, the phenomenologist joins with the linguist in underlining the folly of the naive acceptation of the sign as a "verbal representation," although he is much more inclined than the linguist to associate it with thought processes. We have learned in Saussure, says Merleau-Ponty, that signs by themselves signify nothing, that taken separately the sign seems above all to indicate a diversion or separation of meaning between itself and the others. Languages seem to be composed of endless differences. The refusal to accord the sign any meaning other than a "diacritical" one entails for Saussure the impossibility of grounding *la langue* in a system of positive ideas: the unity of his *langue* is a unity of coexistence, exemplified by the "relating" and "contrasting" principles of linguistics, components of language whose sole function is to allow the discrimination of signs. Take the case of the infant learning to speak:

> . . . the important thing is that the phonemes, as soon as they are uttered, are variations of a single speech instrument and that with them the child seems to have "caught" the principle of a mutual differenciation of signs and in the same breath acquired *the meaning* (*sens*) of the sign (*Signes,* édition Gallimard, p. 50).

These first phonological contrasts intiate the child to "the lateral linking of the sign to the sign as the base of an ultimate relationship of the sign to meaning" (*Signes,* p. 57). At this level, the child anticipates the complete *langue* as a style of expression. Only by visualizing the *langue* as a whole can we understand how the child enters into the domain of language, seemingly closed to those who do not know it: "Because the sign is instantaneously diacritical, because it forms itself and arranges itself with itself, it has an interior and it ends up claiming a meaning" (*Signes,* p. 51).

This initial invocation of Saussure serves two main purposes. First, Merleau-Ponty adduces a historical truth. Citing among other examples the complexities of the transformation from Latin of Modern French, he observes that the attainment of an explicit meaning regularly follows "a long incubation in an operative meaning" (*sens opérant*). The philosopher and the historian must recognize that culture never engenders absolutely transparent meanings: "the birth of meaning is never finalized" (*Signes,* p. 52). On the other hand, the lateral relationship of sign-to-sign leads back to the basic impossibility for Merleau-Ponty of separating language from its meaning. In fact, meaning seems to appear at the intersection of the signs, as if located in the interval between them. "If the sign means something only insofar as it stands out on the other signs, its meaning is entirely caught up (*engagé*) in language, *la parole* always plays on a stage of words, it is never anything but a fold in the immense fabric of speaking" (*Signes,* p. 53). The opaqueness of language reappears in the intersection of signs, for the individual sign, taken out of context, is banal or equivocal, only a grouping of signs has meaning. Recalling his analyses of thinking, Merleau-Ponty again observes that no language precedes language, says that language is more like a being than an instrument in that meaning is the "total movement of *la parole*," is even something like a universe, "capable of housing in itself things themselves,—after having changed them into their meanings" (*Signes,* p. 54).

At this point, Merleau-Ponty states the basic theme of the essay: all language is indirect and allusive, thus, in a sense, is silence. In a remarkable analysis of the relationship between meaning and *la parole*, the phenomenologist reconsiders Saussure's comparison of "the man I love" and *"l'homme que j'aime,"* showing that the absence of a sign may be a sign and that expression is an operation of language upon language. Returning to the distinction between *la parole originaire* (authentic) and *la parole secondaire* (empirical), Merleau-Ponty says that the former, in relation to the latter, is silence, since it avoids the common name of the thing it translates. Language is of itself oblique and autonomous, it expresses as much by what is between words as by the words themselves. To understand the *parole originaire*, which gropes around an intention to make meaning, we must consider other expressions which might have taken its place and the threads of silence intertwined with its words. Our understanding of the expressive intention may be deepened by detailed exploration of the differences between language and other arts of expression, a necessarily lengthy series of analyses leading principally to a meditation on literary communication (with a sort of manifest advocating a criticism which recognizes that its own explicit formulations cannot replace the work of an artist "who reveals what is true or makes it show through and does not touch it"—*Signes*, 98) and a concluding section on philosophical language. Seeking only to situate this latter problem in the proper context, Merleau-Ponty summarizes his position thus:

> . . . in any case no language detaches itself entirely from the precariousness of the mute forms of expression, nor reabsorbs its own contingency, nor consumes itself to make the things themselves appear, and in this sense the privilege of language over against painting or the image of life remains relative, and finally expression is not one of the curiosities that the mind can propose to examine, it is the mind's existence as act (*Signes*, p. 98).

Returning to the Saussurian distinction by which he opened the essay, Merleau-Ponty notes that, given the demonstration showing that meaning arises when we differentiate linguistic gestures, the marvel is that we ignored this before Saussure and forget it whenever we speak, forget it even when discussing Saussure. The point is, then, that a partial act of expression is not limited to expending a certain expressive power held by *la langue*, that it recreates both this power and *la langue* by virtue of man's capacity to transcend signs toward meaning. Expression, then, is not merely the realization of a possible grammatical sequence, and the relationship of sign to sign fits into the scheme we have seen before in which language provides for transcending itself, in which what we want to say is "the excess of what we live over what has already been said" (*Signes,* p. 104).

The succeeding essay, Merleau-Ponty's last important pronouncement on language, is entitled "On the Phenomenology of Language," a relatively inauspicious heading which clearly does not imply that a phenomenological reduction of the term "language" will be attempted. The author insists here, as elsewhere, on the later writings of Husserl, wherein the early idea of a fixed, universal language, susceptible to explicit representation of its total structure, has been abandoned in favor of a new conception, of a language which is the core of thought and the operation which confers upon thoughts their intersubjective value. The phenomenological point of view is defined as that of "the subject who makes use of his language as a means of communication with a living community," (*Eloge,* p. 86),[3] after which we are presented simply with a series of topical elucidations.

When Saussure distinguished a synchronic linguistics of *la parole* and a diachronic linguistics of *la langue,* he merely juxtaposed two irrevocably separated perspectives. Phenomenology, on the other hand, immediately institutes a dialectic to bring the diachronic and synchronic views into communication. By a transversal cross-section, the latter envelops the former, placing the series of fortuitous linguistic facts within a system of internal development. By a longitudinal cross-section, the diachronic envelops the synchronic—the synchronic system contains at every moment openings in which the crude linguistic event can intrude. Hence, a double task is conceived: find a meaning in the development of language, conceived as an equilibrium in movement, and recognize the changes that are latent or incubating, i.e., distinguish "an ensemble of convergent linguistic gestures, each one of which will be defined less by a signification than by an instrumental

---

[3] The references to "On the Phenomenology of Language" are to an edition of *Eloge de la philosophie et autres essais* in the NRF "Collection IDEES" (1960).

value" (*Eloge,* p. 90). History consists of succeeding synchronisms. Phenomenology's lesson?

> . . . a new conception of the being of language, which is now logic within contingency, an oriented system, and which never the less always elaborates chances, recapture of the fortuitous within a totality which has a meaning, incarnate logic (*Eloge,* p. 91).

The structuralist must ask, of course, what notion of structure, if any, can be applied within this vitalized system, where the assumption of linguistic stability is clearly discarded. One possible reply may be obtained from psychology, for Merleau-Ponty had faced an analogous question in regard to the nervous system in *The Structure of Behavior* (1937): "We shall say that there is *form* wherever the properties of a system modify themselves for every change effected upon a single one of its parts, and on the contrary, conserve themselves when they all change by maintaining the same relationship between themselves" (*La Structure du comportement,* Presses Universitaires, p. 50). This definition apparently satisfies the need for a dynamic conception of structure.

Always at the base of Merleau-Ponty's dynamically conceived language lies the intention toward meaning, whose nature is such as to preclude the complete expression which Saussure correctly saw that we naively believe to attain. Representing this intention as the "significative" (*signifiant*) and the achieved expression as the signified (*signifié*), a jargonized definition can be formulated: expression is "the transcendence of the 'significative' by the 'signified' that it is the character of the 'significative' to make possible" (*Eloge,* p. 96). Within what is clearly little more than a rehashing of his previously formulated work, Merleau-Ponty arrives suddenly at a tenet of modern criticism, stated as a consequence of language's self-transcending power: "We who speak do not necessarily know what we express better than those who hear us" (*Eloge,* p. 99). When we claim to know an idea, we really claim no more than to be able to organize coherent statements around it, a capacity which depends on a certain style of thinking. Original thinking may thus involve what Malraux terms the "coherent distortion" of available meanings. Now, once expression is attained, the preparatory steps precedent to it, e.g., the stanzas of a sonnet, are reinterpreted according to the final meaning of the whole; author and reader may henceforth derive the meaning of the whole from any part, a personal and interpersonal tradition is born, a new item has been added to the culture's stock of available meanings.

The latter half of the essay is devoted to the consequences of Merleau-Ponty's understanding of language for phenomenological philosophy. In this context, we confront once again the motif conveyed by the title of this section—the "meaning-power" of *la parole* appears as an aspect of the body's role of mediating our relationship with objects and other people. *La parole* operates in an intercorporeal or intersubjective region, and phenomenology contends that we may understand it only if we account for this omnipresent, irreducible intentional connection. It admits the study of language as an objectified phenomenon only to the extent that the latter may be reintegrated into the only system in which it can be part of human experience. Indeed, *la parole* reveals the most fundamentally human activity at that moment when it seeks to understand itself. Merleau-Ponty's work, over and beyond purely theoretical considerations, makes it clear that the phenomenologist unhesitatingly brings to bear the results of both structuralist and behaviorist inquiries in his study of language. Yet he refuses to lose sight of a larger human context, within which *la parole* is "an eminent case of those 'conducts' which overthrow my ordinary relationship with objects and give to certain of them the value of subjects" (*Eloge,* p. 105). And his focus upon meaning as the principal problem of linguistics reflects the humanist's concern for understanding: the sedimentation of meanings is but another name of truth itself and "the presence of all presents in our own" (*Eloge,* p. 109). We are hardly surprised to see the philosopher advocate a type of textual criticism which is grounded in the determination of original meanings—the idea certainly is not new. But Merleau-Ponty calls for something more—contrasting meaning with what is not meant, and formulating meaning in human rather than lexical terms. The deepest meaning, and the most difficult to bring to light, will indeed be that communicative nugget which resists trans-

lation into a thesis, which retains an element of chance or
ambiguity, "which introduces us to unfamiliar perspectives,
instead of consolidating our own" (*Signes,* p. 97).

Overture to *le Cru et le cuit**

Claude Lévi-Strauss

(The following text is taken from the opening chapter of
Professor Lévi-Strauss' most recent book [Plon, 1964]. Certain
devices [e.g. M_1] in the text refer to a list of myths and their
variants which is appended to Professor Lévi-Strauss' book
[p. 367-71]. The translator wishes to thank Professors F. G.
Lounsbury and Harold Scheffler of the Department of
Anthropology in Yale for their valuable help.)

The aim of this book is to show how certain categorical opposites drawn from everyday experience with the most basic
sorts of things—e.g. "raw" and "cooked," "fresh" and "rotten,"
"moist" and "parched," and others—can serve a people as
conceptual tools for the formation of abstract notions and for
combining these into propositions. (The values of such categorical terms can be defined with any necessary degree of
precision, and of course always from the point of view of a
particular culture, by means of quite simple acts of ethnographic observation.)

The form of this hypothesis requires one's starting point
to be at the level of the most concrete; that is to say, one must
proceed from some particular social group, or from a cluster of
such groups as are reasonably close to one another in habitat,

* "Overture to le cru et le cuit" by Claude Lévi-Strauss, translated
by Joseph H. McMahon, in *Yale French Studies.* Copyright © 1966 by
Yale French Studies. Reprinted by permission of Harper & Row, Pub-
lishers, who will publish a complete English translation in August,
1969, under the title of *The Raw and the Cooked,* translated by John
Weightman.

history, and culture. This is a precaution of methodology, necessary to be sure, but one that need neither conceal nor restrict the goals of our project. By means of a small number of myths taken from certain aboriginal societies which will serve as our laboratory we hope to construct an experiment whose significance, if we succeed, will be of a general order; for we anticipate that it will demonstrate the existence of a logic of perceived attributes: one that occurs over and over again, and that reveals its own inherent laws.

We take off from a single myth, one deriving from a single society, and we analyze it by having recourse first to its ethnographic context, and then to other myths from the same society. Our area of interest widens as we move along; once we have placed them in their appropriate ethnographic context, we will move on to study the primitive myths of neighboring societies. Gradually, we reach even more distant societies. But one basic condition remains: between these societies there must either be genuine historical or geographical connections or else such connections can be reasonably postulated. This work describes only the first steps of a long excursion through the myths native to the New World. The excursion begins in the heart of tropical America and will probably carry us to the northern regions of North America. From start to finish, the guiding line is furnished by the myth of the Bororo Indians of Central Brazil. This choice has been made, not because the myth is more archaic than others we will subsequently study, nor because it is an easier or more complete one. The causes which brought it to our attention are in large measure contingent. Our hope has been to present a systematic account which will reproduce as thoroughly as possible the analytic procedure used. In so doing, it is possible to show the close tie between the empirical and systematic aspects which is found in such materials. If the method chosen to demonstrate this tie embodies that kind of connection the demonstration will be all the more effective.

As we shall try to show, the Bororo myth—which we will henceforth refer to as the *reference myth*—is a more or less extended transformation of other myths which have originated either in the same society or in other near and distant societies. Because of this, it would have been quite possible to take our point of departure from any single representative of the group. What is of interest in the reference myth does not depend on its typical character; rather it depends on its irregular position within the group. And, because of the problems in interpretation which it brings up, the myth is especially thought-provoking.

Despite these cautionary statements, we can reasonably fear that this undertaking will knock up against prejudicial objections from mythographers and specialists of tropical America. And it is unquestionably true that this undertaking does not respect territorial limits or even the contexts of a single classification. From whatever viewpoint we look at it, it is seen to develop nebulously. Like a nebula it never brings together in a durable or systematic way the sum total of the elements from which it blindly derives its substance. Yet we are firmly convinced that the real serves as its guide and indicates a surer path than any the book might have plotted out synthetically. We begin, then, with a myth which has not been chosen arbitrarily; rather it has been selected because of an intuitive feeling that it is promising and productive. We analyze it according to rules we have set forth in earlier works,[1] and establish for each sequence the group of its transformations either as they are manifested within the myth itself or as they are elucidated in isomorphic elements of sequences taken from a number of myths belonging to the same population. From the consideration of particular myths, we move, therefore, to the consideration of certain major diagrams which are ordered about a common axis. At each point on this axis where a schema is indicated, we subsequently trace out the other axes which are produced by a similar operation. The operation, however, is no longer the result of a single population's myths—myths which had all seemed different. Rather the operation results from a realization that the myths, though they come from neighboring popu-

[1] Lévi-Strauss, Claude. *Anthropologie structurale,* Paris, 1958; "Le Geste d'Asdiwal," *Ecole Pratique des Hautes Etudes, Section des Sciences Religieuses,* Annuaire (1958-1959), Paris, 1958; *Leçon Inaugurale* delivered Tuesday 5 January 1960 on assuming the Chair of Social Anthropology in the Collège de France, Paris, 1960; *La Pensée sauvage,* Paris, 1962.

lations, offer certain analogies to the first. Because of this, the
leading schemas are simplified, enriched, or transformed. Each
becomes a source of new axes which are perpendicular to
those on the other planes. There, by a movement which is
both prospective and retrospective, we see outlined sequences which have been extracted from myths belonging to
more distant populations or myths which have been neglected
in the past because they seemed of no use or were impossible
to interpret despite the fact that they belonged to a people
who had already been studied. As our nebula spreads out, its
nucleus condenses and becomes organized. Sparse filaments
are soldered; lacunae are filled; connections are established;
something resembling order is visible behind the chaos. As
though clustering around a germinal molecule, the sequences
which have been ranked in transformation groups are incorporated into the initial group and reproduce its structure
and determinations. A multi-dimensional body is born whose
central parts reveal a pattern or organization, though uncertainty and confusion continue to rule on the periphery.

We do not anticipate a point where the mythical material,
having been dissolved by analysis, will crystallize into a mass
and offer in all respects the image of a stable and well-
determined structure. We must recognize that the science of
myths is still in its infancy and should be satisfied with the
sketchiest of results. But beyond that we must also recognize
that the final step will never be taken simply because no
population or population group now exists or will exist whose
myths and ethnography—and without these there can be no
study of myths—can be the object of exhaustive knowledge.
There would be no point to holding such ambitions anyway.
We are dealing with a reality in process, a reality which is
perpetually under the attack from a past which ruins it and a
future which changes it. Each case in the literature illustrates
how distant such a goal is and we must content ourselves with
samples and remains. We have shown that the starting point
of the analysis must inevitably be chosen haphazardly because the organizing principles of the mythic material are in
the material and will only be revealed progressively. It is inevitable that the finishing point will also impose itself in an
equally unexpected way. That will come when the undertaking

arrives at the point where its ideal object has acquired adequate form and consistency. There will then be no possibility of doubting its existence as an object properly considered as such nor of certain of its latent properties. Here, as with the optical microscope which cannot reveal matter's ultimate structure to the observer, our only choice is between certain enlargements; each manifests a level of organization whose truth is relative; each, while in use, excludes the perception of other levels.

To some extent these remarks explain the characteristics of a book which otherwise might seem paradoxical. It is a complete work, which presents conclusions designed to answer the questions raised at the outset; yet it makes frequent references to a second work in whose shadows a third work is probably beginning to take shape. If they ever come to fruition, these other volumes will not be a continuation of this one; rather they will pick up the same materials and will offer a different attack on the same problems in the hope of accentuating properties which have remained confused or have not been perceived. They will do this by resorting to new ways of seeing or by coloring historical cross-sections in another manner. If the inquiry proceeds according to these hopes, it will not develop along a linear axis but rather as a spiral: it will return regularly to the earlier results; it will embrace new objects only when knowledge of them will make it possible to understand better the fragmentary knowledge previously acquired.

The reader should not be astonished that this book, which by its own statement of purpose is devoted to mythology, reaches into tales, legends, and pseudo-historical traditions, nor that it calls on a wide variety of ceremonies and rites. We reject all hasty judgment about what is properly considered mythic and claim, as appropriate to our interest, every manifestation of social and mental activity which can be discerned among the populations under study. As the movement of our analysis will show, this allows us to round off the myth or clarify it even in those instances where such manifestations do not amount to what musicians call an obligato.[2] Even

---

[2] Cf. Lévi-Strauss, Claude. *Anthropologie structurale*, Paris, 1958, ch. XII.

though the research has been centered on the myths of
tropical America from which the greater number of examples has been drawn, the progressive demands of the
analysis have made it inevitable that we should use contributions culled from more distant regions. The process is very
much like that of those primitive organisms which, although
they are already enclosed in a membrane, maintain a capacity
to move their protoplasm within this envelope and to distend
it extraordinarily in order to emit pseudopodia. Such behavior
is a good bit less strange once we have verified that its object
is to capture or to assimilate foreign bodies. Finally, we have
avoided all preconceived classifications about cosmological,
seasonal, divine, technological, and other sorts of myths. Once
again it is the myth itself, subjected to analysis, which we are
allowing to reveal its own nature and to find its own place
within a type. To the extent that he bases his work on external
and arbitrarily isolated marks, such a goal remains beyond the
mythographer.

The concern of this book, then, is to have no subject.
Since it begins by limiting itself to the study of a single myth, it
must, if it wishes to be complete, assimilate the material of
two hundred myths. While the study does indeed block out a
clearly delimited cultural and geographical region, the possibility of its resembling from time to time a general treatise on
mythology is not excluded. It has no real beginning; it could
as easily have begun in a different fashion. Had it, it would
none the less have developed in an analogous way. It has no
end either; numerous problems are treated only in summary
fashion here and others are given the sparsest space. They
await a better fate. In setting up our map, we have been
obliged to place complex contours in relief. Using the tools
of ethnography and utilizing other myths, we create the
semantic field of a myth. The same operation is repeated for
each of them with the result that the central zone, chosen
arbitrarily, can be crisscrossed by numerous lines; still, the
frequency of the overlappings is reduced in proportion as
one is further separated from it. In order to obtain at all
points an equally dense scanning, the procedure would
have to be renewed several times by tracing new circles at
points situated on the periphery. In the process, the primitive

territory would of course be enlarged. Mythical analysis is very much like Penelope's task. Each step forward offers a new hope which hangs on the solution of a new difficulty. The books are never closed.

Far from alarming us, the odd conception of this book has special significance for us; it indicates that we have perhaps managed to capture certain of the fundamental properties of our object. The discovery is the result of a plan and method which have been imposed on us rather than selected by us. Of the study of myths, Durkheim has written: "It is a difficult subject which must be treated in itself, for itself, and by following a method special to it."[3] He also suggested the reason for this state of things when, further on (p. 190), he mentioned totemic myths "which, beyond any doubt, explain nothing and serve only to displace the difficulty; yet, in displacing it, they appear at least to attenuate their logical scandal." This profound definition could, we believe, be extended to the whole field of mythic thinking by giving it fuller meaning than its author would have admitted.

The study of myths poses a methodological problem if only because such study cannot follow the Cartesian principle of breaking the difficulty down into as many parts as are required for its solution. No term proper to mythic analysis exists; nor is there any secret unity which one can seize hold of at the end of the analysis. The themes can be subdivided endlessly. When we think we have unraveled one from the other and can maintain them separately, we soon find that they are blending together as though under the pressure of affinities we had not foreseen. Consequently, the myth's unity is tendentious and projective; it never really reflects a state or a fixed moment of the myth. It is no more than an imaginary phenomenon implicit in the effort of interpretation. As such its role is to give synthetic form to the myth, to keep it from being dissolved in the war of contraries. We can therefore say that the science of myths amounts to an *anaclasis,* taking this term in the broad sense permitted by its etymology; by definition, it permits us to study reflected rays along with refracted

[3] Durkheim, E. *Les Formes élémentaires de la vie religieuse,* 2nd ed., Paris, 1925, p. 142.

rays. But, in contradistinction to philosophic reflection, which claims it goes directly back to the source, the reflections with which we are here concerned can claim only a virtual source. The diversity of sequences and themes is a fundamental attribute of mythic thought. Such thought manifests itself in a burst of rays; it is only by measuring directions and calculating angles that we arrive at the possibility of a common origin, an ideal point where all the rays reflected elsewhere by the myth's structure would be rejoined. But this does not ever really happen; the rays may very well have come from elsewhere and they have not remained parallel throughout the entire length of their history. As the conclusion of this book shows, there is something quite essential in this multiplicity, for it has to do with the double character of mythic thought: it coincides with its object of which it is an homologous image, but it does this without ever being absorbed into the object since the myth, as image, evolves on another level. The recurrence of themes translates this mixture of impotency and tenacity. Unconcerned with neat beginnings and clear goals, mythic thought does not effect complete courses; it always has something more to achieve. Like rites, myths are *in-terminable.* Our undertaking—which is at once too long and too short—will try to imitate the spontaneous movement of mythic thought; to do so, we have had to bow to mythic thought's demands and respect its rhythm. As a result this book about myths is, in its own way, a myth. Whatever unity might be claimed for it will appear hidden in the recesses of the text and perhaps even beyond it. In the best of circumstances, that unity will only be worked out in the reader's mind.

We shall most probably hear the greatest number of criticisms from ethnographers. Despite our concern with sources of information, some, which were not inaccessible, have been neglected.[4] Those of which we have made use are not always

---

[4] Because of their recent publication certain works like *Die Tacana* by Hissinck and Hahn (Stuttgart, 1961) have been looked at only superficially; others which arrived in France after this book had been completed have not been consulted at all. This has been the case with: J. Wilbert, *Indios de la región Orinoco-Ventuari* (Caracas, 1963),

cited in this final version. In order not to needlessly over-
burden the account, we have had to sort out myths, choose
certain versions, prune the motifs of their variations. Some
will accuse us of shaping the material used to fit the needs of
our project. But if, from the vast mass of myths, we had
retained only those most favorable to our intentions much of
the force of this book would have been lost. Yet surely the
converse is not true: that in order to touch on a comparison
of myths one must work with and mix together the totality of
known myths derived from tropical America.

This particular objection is especially pertinent in light of
the circumstances which have delayed the appearance of this
book. It was almost completed when the publication of the
first volume of the *Encyclopédie Bororo* was announced.
We waited until the book had arrived in France and inspected
it before putting the finishing touches to this text. Yet couldn't
this sort of practice be pushed even further, and shouldn't we
be obliged to await the publication two or three years hence
of the second volume of the *Encyclopédie* which will be devoted to the myths? And, after that, for a third volume which
will treat proper names? Oddly, and despite its many riches,
the study of the first volume taught quite another lesson. For
the Salesians, whose changes of mind are recorded with great
placidity when they are not passed over in silence, are quite
willfully acerbic when they come across a study prepared by
hands other than theirs and which does not coincide with their
own most recent work. When one study contradicts another,
we have a problem but not a solution. We have a good bit
more respect for sources, whether they be ours or those used
by the missionaries. Their evidence possesses a special value.
The Salesians' merits are so outstanding as to allow one to
reproach them, without denying any of the recognition due
them, for one slight practice: they have an unfortunate
tendency to believe that the most recent inquiry cancels out
all others.

Warao Oral Literature (id., 1964), and N. Fock, *Waiwai, Religion and
Society of an* Amazonian Tribe (Copenhagen, 1963). In the last book
we came across a sargus myth which verifies our analyses in the third
and fourth parts of this book. We will profit from these new materials
in a future volume.

Study of other documents which have already appeared and of those which will appear in the future will always influence our interpretation. Those put forward with care will perhaps be confirmed; others will have to be abandoned or modified. But these are not really obstacles. In a discipline like ours scientific knowledge advances with hesitant steps, driven along under the whips of contention and doubt. It leaves to metaphysics the impatience for all-or-nothing solutions. In order for our understanding to be valid, it is not necessary to have the guarantee that, over the years, we can be assured of the truth of every detail of our work. It will be quite enough if we can have the more modest assurance of having left difficult problems in a less bad state than they inhabited when we began working with them. Nor should we ever forget that in science established truths do not exist. The scientist does not supply true answers; rather he asks true questions.

We can be even more firm about this. Critics who may reproach us for not having made an exhaustive inventory of South American myths before proceeding to our analysis of them will be seriously misconstruing the nature and role of the document in question. The ensemble of a population's myths belongs to the realm of discourse. Unless the population is morally or physically extinct the ensemble is never fully rounded off. We do not think of criticising a linguist when he writes the grammar of a language without having included the totality of all the words used since the language's beginning and without knowing the verbal exchanges which will take place so long as the language remains in existence. We know from experience that even a ridiculously small number of phrases, only a sampling of those he might theoretically have had at his disposal, permit the linguist to work out a grammar of the language he is studying. (And we need not tarry over the problem of words he cannot know either because they were not at his disposal or because they have not yet entered the language.) Even a partial grammar, or the sketch of a grammar, represents a valuable acquisition where an unfamiliar language is concerned. We do not have to wait for a tally of a theoretically limitless series of events in order to see syntactical processes at work, especially since syntax consists of the body of rules which governs the engen-

dering of those events. The sketch we have tried to make is of
the same ilk; it is a syntax of South American mythology.
When and if new texts come to enrich mythic discourse, there
will be occasion to check or to modify the manner in which
certain grammatical laws have been formulated. Some will be
given up; others will be discovered. But in no case can the
argument of the need to possess a total mythic discourse have
any relevance to this undertaking. As we have just seen, such
a demand makes no sense.

Another possible objection is more serious. Our right to
choose our myths here and there and to illuminate a Chaco
myth by a Guyanian variant, or a Ge myth by its Colombian
analogue might be contested. Yet, though it is respectful of
history and anxious to profit from its lessons, structural analysis refuses to be enclosed in the already circumscribed perim-
eters of historical investigation. On the contrary, by demonstrating that myths of very diverse origins objectively form a
group, structural analysis raises a problem for history; it
invites history to go looking for a solution. We have constructed a group, and we hope to have supplied proof that
such a group is indeed real. It is incumbent on ethnographers,
historians, and archeologists to show how and why this is the
case.

They can be reassured. In order to explain the group character of the myths drawn together in our enquiry—and drawn
together for this reason alone—we are not counting on historical criticism to restore one day a system of logical affinities to the enumeration of a multitude of successive or
simultaneous borrowings that contemporary or ancient populations have made from one another across distances and
lapses of time which are sometimes so considerable as to
make all such interpretation highly implausible. In any case,
such interpretation could not be verified. We begin simply
by inviting the historian to look on Indian America as a phenomenon whose Middle Ages had no Rome: it is a confused
mass, issuing from an older syncretism of unquestionably
loose texture; at its center and over a period of centuries
there subsist centers both of high civilization and barbarous
people, both centralizing tendencies and disruptive forces.
Although the latter finally carried the day because of the

play of internal causes and because of the arrival of the European conquerors, it is none the less certain that a group—much like the one we are investigating—owes its character to the fact that it was crystallized in an already organized semantic milieu whose elements had served for all kinds of combinations. Without doubt this was less the result of any concern with imitation than it was of a desire to allow smaller, less populous societies to affirm their respective originality by exploiting the resources of a dialectic of oppositions and correlations within the framework of a common conception of the world.

Such an interpretation, which we present in sketchy fashion, clearly rests on some historical conjectures: the great antiquity of tropical American settlements, repeated displacements of numerous tribes in many directions, demographic fluidity, and phenomena of fusion. The last created the conditions of a very ancient syncretism from which the differences observable among the groups were created. These reflect nothing, or practically nothing of the archaic conditions which most often are secondary or derived. Despite the formal perspective it adopts, structural analysis validates the ethnographical and historical interpretations we advanced twenty years ago. Though they were considered adventurous then, they have continued to gain ground.[5] If an ethnographic conclusion emerges clearly from this book, that is because the Ge, far from being those "marginal people" they were imagined to be in 1942 when the first volume of the *Handbook of the South American Indians*—we objected to the suggestion at that time—actually represented a pivotal element in South America. Their role is comparable to that played in North America by the very old cultures whose survivors were established at the basins of the Fraser and Columbia rivers. When our inquiry gets to the southern regions of North America the bases of this rapprochement will be more evident.

It has been necessary to cite these concrete results of structural analysis—others, limited to the cultures of tropical

---

[5] Cf. Lévi-Strauss, Claude. *Anthropologie structurale*, Paris, 1958, p. 118 sq. and all of ch. VI.

America, will be pointed out in the course of the book—in order to put the reader on his guard against the reproach of formalism, indeed of idealism, which we sometimes hear. Does not this present work, even more than its predecessors, push ethnographical research into the realms of psychology, logic, and philosophy—paths which should be forbidden to it? Are we not then distracting ethnography, in part at least, from its genuine tasks: the study of concrete societies and of the problems raised in those societies by the social, political, and economic conditions which governed the relations between individuals and groups. These oft-expressed worries strike us as resulting from a complete misunderstanding of the task we have taken on. But—and this is much more serious—they cast doubt on the continuity of the program followed methodically since *Les Structures élémentaires de la parenté*. Certainly no such criticisms can be reasonably directed against that work.

While *La Pensée sauvage* does represent a pause in our attempt, the pause was needed in order to catch breath between two efforts. There was no doubt about the profit derived from looking closely at the panorama spread before us or of seizing that occasion to measure the distance which had been covered, to take bearings on the remainder of the itinerary, and to get some idea of the unfamiliar countries still to be traversed. We were determined none the less never to stray long from our route and, except for some minor poaching, never to go adventuring into the securely guarded grounds of philosophy. *La Pensée sauvage,* though some thought it was a terminus, was only a stop. It was meant to be no more than a temporary halt between the first step ventured in *Les Structures* and the second which this book is undertaking.

Most important of all, the destination has not changed. From the very beginning of the ethnographic experience, it has always been a question of setting up an inventory of mental enclosures, of reducing apparently arbitrary data to order, of reaching a level where necessity reveals itself as immanent in the illusions of freedom. In *Les Structures* we had disentangled a small number of simple principles from the apparently superficial contingency and incoherent diversity of the rules of marriage. Because of those principles a very complex ensemble of usages and customs was drawn together into a meaningful system, though at first they seemed absurd and had generally been so judged. There was nothing meanwhile to guarantee that these constraints were of internal origin. It was quite possible that they only reflected, within the minds of men, certain demands of social life which had been objectivized in institutions. Their reverberations on the psychic level would then have been the effect of mechanisms whose mode of operation alone remained to be discovered.

The experiment in mythology which we are now undertaking will be even more decisive. Mythology has no evident practical function; unlike the phenomena previously examined, mythology is not in direct contact with a different reality, endowed with an objectivity higher than its own whose orders it transmits to a mind which seems perfectly free to abandon itself to creative spontaneity. If, as a result, we were able to demonstrate that, here too, the arbitrary appearance, the apparently free outsurge, and a seemingly unbridled inventiveness presuppose laws which operate at a deeper level, we could posit as ineluctable the conclusion that the mind, freed for conversation with itself and rescued from the obligation of dealing with objects, finds itself reduced in some way to imitating itself as an object. Since the laws of its operations are no longer fundamentally different from those it manifests in its other functions, it avers its nature as a thing among things. Without pushing this line of reasoning too far, we need only to have acquired the conviction that the human mind appears as determined even in its myths; if that is so, then a fortiori it must be determined in all its manifestations.[6]

Since what we are positing is a process which would allow itself to be guided by a search for mental constraints, we see that it is not unlike Kantianism, though we are indeed making our way along other roads which do not lead to the same kind of conclusions. Unlike the philosopher, the ethnologist does not feel obliged to accept as the basis for his reflections the working conditions of his own thought or of a science

---

[6] ". . . if there are laws in some areas, there must be laws everywhere." This was the conclusion of one of Tylor's passages which, seventeen years ago, we used as the epigraph for *Les Structures élémentaires de la parenté*.

which belongs to his society or his times in order to extend his particular statements to a judgment whose universality would be only hypothetical and virtual. Preoccupied with the same problems, he adopts a doubly inverted procedure. Rather than the hypothesis of universal judgment, he prefers the empirical observations of collective judgments. Their properties, solidified in some way, are manifested to him by innumerable concrete systems of representation. Since he is a man of one social milieu, of one culture, one region, and one period of history, these systems represent the whole gamut of possible variations within a genus; he chooses those whose divergencies strike him as most noticeable. His hope is that the methodological rules which will be imposed on him will translate these systems in terms of his own and, reciprocally, will bare a network of fundamental and common constraints. This is a very high form of gymnastics indeed since it pushes the exercise of reflection to its objective limits—and the limits have initially been marked and inventoried by the ethnographic inquiry itself—flexes each muscle, and reveals all the skeleton's joints, thereby exposing the lineaments of the general anatomical structure.

What we are attempting to do is well described in Paul Ricoeur's qualification of our effort as "Kantianism without a transcendental subject."[7] We see no indication of a lacuna in this restriction; instead we see the inevitable consequence, on the philosophical level, of the ethnographic perspective we have chosen. By pursuing conditions where systems of truth become mutually convertible and can therefore be simultaneously admissible for several subjects, the ensemble of

[7] Ricoeur, Paul. "Symbole et temporalité," in *Archivio di Filosofia,* no. 1-2, Rome, 1963, p. 24. See also p. 9: "More a Kantian unconscious than a Freudian one; a categorical, unifying unconscious . . ." and on p. 10: ". . . a categorical system without reference to a thinking subject . . . homologous to nature; it might even be nature . . ."

With his usual finesse and perspicuity, Roger Bastide ("La Nature humaine: le point de vue du sociologue et de l'ethnologue," in *La Nature humaine,* Acts of the XIth Congress of the *Sociétés de Philosophie de langue française,* Montpellier, 4-6 September 1961, Paris, 1961) anticipates the preceding argument. This coincidence is all the more indicative of his clear-thinking since I had no knowledge of his text until he kindly sent it to me while I was correcting the proofs of this book.

these conditions acquires the character of an object endowed
by a reality proper to itself and independent of any subject.

More than any other phenomenon, mythology allows us to
illustrate this objectified thought and to demonstrate its reality
empirically. We do not exclude the possibility that the speaking subjects, who produce and transmit the myths, may be
conscious of their structure and their mode of operation;
such an occurrence, however, is more partial and intermittent
than it is routine. The situation with myths is very much the
situation we find with language. Any speaker who consciously
applies phonological and grammatical laws in his speech—and
we are presupposing, of course, that he has the requisite
knowledge and virtuosity—would not be able to pursue the
line of his argument very long. In the same way, the exercise
and practice of mythic thought demands that its properties
remain hidden; if they are not, one would find himself in the
position of the mythologist who cannot believe in myths because he spends his time expounding about them. Mythic
analysis does not and cannot have as its object to show how
men think. In the special case with which we are concerned
here, it is at least doubtful that the natives of Brazil go beyond
the delight with which they listen to narratives and conceive
openly the systems of relations to which we are reducing
these myths. When, using these myths, we validate certain
archaic or highly imaged turns of phrase found in our own
popular language, the same observation imposes itself: we
make these discoveries under the influence of a foreign mythology; our discovery is the result of an awareness which
works retroactively. We are not, therefore, claiming to show
how men think the myths, but rather how the myths think
themselves out in men and without men's knowledge.

We have already suggested that it may be appropriate to
go even further and, setting aside consideration of the subject's
role, weigh the possibility that, in a certain way, the myths
think themselves out among themselves.[8] This is not so much
a question of extricating what is within the myths without

[8] The Ojibwa Indians consider myths as "being endowed with con-
sciousness, capable of thought and action." W. Jones, "Ojibwa Texts," in
Publications of the American Ethnological Society, vol. III, pt. ii, New
York, 1919, p. 574, n. 1.

necessarily being held in the consciousness of men; rather it is a question of extricating the system of axioms and postulates which define the best possible code, a code capable of giving a common sense to the unconscious elaborations which are the actuality of minds, societies, and cultures which, set off one against the other, offer the greatest separation. Since the myths themselves depend on codes of the second order—codes of the first order are those of language—this book is offering the sketch of a code which would belong to a third order, an order designed to assure the reciprocal translatability of several myths. For this reason, a reader would not be wrong if he took the book itself as a myth: the myth of mythology.

But, in common with the other two, this third code has neither been invented nor hunted for elsewhere. It is immanent in the mythology itself; we only discover it. An ethnographer working in South America was astonished by the way in which the myths came to him: "Practically every narrator told the stories in his way. Even in important details, the margin of variations is enormous . . ." Still, the natives seem not to be bothered by this state of things: "A Caraja who accompanied me from village to village heard a great number of these kinds of variations and greeted them all with an almost identical trust. It wasn't that he didn't perceive the contradictions. But they had no interest whatever for him."[9] A naive commentator, one who came from another planet, might have a better right to be astonished—since he would be dealing with history and not with myth—by the mass of works devoted to the French Revolution. In them, authors do not always make use of the same incidents; when they do, the incidents are revealed under quite different lights. And yet these are variations which have to do with the same country, the same period, and the same events—events whose reality is scattered across every level of a multi-layered structure. The criterion of validity clearly does not depend on the elements of history. Pursued in isolation, each element would show itself to be beyond grasp. But certain of them derive

[9] Lipkind, W. "Caraja Cosmography," in *Journal of American Folklore,* vol. 53, 1940, p. 251.

consistency from the fact that they can be integrated into a system whose terms are more or less credible when set off against the overall coherence of the series.

In spite of worthy and indispensable efforts to bring another moment in history alive and to possess it, a clairvoyant history should admit that it never completely escapes from the nature of myth. Mythic schemes offer in the highest degree the character of absolute objects; if they were not subject to external influences they would neither lose nor acquire other elements. The result is that when a schema undergoes a transformation the transformation affects the myth in every aspect. Whenever some aspect of a myth appears unintelligible, we are justified in treating it, in a hypothetical and preliminary way, as a transformation of the homologous aspect of another myth which has been attached to the same group because it lends itself better to interpretation. We have done this several times. For example, in resolving the episode of the covered jaw of the jaguar in M_7 by using the universe episode of the open jaw in M_{55}, or that of the real obligingness of the carrion vultures in M_1 by looking at the manifestations of their deceptive obligingness in M_{65}. Contrary to what one might believe, the method does not fall into a vicious circle. It implies only that each myth, considered by itself, exists as a restrained application of a scheme which can be progressively extricated with the aid of those relations of reciprocal intelligibility which are perceived among several myths.

We shall probably be accused of over-interpreting and over-simplifying in the use we make of the method. By way of reply, we can only point out once again that we have never claimed that all the solutions suggested have an equal value; to this we can add that we have at times pointed out the precarious value of some of them. Still, such a reply would be a hypocritical evasion of a declaration of the full weight of our thinking. To such eventual critics, we offer an immediate answer: what difference does it make? If the final goal of anthropology is to contribute to a better knowledge of objectivized thought and its mechanisms, then in the end it does not make much difference whether the thought of Latin American natives finds its form in the operation of my thought or if mine finds its in the operation of theirs. What does matter is that the human mind, unconcerned with the identity of its occasional bearers, manifests in that operation a structure which becomes more and more intelligible to the degree that the doubly reflexive movement of two thoughts, working on one another, makes progress. It is a process in which now one, now the other can be the wick to a glimmer of rapprochement from which their common illumination will spring forth. If a treasure is uncovered in the process, we will have no need of an arbiter in order to move on to the division of the riches; from the very start we have recognized that the inheritance is inalienable and that it must remain undivided.[10]

At the outset we said that we were seeking to transcend the opposition of the perceptible and the intelligible by straight-away placing ourselves on the level of signs. Through signs the one is conveyed by means of the other. Yet, even when restricted in number, they lend themselves to rigorously grouped combinations which can translate, in their most discrete nuances, the whole diversity of perceptible experience. Our hope is to attain a level where logical properties will be manifested as attributes of things quite as directly as savors and perfumes. Their special nature, excluding all error, can still evoke a combination of elements which, were they selected or disposed in other ways, would evoke awareness of another perfume. Because we have the notion of the sign, our task is that of bringing secondary qualities to the business of truth at the level of the intelligible; we are no longer exclusively limited to the perceptible.

This search for a middle way between the exercise of logical thought and esthetic perception should naturally be inspired by the example of music which has always followed the middle way. Something more than a general point of view suggests the rapprochement. Almost as soon as work on this book had started, it was evident that it would be impossible to arrange its materials according to any plan which respected traditional norms. Chapter divisions would not only have done violence to the movement of its thought but would have brought impoverishment and mutilation; all the bite would

---

[10] Lévi-Strauss, Claude. *La Pensée sauvage*, Paris, 1962.

have been gone. If the presentation was to appear decisive, then, paradoxically, more freedom and suppleness would have to be conceded to it. We noticed, too, that the order chosen for the presentation of documents could not be linear; the sentences in the commentary could not be connected by a simple before and after relationship. If the reader were to have from time to time a sense of simultaneity, then artifices in composition would be essential. His sense of simultaneity would, of course, be illusory, for he would still be tied down by the order of the narrative. Yet a close equivalent could be hinted at through alternation of a lengthy discourse with a diffuse one, by speeding up rhythms which had been slowed down, by heaping up examples at some points and, at others, by keeping them separated. We noticed thus that our analyses were situated on several axes. One was the axis of succession; but there was also the axis of relative density which demanded that we have recourse to those evocative musical forms, the *solo* and the *tutti*. Furthermore, there were the axes of expressive tensions and replacement codes which produced, as the book was being written, oppositions comparable to those between song and recitative, between the instrumental ensemble and the aria.

In choosing this free recourse to a multi-dimensional approach which would best display our themes, we had to give up something. The usual division of a book into isometric chapters had to give way to a division into less numerous parts. These, as a result, are more voluminous and complex; they are also unequal in length. But each forms a whole by virtue of its internal organization which is the outflow of a certain unity in inspiration. For the same reason these parts could not be poured into a single mold; rather each has had to obey the rules of tone, genre, and style required by the nature of the materials being used and by the nature of the technical means employed for each case. The result was that musical forms once again offered the resources and diversity already gauged by experience. Comparisons with the sonata, the symphony, the prelude, the fugue, and other forms permitted easy verification of the fact that problems of construction analogous to those posed in the analysis of myth had

already cropped up in music where solutions had already
been invented for them.

At the same time there was no way of eluding another problem: what deep causes were behind this at first surprising
affinity between music and myths? (Structural analysis limits
itself to pointing out their value, simply taking them into
account and transporting them to another level.) Certainly a
major step towards an answer had already been taken once
we could evoke a constant element in our personal history
which no sudden event could shake. We speak of the service
we had rendered since childhood at the altars of the "god
Richard Wagner," a devotion in no way shaken either by hearing *Pelléas* as an adolescent or, later, *Les Noces*. If one must
see in Wagner the unimpeachable father of the structural
analysis of myths (and, in the case of *Meistersinger*, of tales),
then it is highly revealing to note that such analysis was first
made *in music*.[11] In suggesting that the analysis of myth was
comparable to the perusal of a great score, we were only
drawing the logical consequence of the Wagnerian discovery:
the structure of myths is revealed through means of a score.

This prefatory homage does more to confirm the existence
of the problem than to resolve it. The true answer is found,
we believe, in the character common to the myth and the musical work: each after its fashion is a language which transcends
the level of articulated language; each requires at every instance a temporal dimension in order to become manifest;
the same is true with language but is not true with painting.
This relationship to time is of a very special nature: everything
takes place as though music and mythology needed time only
in order to deny its place. Both, in effect, are mechanisms designed to do away with time. Underneath the sounds and
rhythms, music operates on a rough terrain which is the
physiological time of the listener; that time is irremediably
diachronic because it is irreversible; music none the less

[11] While acknowledging this paternity we would be guilty of in-
gratitude if we did not admit other debts: first of all to the work of
Marcel Granet which glitters with brilliant intuitions; then—and if last
not least—to the work of Georges Dumézil and to the *Asklèplos,
Apollon Smintheus et Rudra* of Henri Grégoire (*Mémories de l'Aca-
démie Royale de Belgique, classe des Lettres,* t. XLV, fasc. 1, 1949).

transmutes the segment of that time which is devoted to listening into a totality which is synchronic and enclosed in itself. The act of listening to the musical work has immobilized the passage of time because of the work's internal organization; like a cloth billowing in the wind, it has caught up and infolded it. In listening to music—and while we are listening—we have achieved a kind of immortality.

It is clear now in what way music resembles myth; myth, too, overcomes the antinomy of historical and elapsed time; it has also overcome the limitations of a permanent structure. In order to justify the comparison fully, it must be pushed further than in one of our earlier works.[12] Like the musical work, the myth operates with a double continuum as its starting point: One is external; in one case its matter is made up of occurrences which are either historical or believed to be historical; these form a theoretically unlimited series from which each society extracts a restricted number of pertinent events in order to elaborate its myths. In the other case, it is made up of an equally unlimited series of physically possible sounds from which each musical system appropriates its scale. The second continuum is of an internal order. It has its seat in the psycho-physiological time of the listener whose factors are very complex: the periodicity of the cerebral waves and the organic rhythms, the capacity of memory, and the power of attention. These are neuro-psychical aspects which mythology especially challenges by the length of the narration, by the recurrence of the themes, and by the other forms of recurrence and parallelism. In order to be properly taken in, mythology demands that the mind of this listener sweep thoroughly back and forth across the field of the narrative as it spreads out before him. This applies equally to music. But, aside from psychological time, music addresses itself to physiological and even viscereal time. Mythology does this, too; we do not hesitate to say that a told story has been "breathtaking." But in mythology it does not play the same essential role as in music: all counterpoint contains a mute part to be filled in by the cardiac and respiratory systems.

[12] Lévi-Strauss, Claude. *Anthropologie structurale*, Paris, 1958, p. 234.

In order to simplify this line of reasoning, we shall limit our discussion to visceral time. We will say that music operates through two grids. One is physiological and therefore natural; its existence is connected to the fact that music exploits organic rhythms and thereby gives pertinence to discontinuities which would otherwise remain in a latent state as though drowned in duration. The other grid is cultural; it consists of the scale of musical sounds whose number and deviations vary according to cultures. This system of intervals supplies a first level of articulation to music, not by function of relative pitches—which result from the perceptible properties of each sound—, but by function of the hierarchical rapports which appear between the notes of the scale: whence their distinction into fundamental, tonic, dominant seventh, and dominant to express the rapports which polytonal and atonal systems enmesh without destroying.

The composer's mission is to adulterate this discontinuity without revoking its principle; at times, melodic invention hollows out momentary lacunae in the grid; at other times, but again only momentarily, it plugs up the holes or reduces their circumference. At times it perforates; at other times, it stops up a gap. What is true of melody is also true of rhythms since, by this second means, the times of the physiological grid which are theoretically constant are overlooked or accelerated, anticipated or overtaken by retardation.

Musical emotion stems precisely from the fact that the composer at each instant removes or adds more or less than the listener anticipated on the basis of his faith in a project which he believes he is incapable of penetrating genuinely because he is subject to a double periodicity: that of his thoracic cage, which stems from his individual nature, and that of his musical scale which is a function of his education. If the composer holds back even more, we experience a delightful impression of having fallen; we feel we have been torn away from the stable point of the sol-fa and thrown into the void, but only because the support which will be offered, did not come at the expected place. When the composer holds back less, the opposite happens: he forces us to more able gymnastics than we have been accustomed to. At times we are stirred; at times we are constrained to stir ourselves; but we always move beyond what on our own we would have thought ourselves capable of achieving. Esthetic pleasure is made up from this multiplicity of excitements and respites, expectations which are deceived only to be rewarded beyond expectation; these result from the challenge which the work delivers. They result, too, from the contradictory feeling music provides: the tests to which it submits us are insurmountable even at the moment when the work is preparing to offer us marvelously unforeseen means which will allow us to triumph over it. Though it is equivocal in the score which delivers it to us,

> . . . irradiant un sacre
> Mal tu par l'encre même en sanglots sibyllins,

the composer's design assumes reality, as does myth, through the listener and by him. In both cases, we are effectively observing the same inversion of the relationship between the sender and the receiver since, in the end, the receiver reveals himself as signified by the message of the sender. The music lives out its life in me; I listen to myself through the music. The myth and the musical work thus appear to be like orchestral conductors whose listeners are silent members of the orchestra.

If we ask where the real home of the work is, we find that no precise answer can be given. Music and mythology confront man with virtual objects whose shadow alone is real; they offer conscious approximations—a musical score and a myth can be nothing else—of ineluctably unconscious truths which are consecutive to them. In the case of myth, we conjecture as to the why of this paradoxical situation. It has to do with the irrational relationship which prevails between the circumstances of the creation, which are collective, and the individual nature of consumption. Myths have no author; from the moment when they are perceived as myths, and despite their real origin, they exist only as they are incarnated in a tradition. When a myth is recounted, individual listeners receive a message which in a very true sense comes from nowhere. It is for this reason that a supernatural origin has been assigned to it. It is therefore understandable that the unity of the myth should be projected on to a virtual home: beyond the conscious perception of the listener which it only traverses to a point where the energy it radiates will be consumed by the unconscious reorganization it has previously released. Music raises a much more difficult problem because we are thoroughly ignorant of the mental conditions behind musical creation. In other words, we do not know what the difference is between the small number of minds which secrete music and those, vastly more numerous, where no such phenomenon occurs even though such minds show musical sensitivity. The difference is so clear and manifests itself with such precocity that we suspect it implies properties of a special nature which are doubtless to be found at the deepest levels. But that music is a language by whose means messages are elaborated, that such messages can be understood by the many but sent out only by the few, and that it alone among all the languages unites the contradictory character of being at once intelligible and untranslatable—these facts make the creator of music a being like the gods and make music itself the supreme mystery of human knowledge. All other branches of knowledge stumble into it, it holds the key to their progress.

It would be wrong to invoke poetry in order to pretend that it causes a problem of the same order. Not everyone is a poet, but poetry utilizes a vehicle which is a common good: articulated language. It is satisfied with decreeing certain special constraints on the use of language. Music by contrast uses a vehicle which belongs properly to it and which otherwise does not lend itself to any general usage. By right if not by fact, any reasonably educated man could write poems, be they good or bad. Musical creation presupposes special aptitudes which can not be brought to flower unless the seeds are already there.

Translated by Joseph H. McMahon

Structuralism in anthropology

Harold W. Scheffler

Most men do not take the universe or their experiences of it, which they confound with it, to be disorderly. Few of us are given even the opportunity to do so, for our societies provide us with ready-made orders which we at first learn as best we can and then later perhaps contribute to or modify, thus sometimes discovering something of the arbitrariness in the relatively serviceable orders we habitually recognize.

These ready-made orders, or sets of "models" of and for experience, we may call a society's *culture,* and the anthropologist assumes, from profitable experience with the assumption, that culture is one of the most powerful constraints on human behavior. This is not to suggest that culture is the sole determinant of human-behavior-in-society. It is simply that men act in accord with their "definitions of situations" and their "rules" for dealing with those situations; in the light of such definitions and rules their behavior may be seen to be rational and therefore comprehensible to us. Most of the supposed "irrational" or "illogical" behavior of so-called primitive people has, on closer inspection, proven to be no more than behavior which differs from what we would expect in a given situation, and the behavior differs because the participants define or conceive of the situation differently than we would.

We have found then that if we can isolate and describe a people's models for perceiving, relating and otherwise interpreting their experiences we have gone a long way towards accounting for their behavior. Such accounts are by no means exhaustive, but they are essential components of any explanation of human social behavior. They invite rather than exclude other modes of explanatory synthesis.

To present such an account is not a simple unproblematic task; the pitfalls are numerous. In order to do so, we must first develop methods for isolating and describing other people's models (ethnographic methods), and these must minimize the danger of foreshortening the process and uncritically imposing alien models. (There is a complementary danger, less well recognized, of refusing to admit that other people's models may at times be very much like our own in some respects.) At the same time, we are confronted with the inherent difficulties of translation. We must avoid distorting other people's models in the process of reporting them in a language different from that in which they are normally expressed. Finally, it would seem that many indigenous models are rather like icebergs, with much of their mass lying below the surface phenomena of language. As Lévi-Strauss would have it, they are in large part "unconscious" or at least "unconsciously structured" and, in the strict sense of the term, not "known" to and certainly not readily verbalizable by those people who live with them. They are then difficult to discover, and validation of our formulations of them is equally problematic.

Linguists are, of course, accustomed to dealing with difficulties like these and it is, therefore, not surprising that many significant contributions to the anthropologist's task have been made by anthropological linguists or anthropologists who have been ready and willing to put the linguist's findings and methods to use. There are, however, several kinds of linguistics, even so-called structural linguistics, as well as several kinds of anthropological structuralism, the latter label now generally signifying a concern for the isolation, description and, ultimately, comparison of the content and *integral* organization of indigenous cultural systems. Of the several varieties of anthropological structuralism, I consider only two, Lévi-Strauss' "structural anthropology" and what has come to be known as "formal ethnography" in the United States. Both have borrowed extensively from the works of linguists, but they have done so differentially and have been led, for that and other reasons, in diverse though perhaps complementary directions.

LÉVI-STRAUSS' STRUCTURAL ANTHROPOLOGY

Through their cognitive and intellectual processes and through
the exchange of linguistic signs and their meanings, the members of a society produce, maintain, and occasionally modify,
elaborate conceptual schemes, plans or models (compare
Durkheim's "collective representations") which are logically
ordered and which mediate and constrain social transactions
in complex ways. Interpersonal transactions may thus be said
to "express" such models, just as an utterance expresses the
grammar of the language in which it is phrased. But just as a
particular utterance does not exhaust the grammar of its
language, so any particular transaction between persons is a
partial expression of the model or models underlying all
transactions between members of a society. Moreover, a particular utterance may be an imperfect (e.g. slurred) realization of the sound units and rules if its language, and similarly
a particular social transaction may be a permuted expression
of some part or parts of a people's model of social order. Such
models are also expressed in verbal behavior, but again only
partially, and it must be the anthropologist's task to recon-
struct them *in full* (to build his own models of them) from
their partial or permuted expressions in verbal and other
forms of behavior.

It is possible for the anthropologist to do this because
these models are all products of human minds which presumably operate in much the same way as his does. But a
naive imaginative apprehension of other people's models will
not do as an anthropological method; our apprehension of
other people's models must be by means of some systematic,
replicable method. Now since these models are all products
of human minds, they must, perforce, share the "structure"
of the mind, and the anthropologist's task would be facilitated
by a knowledge of that structure. Given such knowledge he
could proceed to use the "code" or "logic" of the processes
of the mind to "decode" any particular product of it, for that
same "code" must have been utilized to construct the model
in the first place.

The structure of the mind is not, however, given to immediate observation. It must be inferred from empirical observations, and the best place in which to begin to look for this structure, or so Lévi-Strauss argues, is in language. This is because, in most societies, there are no indigenous theories of the language spoken, no "grammars" as "conscious models" or explicit sets of rules, so that linguistic behavior is governed entirely by "unconscious models" or "rules." Linguistic behavior is thus that behavior *par excellence* which is governed by rules and structures which are "unknown" to the actors. When expressed in scientifically constructed grammars, these rules and structures are the more accurate representations of the relatively simple order underlying the diversity of observed behavior (utterances) precisely because they are unknown to the speakers of the languages concerned. As already intimated, Lévi-Strauss supposes that people's models of and for experience have also this property of an unconscious structure (as well as an apparent or phenomenal order) and that it is one of the anthropologist's tasks to construct his own models of these unconsciously structured indigenous models, just as the linguist constructs a grammar.

This task is complicated by the fact that people usually have conscious models ("folk grammars," so to speak) of or for their behavior in society, and anthropologists have sometimes taken these to be the *totality* of their culture. As Lévi-Strauss sees it, these conscious models are often only the products of "reinterpretation" or "secondary rationalization." They may be designed to "perpetuate" an established order rather than to explain it, and, therefore, may be seriously misleading if taken as representations of the order in concrete transactional relations or as representations of an ideal order. Moreover, neither the conscious or unconscious models nor the apparent statistical order in transactional relations may be said to constitute *the* structure of the society concerned. These various forms of order, like the anthropologists' representations of them, are not *the* structure itself; they are, all of them, only *variant expressions of structure,* which is, again, in Lévi-Strauss's view, the "logic" or "code" whereby the human mind operates. This same structure must underlie and be expressed in not only a people's conscious and unconscious models but also in their concrete social transactions. It must be expressed in the anthropologists' representations of these models, and we shall not be able to make systematic sense of or integrate the different forms and levels of order in human-behavior-in-society until we know and make use of our knowledge of that structure.

Since, in Lévi-Strauss' view, structure, once discovered, must be a tool of analysis, ethnographic analysis is not seen as a procedure for discovering structure. Structural analysis is rather a procedure for sorting out levels of social phenomena, for learning about relations between phenomena at the same or different levels and for relating the conscious and unconscious models of the same or different peoples to one another. In the process of structural analysis the anthropologist will discover unsuspected unconscious models, and his understanding of the phenomenal order in each model, system of models, and system of social transactions should be considerably enhanced. He will discover nothing new about structure itself, but only about the ways in which it may be "expressed."

It should be emphasized that Lévi-Strauss' argument is neither reductionistic nor idealistic (in the philosophical sense), though some have understood it to be. He does not argue that structure is the only "reality" and he is not concerned to reduce sociological facts to psychological facts. He argues: "To derive from language a logical model which, being more accurate and better known, may aid us in understanding the structure of other forms of communication, is in no sense equivalent to treating the former as the origin of the latter" (*Structural Anthropology*, 1963, p. 83).

This passage alludes to a fundamental feature of Lévi-Strauss' approach to the study of human-behavior-in-society. Anthropology, he argues, should seek to become a science of relationships, like economics and linguistics, and these sciences should view themselves as concerned with different forms of *communication*. The consequence would be an ability to relate the findings of these various sciences to one another in terms of the "rules of communication." Thus, it might be possible to demonstrate, for example, that the "rules of kinship and marriage," the "economic rules" and the "linguistic rules" of the same or different societies are all systematically interdependent. To do this, it would not be necessary to reduce each of these types of communication (of women, of goods and services, and of messages, respectively) or their rules to one another. We might instead find that the rules ordering or regulating these different types of communication are best conceived as variant expressions of one another. Though each regulates the circulation or communication of a different kind of "material," the rules for each type of circulation could be at least *formally* similar and perhaps identical. One task would then be to formulate further rules for transforming the rules for one type of communication into the rules for another type. We would also be in a position to discern whether or not the rules regulating a particular type of communication, say "marriage," in different societies are understandable as variants of one another. If all of this could be demonstrated, then, as Merleau-Ponty observed: "It [would be] sound practice to envision at the limit the program of a universal code of structures, which would allow us to deduce them from one another by means of rules of transformation, and to construct possible systems different from the existing ones—if it were only to direct empirical observation, as it has already been directed, toward certain existing institutions which would remain unnoticed without this theoretical anticipation" (*Signs,* 1964, p. 181).

In Lévi-Strauss' view, no society or social system can ever be grasped as a whole. Each society must be seen as composed of diverse and perhaps only more or less interdependent "orders" of relationships between persons, or between persons and objects, or between objects as conceived by persons. These orders differ in the "materials" being interrelated (e.g., women, kinds of objects, events, etc.) or in the ways in which the same materials are conceived as interrelated. Yet each order must have the same ultimate structure as all others. Because of this we may, again, find that each order is but a conditioned variant of some other, the conditioning variables being the kinds of materials involved and the "dialectical" rules governing the number of possible permutations or variations. As noted above, this possibility of viewing "orders" (such as models of and for experience) as conditioned variants of one another applies cross-culturally as well as within the boundaries of a single society.

Cross-cultural comparisons are possible not only because we use the same method (the method of structural analysis) to analyze models from different societies, but for other reasons as well. The content and organization of any particular model is seldom created wholly anew and is usually but a conditioned variant of the content and organization of another model, perhaps simply one held by the same people at an earlier time. Since societies are historically interrelated it therefore follows that their models may be genetically related, though perhaps via complex chains of transformations or permutations which it is the anthropologist's task to work out.[1] Moreover, it will be found that models from historically unrelated societies will sometimes be quite similar since the nature of the materials being ordered is determinate, if not wholly determinable. Finally, men everywhere face many of the same problems in imputing meaning and order to their experiences, often coming to the same or substantially the same kinds of solutions to such problems.

A fundamental question of interest is then, what does the study of linguistic behavior teach us about the structure of the human mind? A difficulty here is that few linguists have much to say on this matter and what the few have to say is vigorously denied by other linguists. Lévi-Strauss appears, however, to accept as established the position of Roman Jacobson (and others) as expressed in the latter's theory of a universal set of distinctive phonological features.

LINGUISTICS AND THE STRUCTURE OF THE MIND

For the speakers of most languages, the constituent units of their languages are "words," but the linguist, in his effort to reduce the continuous flow of speech sounds constituting utterances to a few elementary components and their orderly

[1] For some examples of this, see *Le Cru et le cuit* and "The Bear and the Barber," *Journal of the Royal Anthropological Institute,* Vol. 93, 1963.

relations, is forced to go further than this. He finds it useful to describe a language in terms of, for example, its morphemes, phonemes and, ultimately, those articulatory "distinctive features" which in various combinations constitute the phonemes.

Jacobson's theory holds that all articulatory distinctive features may be described as the values, or "terms," of two-valued dimensions of opposition. Furthermore, he argues that all phonemic systems may be most economically and, at the same time, satisfactorily described in terms of a single and small set of some twelve or so kinds of binary opposition. In Jacobson's view, this scheme is more than just an economical and fairly satisfactory descriptive device. The fact that it is possible suggests to him, and to others, that it reflects something inherent in the nature of language itself: "a set of binary selections is inherent in the communication process itself as a constraint imposed by the code on the participants in the speech event, who could be spoken of as the *encoder* and *decoder*" (*Preliminaries of Speech Analysis*, 1963 ed. p. 9; with Fant and Halle).

Furthermore, perhaps this situation reflects something inherent in the nature of the "encoder" and "decoder." Halle, for example, suggests: "If it is true that a small set of attributes suffices to describe the phonetic properties of all languages of the world, then it would appear quite likely that these attributes are connected with something fairly basic in man's constitution, something which is quite independent of his cultural background." Halle continues, with proper caution, to venture that "these attributes will prove to be productive parameters for describing man's responses to auditory stimuli in general."[2] Elsewhere, however, Jacobson and Halle are somewhat more expansive in their suggestions. In reply to queries as to whether the "dichotomous scale" is indeed inherent in the structure of language, they reply that it must be. For a system of distinctive features based on binary oppositions is the "optimal code" that can be used, and "it is unwarranted to assume that the speech participants in their encoding and decoding operations use a more complicated

[2] M. Halle. "On the Bases of Phonology," in Fodor and Katz (eds.), *The Structure of Language*, 1964, p. 329.

and less economic set of differential criteria." Also, they argue, the phonemic code "is acquired in the earliest years of childhood and, as psychology reveals, in a child's mind the pair is anterior to isolated objects. The binary opposition is a child's first logical operation." (*Fundamentals of Language,* 1956, p. 47)

There is, however, room for doubt. It is, first of all, by no means a certainty that all phonemic systems can be satisfactorily described in the terms of Jacobson's distinctive features (though some linguists will contradict me and maintain that it is). Secondly, a scheme admitting only binary discriminations at the elementary level of language structure may be the most economical in the abstract, but it is not necessarily so in practice. Some linguists find that Jacobson's scheme yields relatively uneconomical and formally unsatisfactory results for some languages. While not denying that most dimensions of opposition are indeed best treated as two-valued, they see no reason to rigidly impose this pattern on all dimensions and find that admitting at least some three-valued dimensions of opposition (as Jacobson did at first) may yield the most economical and satisfactory results for some phonemic systems.[3] Also, it would seem that psychology's testimony on the matter of the organization of human thought processes (the human mind) is a mixed one. Certainly, Paiget, for example, makes much (and rightly so) of the logical operation of binary opposition, yet other psychologists manage to discuss thinking and linguistic behavior without appeal to any such process, or they relegate it to a less important place as one among several basic processes.[4]

Most importantly, where is the warranty for assuming that *all* levels of language organization—especially those most charged with the duty of carrying meaning—are structured in terms of bipolar oppositions, even if the phonemic level were so structured? Isomorphism of structure (in Lévi-Strauss'

---

[3] Curiously, almost all of this discussion has been oral, much of it in the form of papers presented at linguistic professional meetings, and relatively little has appeared in print so far.

[4] See especially W. Garner, *Uncertainty and Structure as Psychological Concepts,* 1962, and D. Berlyne, *Structure and Direction in Thinking,* 1965.

sense) at all levels cannot be merely assumed, unless, of course, one is prepared to accept that the structure of phonemic systems most directly reflects the structure of the mind, which is imposed on all its products. But as we have just seen, it is not at all certain that the structure of phonemic systems and the structure of the mind are identical.

Lévi-Strauss' analyses of cultural systems depend, however, on the principle of binary opposition. This principle, he assumes, is not only that which orders human thought processes, it is that which orders all of nature: man's mind and nature have the same structure. Lévi-Strauss' procedure is to search out all binary oppositions relevant to one another in a particular cultural system. He feels that a satisfactory analysis has been achieved when he is able to comprehend and represent a system or sub-system of norms, ideas, ideals (and actions) as one composed of a set of bipolar oppositions, though perhaps a rather elaborate set, and of features not always very obvious. To those familiar with the ethnographic data under analysis, Lévi-Strauss' interpretations frequently appear rather forced and his emphasis on bipolar oppositions too constraining.[5] But even his critics have to admit that his method of analysis may bring out previously unperceived details and, better yet, point to alternate and highly suggestive lines of inquiry. Clearly then, there is much of value in what Lévi-Strauss has to say, and his writings have revived, in social anthropology at least, a concern for the strategic significance of symbols and symbolic systems in human social behavior. Yet rigid adherence to his method could, in the end, block rather than advance that concern. There is good reason to believe that in anthropology, as in other sciences, and perhaps more so than in the physical and biological sciences, there can be no set of first principles for analysis which, if rigidly adhered to, will inevitably yield the proper results.[6]

[5] See e.g., E. R. Leach, "Telstar et les aborigenes," *Anales Economies, Societes, Civilisations,* Vol. 19, 1964; "Anthropological Aspects of Language: Animal Categories and Verbal Abuse," in E. Lenneberg (ed.), *New Directions in the Study of Language,* 1964.

[6] See J. Bronowski, "The Logic of the Mind," in *American Scientist,* March 1966; also Bronowski's *The Identity of Man,* 1965.

AMERICAN FORMAL ETHNOGRAPHY

Although Lévi-Strauss practices something he calls structural analysis, this bears only a superficial resemblance to what American anthropologists, who also think of themselves as "structuralists," have come to call "descriptive" or "structural semantics" and "formal ethnographic description." It must be admitted, however, that descriptive semantics is hardly an American or an anthropological invention. Jacobson's early work on the semantics of case systems and Trubetzkoy's on phonology are often credited as being ancestral to this endeavor, and much of value has been taken from Charles Morris' "theory of signs," formal logic, the psychology of cognition, and even Malinowski's early work in ethnographic semantics.

The goals of formal ethnography are much the same as those of Lévi-Strauss' structural anthropology: to isolate, describe, compare and generalize about people's conceptual models and their significance for human-behavior-in-society.[7] The methods and some of the assumptions are, however, quite different. Practitioners of formal ethnography have been concerned to develop the methods and assumptions for the structural analysis of words and natural sets of words (something Lévi-Strauss once thought impossible, though I am sure he would now admit its feasibility and utility), while Lévi-Strauss has been concerned with the development of a much more broadly applicable analytical system. Although formal ethnographic analysis has so far been confined largely to the study of kinship terminological and other indigenous classificatory systems (e.g., animal and plant taxonomies), its procedures are, however, of considerably greater relevance. Some practitioners are now extending the method to the

---

[7] On descriptive semantics see F. G. Lounsbury "Linguistics and Psychology," in S. Koch (ed.), *Psychology: A Study of a Science*, Vol. 6, 1963. On formal ethnography see K. Romney and R. D'Andrade (eds.), *Transcultural Studies in Cognition, American Anthropologist*, Vol. 66, No. 3, Part 2, 1964, and E. Hammel (ed.), *Formal Semantic Analysis, American Anthropologist*, Vol. 67, No. 5, Part 2, 1965.

construction of large-scale ethnographic statements which integrate findings about the content and organization of numerous distinguishable models from a single culture and others are exploring the ways in which models from different cultures may be assimilated to one another.

The practitioners of formal ethnography begin with structural semantic analyses of linguistic signs: they abstract from the objects which certain linguistic labels denote those common distinctive inherent features which make those objects a "kind." They find that to do this successfully it is usually necessary to construct a model of an entire conceptual domain, that is, an indigenous model. Like Lévi-Strauss, the formal ethnographer therefore seeks to build models of models which he hopes to be able to relate to one another. But he differs from Lévi-Strauss not only in methods but also in the choice of criteria of satisfactoriness. For the formal ethnographer, the model he constructs is satisfactory when it is *adequate,* that is, when it enables him to specify the conditions under which particular labeling responses, or other forms of behavior, if relevant, would be judged *appropriate* (which is not to say "right" or "good" in any moral sense) by his informants. He is not determined that the systems of distinctive semantic features he isolates, or the larger organizations he postulates, should be describable as founded exclusively on binary oppositions, though this form of opposition is, it seems, most common. The formal ethnographer is concerned that his analysis be economical, but he recognizes no simple and universally relevant criteria of economy. In short, of the several criteria of satisfactoriness of a formal account or structural analysis—simplicity, consistency, and adequacy—Lévi-Strauss stresses the former two and, in practice, virtually ignores the latter, which is stressed by the formal ethnographer.

Further differences and similarities between Lévi-Strauss' approach and that of at least some American anthropologists may be illustrated through consideration of certain aspects of Lévi-Strauss' structural analysis of "kinship," particularly as set forth in *Les Structures élémentaires de la parenté.* There Lévi-Strauss presents a model of a kind of society which has been the subject of much debate among social anthropologists. The debate is of considerable significance, for it concerns the very nature of kinship and of kinship-based social orders.

KINSHIP SYSTEMS

In the 1940's Lévi-Strauss' attention was focused on kinship and he argued that any "'kinship system' comprises two quite different orders of reality": "a system of terminology," or of recognized categories of kinsmen, and "a system of attitudes," or of prescribed behaviors and sentiments deemed appropriate between the members of the various categories. Since he thought it impossible, at least at that time, to subject the terminological system to structural analysis, and since he thought that the content and organization of these categories is, in any event, not difficult to discern, he ventured to apply the method of structural analysis to "systems of attitudes."

Now in order to begin to deal with the order in a system of prescribed behaviors and sentiments we must specify who the behaviors and sentiments are between, and if we are to compare the orders of such systems of relationships we must be able to specify the units involved in such a way that they will be identifiable cross-culturally. In other words, what are the basic materials that may be differentially ordered from society to society?

The materials are "kinsmen," and thus the problem is to specify what it is that makes people one another's kinsmen *from their point of view*. Yet this must be done in such a way that some essential component of whatever it is that constitutes "kinship" as conceived in a particular society will be found to occur in most, if not all, human societies.

This is a most difficult requirement, and it, or another version of it, has persistently plagued anthropology. To phrase the issue more concretely, the difficulty is that if we argue that kinship as we Western Europeans conceive it consists in relations of biological or, more specifically, "consanguineal" connections between persons, then in many societies there are no "relations of kinship" of and for the members of those societies. For it is true that in some societies people have no knowledge of and no conceptions about "consanguineal" connections between persons. We may, however, generalize the notion of "consanguineal" connection so as to include all concepts of biological connectedness (through the sharing of blood, flesh, bone, etc.) and then speak of all of these as concepts of *genealogical* connection. If genealogical connections are taken as the basis of kinship generally, a great many more societies then fall into our conceptual net. In *Les Structures* Lévi-Strauss practiced just this sort of conceptual expansion, at least implicitly, and conceived of kinship somewhat more abstractly than it is conceived in particular societies, but without misrepresenting or falsely construing people's concepts in the process. He seems to have assumed that in all of the societies he dealt with genealogical connections, of one kind or another, are recognized, and that persons so connected to one another are conceptually aggregated into categories which we may call kinship categories. Furthermore, certain social relationships are deemed proper between the members of these categories and the person relative to whom (Ego) they are so categorized. Although not all members of a given society may be thought to be genealogically connected to one another, non-kin may be assimilated to both kinship categories and social relationships according to various criteria, such as descent group membership. In this way, kin categories and relations may serve as the underlying model for the organization of social relationships throughout the whole society.

Now the kind of social order Lévi-Strauss was concerned with in *Les Structures* was one that, he argued, could be understood in terms of a set of elementary relations of kinship and a set or sets of rules for combining these elementary relations into a larger and complex system, or rather a variety of larger systems each of which could be seen as no more than variant of another in the same series. He also addressed himself to what he took to be the related problem of the *origin* of kinship systems: how did they arise out of nature?[8]

Lévi-Strauss argued in this way: Systems of kinship and

[8] For a brief version of Lévi-Strauss' theory see "The Family," in H. Shapiro (ed.), *Man, Culture and Society*, 1956.

marriage are one in origin and in their contemporary manifestations. Kinship as a social, "integrating" or "communicating" phenomenon came into existence with the prohibition of incest. The incest taboo is a "rule," probably the first cultural rule, and it precludes sexual and therefore marital relations between certain close kinsmen. Moreover, the prohibition on incest automatically forces a man or woman to "marry out" of his or her own "kin group" and it is, therefore, but the negative aspect of a positive rule, that is, the rule of exogamy. The incest taboo, in Lévi-Strauss' view, is essentially a rule relating to "groups" and its effect is to establish relationships of exchange between them, thus literally creating society, by forcing groups to exchange women either directly or indirectly through other groups. (Women rather than men are exchanged because male/female relationships are essentially asymmetrical; men dominate women, at least jurally, in all human societies.) Therefore, a kinship system, as a system of transactions or "exchanges," requires women to be exchanged, men with the rights to exchange them (these rights given by "biological" connection since there could be no other basis for them), other men to accept the women in marriage, and, finally, children of those women to perpetuate the system.

This argument gives us a basis for the determination of the nature of "the atom of kinship," that is, that minimal set of relationships that could be said to be the basic component of any kinship system *as a system of communication based on the exchange of women.* Now although an incest prohibition almost always forbids sexual (and marital) relations between a man, his sister and his daughter, neither this unit nor that consisting of a man, his wife and their children, could be the atom of kinship, in the above sense. For where could the man have gotten his wife, and, via her, his own daughter except from another man and in exchange for his own sister? Thus, in Lévi-Strauss' view, the basic unit of a kinship system again, as a system of exchange, is the set of "biological" (read genealogical) relations brother/sister and mother/child and those cultural relations husband/wife and sister's husband/wife's brother which are set up either directly through men exchanging their sisters in marriage or indirectly through the exchange of the sister of one man for the goods or services of another man. The basic oppositions are thus brother/sister, mother/child, husband/wife and brother-in-law (or wife-giver)/brother-in-law (or wife-taker). Others, such as father/child, were regarded, it seems, as derivative; the father/child relation is one set up by the husband/wife and mother/child relations.

Lévi-Strauss then went on to analyze the ideal orders or "systems of rules" of those societies in which these "elementary structures" received their fullest expression, that is, societies whose normative orders appear to be based on "a rule of cross-cousin marriage." (If direct or indirect exchange of women is assumed as a general rule the overall system that results can be described as one of "preferential" or "prescriptive cross-cousin marriage.") As noted above, Lévi-Strauss wanted to show that although the various empirical systems exhibit considerable apparent diversity they could in fact be demonstrated to bear definite formal relations to one another since all are built, as it were, on the same base. Although we can see from his work that this is probably true, it may be argued that Lévi-Strauss did not demonstrate it in detail, and he left room for disagreement as to the minimal constituents or primitive elements of such systems, the rules for ordering these elements into systems, and the rules for transforming the systems into one another. For these reasons, there is still much discussion of and disagreement about the value of *Les Structures,* and this discussion is bound to flare up once again with the long-awaited publication of the English translation, promised for late 1966.

The basic issue is the nature of those categories whose members are linked by "cross-cousin marriage" or, as some anthropologists prefer, "prescriptive alliance." Are they constituted of kinsmen, either wholly or at least in part and in such a way that genealogical connections are essential components of any analytical models of these systems? Or are these categories defined by reference to some other criteria, such as group affiliation, so that genealogical connections, though they may be present and recognized in the societies, are none the less substantially irrelevant to an understanding of their plans of or for social order? For those who take the latter view, the appellation "cross-cousin marriage" is utterly mistaken and Lévi-Strauss' treatment of these systems as though their rules were primarily, if not entirely, phrased in terms of genealogical connections thoroughly distorts their true nature by imposing alien concepts upon them.

This is a difficult issue to resolve since the indigenous models of social order of which these categories are components are by and large "unconsciously structured" or at least not readily verbalizable. Therefore, much of any analysis must be founded on inference. The anthropologist must indeed construct, from disparate materials, a model which matches as closely as possible the indigenous models he is concerned to understand. Thus the anthropologist must resort to structural analysis and to the use of methods borrowed most immediately from linguistics. Moreover, since we are concerned here with the meanings of words (category labels), and especially with the perceived properties of persons, or of relationships between persons, which are the criteria of their categorization, we must also employ a semantic theory, a theory of the relations between signs and their objects. In order for this issue to be satisfactorily resolved it is essential that we be able to subject the terminological systems in which these category labels occur to structural (semantic) analysis. And this, it will be recalled, is precisely what Lévi-Strauss found so impossible to do in 1945, and presumably at the time he was writing *Les Structures.*[9] Thus there is a critical flaw in *Les Structures:* its lack of structural semantic analysis of those categories and sets of categories, the content and interrelations of which constitute the social orders Lévi-Strauss was concerned to comprehend. Yet another and related flaw is Lévi-Strauss' utilization of an essentially unanalyzed, though not wholly mistaken, concept of "kinship," and before we can proceed any further this concept must be clarified.

Kinship as a socializing, integrating or communicating agent, as the basis of a mode of exchange, as Lévi-Strauss well knows, has its roots in both nature and the human mind. Kinship in its elementary cultural form is a "purely con-

[9] See *Structural Anthropology*, 1963, p. 35-37.

ceptual" phenomenon and its analysis as the basis of a mode of communication must begin at that level, that is, at the level of people's concepts that may be called their concepts of kinship. These relate to but are not the same as kinship as a biological or "natural" phenomenon, and the latter has an ultimate relevance for the anthropologist since it sets certain limits to the forms that such concepts may take. One of the themes of *La Pensée sauvage* is the extent to which the content of verbal categories may be constrained by the nature of the real objects or events which are being categorized: Empirical biological science tells us that a mature man and woman having sexual intercourse are always required for reproduction, and their offspring share with them and one another certain of their features as a consequence of genetic transmission and genetically controlled developmental processes.

Despite some ethnographic reports to the contrary, it would seem that all people have theories of the reproductive process. These theories always require the existence of a mature man and woman having sexual intercourse, and they always hold that, as a consequence of bisexual reproduction, the offspring share certain features with one or the other of their parents and perhaps one another (e.g., blood, bone, and flesh, *but also* appearance, soul, etc.). In the great majority of instances, it is also held that these, again let us call them, genealogical connections naturally entail certain normative social relationships between the persons so connected (just as our "fathers," whose "blood" we share, are "naturally" affectionate towards and protective of us). Certainly, different societies perceive "the facts of procreation" differently; there is a very real sense in which the "facts" may be said to differ from society to society, but they differ only within certain clear limits and have, it seems, always much the same formal organization. All such theories provide for the existence of a "genitor" and a "genetrix" (parents), their offspring, who are related to one another (as "siblings"), and, of course, for the existence of what may be called genealogical connections between such persons. It would seem that the relationship between kinship in nature and kinship in culture is that if people are to explain the former to themselves in anything like a satisfactory fashion there are certain rather narrow and naturally imposed limits to the forms their theories may take.

Kinship as a cultural phenomenon has to do first and foremost with any particular person's (Ego's) relationships with other persons as these are given by and conceived to result from what his culture takes to be "the facts of procreation." From the point of view of any particular Ego, he, his mother, and her brother do not constitute a procreative or socially self-sufficient unit. His father (genitor) is as necessary to his existence as is his mother (genetrix), so that from this perspective it is the triad self-genitor-genetrix that should be considered to be the "atom" of kinship. For it is that unit which "generates" the elements "brother" and "sister" who, in Lévi-Srauss' theory, are forbidden to one another precisely because of their common origin which defines them as "brother" and "sister." Clearly then, the elementary relations of a kinship system are: parent/child, husband/wife, and sibling/sibling (though the parent/child relation may be more fully expressed as father/child and mother/child, and the sibling/sibling relation as brother/brother, brother/sister and sister/sister). These are of course the constituent relationships of the nuclear family.

Now although the nuclear family as a domestic unit may not be present in every human society—it is present as such in better than ninety-nine per cent—recent advances in our understanding of man's nature as a primate have established that the nuclear family has its roots in that nature. The pervasive recurrence and durability of the nuclear family as a human social institution is the product of several factors: the extreme and prolonged dependency of human infants and children upon both male and female adults; the division of labor between the adult sexes which arises out of behavioral differences related to the sexual differences; and the enduring unions that tend to form between adults of the opposite sex in order to rear children, in order to subsist, and because of the continual sexual receptivity of the human female. Yet the internal organization of each family contains within itself the sources of that family's undoing. Children mature and seek their own identities and rewards as adults, and to do this they must become psychologically independent of their parents.

This psychological separation from the natal family is, in part at least, facilitated by the fact that the rearing of children by adults appears to establish behavioral patterns and attitudes between them which are substantially, though not wholly, incompatible with the adult sexual response. Moreover the rearing of children *together* may have much the same effect. Men and women are thus perhaps psychologically predisposed, not innately but because of the elementary learning situation and experiences within it, to look outside their nuclear families for mates. Moreover, it is essential to human survival that they do so, for nuclear families can survive only in cooperation with one another.[10]

These are, however, only tendencies imposed by certain features of man's particular primate nature, and these tendencies have their strongest and most direct expression only under certain external conditions—those physical environmental and technological conditions of human existence which give rise to band organization. Elsewhere, and even there, they require a certain amount of *normative* reinforcement precisely because they are not instinctual and have such enormous adaptive values. It is for these reasons, it would appear, that men so often and so strongly insist upon wedlock (which unites groups as well as individuals) as a precondition for the legitimate engendering of children while continuing to recognize, as observant men must, that it is not a natural precondition and therefore not one of the bases of kinship proper. (Thus where I wrote, above, of the husband/wife relation as an elementary kinship relation, "husband" and "wife" were merely convenient labels for the parties to what might be better described as a "co-contributor" relationship.)

It should not go unnoted that the range of the incest prohibition is not necessarily coextensive with the boundaries of the exogamous unit in all human societies. It is sometimes permitted to have sexual relations with persons whom one is not free to marry. This suggests that although the rule prohibiting incest and the rule requiring exogamy may be, in origin, but the negative and positive aspects of one and the

---

[10] For additional discussion see J. R. Fox, "Sibling Incest," in *British Journal of Sociology*, Vol. 13, 1962; Lévi-Strauss, "The Family," 1956.

same rule they are not *now* necessarily so. In many human societies they are functionally differentiated rules and the seeds of this differentiation lie in the difference between the psychological predispositions underlying the incest taboo as opposed to the social value of a rule of exogamy, which has somehow become institutionalized in all human societies through selective processes which are everywhere present.

Now, it will surely be asked, does it really matter that social anthropologists, including Lévi-Strauss, may have been mistaken about the elementary structure of kinship? The answer must be that it most definitely does matter, for if much of the argument of *Les Structures* is to be salvaged from the attacks of its critics, and much of it is by all means worth salvaging, something like this theory of the nature of kinship systems must be adopted. Lévi-Strauss' theory is unacceptable because it deals not with kinship systems proper but with systems of kinship and marriage, and these two systems, though apparently interdependent in all human societies, are none the less discriminable, and the former must be analyzed separately and prior to its use in a more comprehensive analysis. Yet if it is realized that Lévi-Strauss' "atom of kinship" is perhaps the basic unit of a system of communication based on the exchange of women and that the elementary structures of kinship (as here formulated) deal with nothing more than the logically primitive elements of a system of kinship categories, there is, I would argue, no basic contradiction between these two theories; they are, indeed, complementary.

Although the details of the argument cannot be developed here, the theory of kinship systems presented here, or one very much like it, is the only one that will serve as a rational basis for the kinds of American anthropologists are now doing.[11] This view of kinship and analyses of kinship terminological and classificatory systems that recently developed techniques of formal semantic analysis permit us to see that

[11] See especially F. G. Lounsbury, "A Formal Account of the Crow- and Omaha-type Kinship Terminologies," in W. Goodenough (ed.), *Explorations in Cultural Anthropology*, 1964; "Another View of The Trobriand Kinship Categories," in E. A. Hammel (ed.), *Formal Semantic Analysis*, 1965.

Lévi-Strauss was substantially correct in certain assumptions basic to the argument of *Les Structures:* that each of the societies he discussed has a system of categorizing persons on the basis of the form of genealogical connection presumed to exist between those persons and an Ego; and that such connections and categories are the basic elements of these societies' models of their social orders. Coupled with a semantic theory which permits us to argue that certain of the members of these categories are the primary members and that others are included by virtue of specifiable rules of genealogical and/or extra-genealogical extension of category membership, this view of kinship permits us to affirm the basic correctness of many of Lévi-Strauss' analyses. We can now both perceive *and demonstrate* that the kinship systems of most societies are complexly ordered and multi-leveled systems which, as Lévi-Strauss argues, are composed of several distinct kinds of social phenomena. These are, first, concepts which may be called concepts of genealogical connection, and second, norms governing transactional relationships between categories of persons believed to be so connected. Beyond this genealogically-based *conceptual* order there is the order of *transactions* between persons believed to be kinsmen, and beyond this the conceptual and transactional orders of relationships between persons *acting as kinsmen.* In many societies, although the recognized range of kinship proper is fairly narrow, the norms which organize social relationships among recognized kin are metaphorically extended, often in modified form, into the realm of relationships between persons who are known not to be kin (e.g., fellow clansmen and often well beyond). In this way, the model for relationships between kinsmen proper may become the model for social relationships generally.

From this point of view, the rules on which systems of "cross-cousin marriage" are founded are substantially what Lévi-Strauss took them to be: A man is supposed to marry a female cross cousin (of one or another specified sort), or he may be supposed to marry a woman who belongs to the kinship category of which the appropriate cross cousin is, logically at least, the primary member; that woman may or may not be a kinsman, depending upon the principles which determine the genealogical and extra-genealogical extensions of the term for the appropriate cross cousin(s). These systems vary in the cross cousin(s) specified as marriageable and also in the rules of genealogical and extra-genealogical extension of the term for the appropriate cross cousin(s), but all are understandable and formally (and sometimes historically) interrelatable as variants of one another. (Remember, we are here considering the underlying model, not the actual marriages or alliances that are made, for which we would have to construct a much more complex "statistical" model.)

However, it is true, as numerous critics of *Les Structures* have argued, that the label "systems of cross-cousin marriage" is often inappropriate. The reason for this has little or nothing to do with the fact, often pointed out by these critics, that in such societies men often do not marry their closest cross cousins or even genealogically more distant ones, and perhaps not even women who are in the same kin category as their cross cousins. It is rather because in order to argue that such societies are ordered by "a rule of cross-cousin marriage" there must be a category of kinsmen the linguistic label for which is accurately translatable as "cross cousin." Now there can be a category of "cross cousins" only where there is an opposed category consisting of "parallel cousins," and in most of these societies those kinsmen whom we anthropologists would describe as parallel cousins are classified as "siblings." Moreover, structural semantic analyses of such systems have revealed that the inherent opposition is sometimes not "cousin" versus "sibling" but a much less obvious one, such as "a distant kinsman of my own generation" vs "distant kinsman of another generation." The opposition "cross" vs "parallel" (or "same-" vs "opposite-sex") in the parental linkages may be relevant to the differentiation of "close" and "distant" kin, but the terms "cousin" and "cross cousin" are best avoided if one wishes to represent most accurately the indigenous meanings of the relevant category labels.

Recent developments in the structural analysis of cultural systems make it possible to criticize certain aspects of the argument of *Les Structures* and to revise some of its particular analyses. However, these developments also reveal that whatever flaws there may be in *Les Structures* they are attributable more to the state of theory in social anthropology and to the quality of ethnographies in the 1940's than to any lack of anthropological perspicacity on Lévi-Strauss' part. *Les Structures* brought together and ordered in a challenging, and, I am sure Lévi-Strauss would agree, preliminary fashion, a mass of the ethnographic data whose essential interrelations had been previously only vaguely perceived. *Les Structures* achieved a degree of integration of ethnographic data for which it is difficult indeed to cite a parallel, and social anthropologists will of necessity sharpen their wits on it for years to come.

Structural analysis in art and anthropology

Sheldon Nodelman

One of the most striking phenomena of advanced twentieth century thought has been the increasing utilization of the concept of structure as a tool of understanding in the human sciences. The *anthropologie structurale* of which Claude Lévi-Strauss—though he modestly disclaims the role of its founder—is beyond doubt the leading practitioner and most serious theoretician, and the predominantly German school of *Strukturforschung* in the plastic arts, whose most distinguished representative has been the late Guido von Kaschnitz-Weinberg, have developed their methods spontaneously and independently, and out of intellectual sources which are, at least overtly, quite different. The concept of structural analysis held by Lévi-Strauss is founded on the functional analysis of society as a global unit carried out by Marx, and upon the example of the modern structural linguistics of Troubetzkoy and Jakobson. *Strukturwissenschaft* developed from the ideas of Alois Riegl, and has been profoundly influenced by the thinking of German romantic and neo-Kantian philosophy, up to and including Husserl. In view of this disparity of overt intellectual origins, it may be asked whether what the two schools intend by structural analysis is in any sense the same thing, whether there is in fact any substantial identity of method between these two methodologically self-conscious disciplines. Such an inquiry must take into account the quite different objects of investigation in each case: on the one hand, the structure of a social organism or institution; on the other, that of a work or group of works of plastic art. Lévi-Strauss' various treatments of the problems of art, extremely interesting as these are, are not of special interest here, for he deals with works of art primarily as instruments within the social process, the structure of which process, rather than the intrinsic structure of the works, he seeks to elucidate.

The *Strukturforschung* school—if such a term be appropriate to so loose a grouping—arose during the 1920's in Germany and Austria but has remained little-known in the United States. Under the leadership of Kaschnitz, its most systematic and most theoretically oriented practitioner, it has had its greatest impact in the field of ancient Mediterranean archaeology, with the adherence of such distinguished scholars as Bernhard Schweitzer, Friederich Matz and others. It has been applied also, in highly individual ways, to problems of later Western art history by Hans Sedlmayr and Theodor Hetzer—in the latter case with conspicuous brilliance. There is perhaps an analogy between Lévi-Strauss' preference for applying his structural-analytic techniques to the study of "primitive" societies, and the predominant concern with the ancient art of the Mediterranean, from prehistoric through classical times, which has so far characterized the *Strukturforscher*. Such culturally remote objects of study appear to have particularly solicited structural-analytic methods of investigation. One reason for this is the handicap imposed by such remoteness in space or time upon the collection of data and more especially upon its interpretation. Not only is the whole matrix of assumptions, values and usages in which the social institution or work of art under study is rooted initially unknown to the observer, but its reconstruction is complicated by the fact that his spontaneous interpretations are founded, consciously or unconsciously, on patterns of behavior and attitude proper to his own culture, and thus must almost always be wrong. These difficulties inspire a desire for more refined and accurate method, which the student of our own culture, with abundant material directly accessible and with a pre-existing pattern of explanatory assumptions already available to him, may not feel so keenly. The very difficulties which encourage the application of structural-analytic techniques to the study of remote societies or their works offer simultaneously a great advantage of method. The observer, as perforce a non-participant in the convention—and value-systems presupposed by the society or work of art in question, is strengthened in his objectivity by the minimization of his tendency to interpret—or indeed even to observe—in terms of affective reactions generated by a naturally biased and partisan position. Even more important, he has the opportunity to stand outside and over against the object of his investigation and to view it, so far as his evidence reaches, as a whole. It is obviously impossible to view as a whole in this sense—in the full range of its actions and in the mutual implication of all its parts—a culture or work of art within whose value-system one is oneself plunged, of which one has an inside perspective, and whose most vital aspects can hardly be brought into explicit consciousness and rationally examined, simply because they are pervasive, forming an unspoken background for conscious activities and opinions.

Both *Strukturforschung* and *anthropologie structurale* assert an integrative and holistic viewpoint, maintaining that the reality of the object consists in the full texture of all its relations with its environment. Both view these relationships in operational terms, as modes of action rather than states of being. Anything which obstructs our view of the unconstrained development of the object in these various relations, whether as the result of ignorance or—as in positivism—of methodological prejudice, flattens out, impoverishes and necessarily falsifies our understanding of it. (Falsifies, inasmuch as a reduced view is not simply a portion of the larger whole, quantitatively diminished but qualitatively unchanged, but a distortion, since the balance between the parts is arbitrarily upset.) The observer must scrupulously avoid the imposition of artificial and limiting categories upon the object, and must frame his tentative theoretical model in the broadest and most inclusive relevant terms. As Lévi-Strauss writes:

> On the observational level . . . all the facts should be carefully observed and described, without allowing any theoretical preconceptions to decide whether some are more important than others. This rule implies, in turn, that facts should be studied in relation to themselves (by what kind of concrete process did they come into being?) and in relation to the whole (always aiming to relate each modification which can be observed in a sector to the global structure in which it first appeared). ("Social Structure," in *Structural Anthropology*, New York-London, 1963, p. 280.)

Thus the observer must at first confine himself to pure description, confident, as in Husserlian phenomenology, that the entire being of the phenomenon is inherent and given in its appearance, if the appearance be permitted to present itself fully and without distortion. He must "bracket out" or "put in parentheses," to use Husserlian terminology, whatever presuppositions may impede his grasp of the essence of the phenomenon—even, Husserl would say, the supposition of the material existence of the phenomenon. This *askesis* of the observer with respect to any practical or indeed "existential" considerations which might affect his view of the phenomenon, this "epoché" as Husserl calls it, is fundamental—though emphatically not final—to the method of structural analysis practiced by Lévi-Strauss and by the *Strukturforschung* school. Both maintain that the thus clarified structure and pattern of implications, as well as the functional significance, of the phenomenon need not—indeed usually will not—correspond to any explicitly formulated and verbalized awareness, in the minds of those who create and sustain them. Lévi-Strauss observes:

> A structural model may be conscious or unconscious without this difference affecting its nature. It can only be said that when the structure of a certain type of phenomenon does not lie at a great depth, it is more likely that some kind of model, standing as a screen to hide it, will exist in the public consciousness. For conscious models, which are usually known as "norms" are by definition

> very poor ones, since they are not intended to explain
> the phenomena but to perpetuate them . . . The more
> obvious structural organization is, the more difficult it
> becomes to reach it because of the inaccurate models
> lying across the path which leads to it (ibid., p. 281).

Kaschnitz objects to the prevailing terminology and methods
of art history, most especially to those of Wölfflin, and to
"style-criticism" in general, that these are concerned solely
with the effect of the work of art upon the beholder, with the
"impression," rather than with the interior structure of the
work itself; it is only *after* this structural description, undertaken with the aid of the bracketing method, that the interaction between work and spectator can usefully be discussed.
All "esthetic" considerations, and all categorizing schemes
which evaluate the work by criteria beyond itself—for instance,
its resemblance or lack of resemblance to "nature"—must
at this stage be eliminated. The result of such an analysis,
radically purified of distorting elements, and shaped solely in
terms of the internal structure and dynamics of the work
itself, aspires to an objective validity which would hold, as
Lévi-Strauss says, "for any possible observer."

The concrete execution of such an objective structural
analysis is of course not so simple, for subjective attitudes
banned from one level of thought have a way of reintroduc-
ing themselves into the argument at another level. Even a
neutral phenomenological description is necessarily concerned
not only with "primary data" but with inter-relationships—it
is not, indeed, the terms themselves which are truly elementary, says Lévi-Strauss, following Troubetzkoy, but the
relations between them—and such relationships obtain at varying levels of generality and structural importance. Indeed
each element, to be properly apprehended at all, must present
itself as utterly impregnated with its formal rank and level
of generality, for these are constitutive of it. The category
"individual element" and the category "relationship between
individual elements" are not genetically or functionally independent of one another, but are mutually implicatory, so
that the initial choice of terms posits a set of structural relations between them. The decision to objectify one or another
aspect of the phenomenon into an independently manipulable

term or attribute immediately polarizes the totality and in effect pre-imposes a particular structure upon it before the analysis proper has begun.

Here as elsewhere, thus, the hermeneutic circle is inescapable. It need not, however, be vicious; and it is one of the virtues of Kaschnitz's and Lévi-Strauss' methodological absolutism that one's attention is forced upon the problem of rationally evaluating the spectrum of possible strategies of analysis. An analytical strategy must of course satisfy the criterion of internal validity: that is, each of its various terms and the relations generated between them must entail the rest by logical necessity. This consideration, however, is purely formal, relating to the design of the inquiry itself, and thus too abstract to seize readily the full substance of the phenomenon. The decisive criterion for the selection of an analytical strategy is that of *meaning*. The phenomenon is understood not merely as a brute existent, but as a system of references beyond itself to the ultimate plane of human reality. "Anthropology," says Lévi-Strauss, "aims to be a semiological science and takes as its guiding principle that of meaning" ("The Place of Anthropology in the Social Sciences," *ibid.*, 364). Kaschnitz conceives of the work of art as a kind of total symbol of the cosmos:

> If one understands works of plastic art as human images of the world and the divine and human realities obtaining within it, then structure is the mode of action of that energy which in art stands symbolically for those cosmic or divine forces as they reflect themselves in our conceptions and in our imagination.

("Bemerkungen zur Struktur der Ägyptischen Plastik," *Kunstwissenschaftliche Forschungen* II, 1933, p. 8).

Not only is another dimension added to the phenomenon by the recognition of its referential nature, but the introduction of the concept of meaning as the ultimate horizon in terms of which such human products as works of art and social institutions are to be interpreted immediately imposes a hierarchical order upon the various possible strategies of structural analysis. The phenomenon may be interrogated in many ways, each exposing one or another of its modes of action, but each strategy of interrogation must situate itself in terms of the highest strategy, whose goal is to allow the fullest self-revelation of the phenomenon in its signification as an image of the world and of man's situation in that world. Thus it becomes possible consciously to adjust levels of inquiry to levels of signification in the phenomenon itself, and to eliminate the confusion of categories and of criteria of evaluation which have handicapped the proper assessment even of individual phenomena, to say nothing of more complex groupings.

The manner in which Lévi-Strauss has applied the consequences of this position to the understanding of social phenomena will be familiar to the reader. The works of Kaschnitz provide the best example of how the *Strukturforschung* school has used them to elucidate the structure of individual works of art and subsequently the historical development of art forms, as exemplifying stages of human consciousness. Once the character of the work of art as a world-symbol has been recognized, and once the specific capacities for particular kinds and levels of symbolic reference inhering in its various formal components are plotted out, it becomes possible to read modifications of structure in the work as indicative of modifications of consciousness in a consistent and readily verifiable way. The superiority of such a coherent and rational hermeneutic system to the prevailing chaos of impressionistic judgments is obvious; equally obvious is that the choice of analytical strategy here is crucial.

The first attempt at a systematic and coherent analysis of works of art in terms of essential categories was carried out by Alois Riegl, who was not only the direct source from which the ideas and method of *Strukturforschung* were developed, but from whose works have been drawn much of the theoretical presuppositions and critical terminology of twentieth century art-historical discourse—often degraded into commonplaces and used in ignorance of their origin and original meaning. Riegl's much-discussed concept of *Kunstwollen,* the superindividual "will to form" which impresses itself upon all the artistic products of a particular age and culture, was created in conscious opposition to the dominant late nineteenth century view of stylistic development, an evolutionary progress, on the Darwinian model, in the techniques of illusionist representation of a presumably constant "nature." By stressing the autonomy of the *Kunstwollen* of each particular period, its susceptibility to criticism and evaluation only in terms of its own immanent intent, Riegl made of it a "bracketing" device in the sense discussed above. In his search for fundamental categories of structural analysis, which would be of sufficient generality to encompass all works of art, and of sufficient specificity to elicit relevant information from them, Riegl departed from the elemental fact that works of plastic art as such are apprehended as phenomena in our visual field. Contemporary empirical psychology was in the process of discovering that ordinary visual experience is in fact a complex synthesis, built up out of the experience of the full gamut of the senses under widely varying conditions of perception, depending on different characteristic life-situations. Riegl proposed to analyze works of art in terms of how they were articulated with respect to certain *basic categories of visual perception,* thus effecting a Kantian revolution in art-critical method; for this purpose he distinguished two categories of privileged epistemological significance, whose interplay most strongly marks our ordinary visual experience: the *haptic* (or tactile) and the *optic,* referring to the kinds of knowledge of the external world fundamentally proper to the senses of touch and of sight. Individual works of art, and historically linked groups of works, might be understood as being articulated according to varying syntheses of these perceptive modes, and of the kinds of knowledge intrinsic to them. In these terms Riegl not only carried out formal analyses of an unprecedentedly rigorous and penetrating kind upon individual works of art, but in his *Spätrömische Kunstindustrie* (1901) mapped out a grandiose developmental scheme in which the structural transformation from Egyptian to Classical Greek to medieval (and in a larger sense to all post-antique) art, consisted in the shift from predominantly haptic to balanced haptic-optic to predominantly optic criteria of artistic formation.

Many aspects of Riegl's thought were marked by the positivistic, mechanistic, and deterministic prejudices of his time and do not withstand criticism. Kaschnitz has acutely differentiated the time-bound and obsolete from the permanently valuable in the thought of Riegl in a review of the second edition of the *Spätrömische Kunstindustrie* (*Gnomon* V (1929), 195 ff.), which is itself a major theoretical exposition of the *Strukturforschung* position. Riegl's fundamental analytical strategy, springing as it did out of a mechanistic psychology which sought to reduce sensory experience to physiological processes in the observer, still depended in a sense on the external appearance of the work of art, thus still on the subjective "impression," though in a far more rigorous form than heretofore. Kaschnitz, while retaining and exploiting the insights afforded by the haptic-optic antithesis, has sought to found it in a deeper, more penetrating analysis, one exposing the objective structure of the work of art and articulating it as an independent, internally focused phenomenon. In so doing he has re-founded the analytical categories at the disposal of *Strukturforschung,* and has immensely expanded and refined them. The resulting instrument is far more rigorous in its elucidation of the consequent, mutually implicatory internal structure of the work, and far more flexible and subtle in its powers of description. The work of art appears as a complex metaphoric (or as Kaschnitz would say, symbolic) structure, in which references to a wide range of human experiences (by no means exclusively, or even mainly, those given in acts of immediate sense-perception) are interwoven both hierarchically and at the same level. The primary field within which the work of art displays itself is not, for the purposes of Kaschnitz's analysis, the subjective, observer-oriented one of the visual field, but the objective one of *space,* which is common to both observer and work, and can thus permit the explication of the necessary relations between them. Space as the medium in which the observer concretely lives and moves, possesses moreover an existential dimension which is lacking in the more specialized and abstract concept of "visual field." The latter is in fact logically and genetically dependent upon the former, as is implied even in Riegl's own basic distinction between "near vision" and "far vision," and as has been repeatedly demonstrated in modern psychology. The work of plastic art, situated in this spatial continuum, modifies it by its very existence and thus generates a particular esthetic space, coextensive with the space of natural life and action, but qualitatively different from it. (Compare Lévi-Strauss' notion of "social space" and "social time" in "Social Structure," *op. cit.,* p. 289).

The spatial continuum includes two classes of existents: so-called "empty" space and solid objects. The relations between these two, the absoluteness or the blurring of the boundaries between them, the susceptibility of each to playing the role of primary object of artistic formation, with the other negative in respect to it, are major objects of *Strukturanalyse*. Only solids, indeed, can be directly worked by the hand of man, and are traditionally regarded as the only "things" *sensu strictu,* with empty space being merely their negative ground. But it is quite possible, as Kaschnitz has stressed in his discussions of Roman architecture and sculpture, for the formed solid to be treated merely as an instrument to mold and shape *spaces* which are dominant over their containers, which are infused with an energy and directionality of their own, and which clearly are here the primary objects of artistic formation.

Natural space, and more especially its solid-object constituents, are not however merely passive and static. In addition to mere extension, they have the property of embodying or being permeated by *forces*. In the natural world the more obvious of these forces are of two kinds: one, omnipresent in all solids, is that of gravity; the other is the vital, animal energy resident in living creatures. One is mechanical, predictable and rational; the other organic, spontaneous and irrational. These energies, singly or in interaction, contain within themselves a repertory of imagery and a structural logic which permeate the work, and radically affect the manner in which it charges and transforms the space of the beholder, making it a space in which certain interactions of force prevail, and certain kinds of action are possible.

A paradigmatic analysis conducted in these terms is Kaschnitz's essay on the structure of Egyptian sculpture (*Kunstwissenschaftliche Forschungen II,* 1933, 7 ff.). There the observed qualities of Egyptian free-standing statuary and relief—massive solidity, enclosure, and isolation of forms; the tyranny of stiff cubic and geometrical modules over the shapes of nature;

painstaking care in the enumeration of naturalistic details and an amazingly life-like "portraiture" combined with absolute exclusion of organic relations and connections between parts of the body; the prevalence of these and other conventions in two-dimensional representation, both in the individual figure and in group composition—which heretofore had been explained, if at all, largely by vague, random, and mutually inconsistent generalizations, were studied as a purposefully organized system and brought into relation with the historically attested function of the work of art in Egyptian culture. Starting from the observed conformity of Egyptian aesthetic space and the solid forms contained within it to an orthogonal grid of vertical, horizontal and depth directions, meeting at angles of 90 degrees, Kaschnitz points out the derivation of this system from the force of gravity which inheres in masses, which alone confers upon the vertical and the right angle their stringency and authority. In Egyptian sculpture, however, all traces of tectonic conflict, of the mutual striving and balancing out of weight and support within the mass, are eliminated. Instead of a more complicated and internally differentiated equilibrium, capable of imaging the reciprocal interactions of organic life, there reigns a simple equilibrium, passive and conflictless, in which the implication of possible action and change are rigorously excluded. The transposition of the forms of life into a world of timeless, static being, at the cost of the suppression of all organic relations and real actions, is characteristic not only of Egyptian sculpture in the round, but of relief, in which the actions engaged in or the burdens borne by the represented figures cause no complementary displacements, no sign of exerted energy, within them, and of Egyptian architecture, in which the great columns, with their spreading capitals, give no hint of bearing any weight from above. The often amazing naturalism of Egyptian sculpture answers to the need to provide a magical surrogate, a facsimile of the dead man, to help sustain his existence in the afterlife. But any suggestion of real movement, of representation of a real event—as distinct from the timeless, fossilized pseudoevent, whose value is exemplary rather than narrative—would subvert the whole purpose of this funerary art. Real action would necessarily reintroduce time and change, and with them inevitably death, into the system; and the entire function of Egyptian monumental art is to exclude death, to conserve existence at the cost of petrifaction, by a process parallel to that of the mummification of the dead. Kaschnitz's account, grossly oversimplified here, is an exemplary fulfillment of the three conditions once enumerated by Lévi-Strauss for an effective structural analysis: it is *concrete*, since it deals with real qualities of the sculpture itself; *simplificatory*, since it provides an intellectually economical rationale for a very diverse set of facts; and *explanatory*, since it exposes the meaning and intent of the phenomenon as a human endeavor. (Cf. Lévi-Strauss, "Structural Analysis in Linguistics and Anthropology," in *op. cit.*, p. 35 ff.)

The advantages of the structural-analytic method are not confined to the penetration with which individual works or classes of works can be studied. It seeks to establish categories of analysis sufficiently fundamental that very different works of art, the products of historically remote cultures, may be effectively and meaningfully compared. Kaschnitz's comparative analyses of Egyptian and Greek sculpture, and his studies of the historical development of the latter (the best example of which, perhaps, is "Über die Rationalisierung der 'mythischen' Form in der klassischen Kunst," *Festschrift Bernhard Schweitzer*, 1954) may be mentioned here, as well as his subtle exposition of the relations between Greek sculpture and that of Etruria and Rome, in which the external form of the one is grafted onto the utterly different fundamental structure of the others, and is inevitably transformed thereby in function and meaning. (For this Italic-Roman sculpture, devoid of any genuine or intrinsic tectonic structure, but upon which the surface appearance of Greek tectonically articulated form is imposed, Kaschnitz coined the adjective "pseudo-plastic.") Out of this method emerges the possibility of a history of art not as a mere chronological enumeration based on external categories, but as a consequent and rational account of the evolution of artistic structure, a project upon which Kaschnitz was engaged, within the limits of the ancient world, at the time of his death.

Such a history of art, with a program of inquiry founded upon the nature of the work of art as a cosmic symbol or metaphor, containing within itself and in the terms proper to itself a global account of the human world which engendered it; and with a set of analytical categories corresponding to the fundamental categories of human existence, would be able to deduce *from the form* of the work of art, the whole range of assertions about being, knowledge and value posited by it.

The structural-analytic method is thus capable, not only of supplying new and independent evidence for the evolution of human consciousness in periods and cultures whose traditions are otherwise accessible to us, but also of rendering accessible, through the surviving material artifacts which are so often our only evidence, the structure and content of consciousness in epochs for which we have no written documents. The account, moreover, which this method renders has the special advantage of representing an unconscious, or not overtly conscious, content: the concrete meaning and value structure which materially informs the work, and which may never be explicitly formulated in verbal terms by the culture concerned, or only in the form of inadequate or deceptive rationalizations. Kaschnitz himself, influenced no doubt by the anonymous character of much of the archaeological material with which he was concerned, and which to a large extent sprang from cultures in which the self-consciousness of the individual, including the individual artist, was far less stressed than in the modern West, has tended to ascribe a super-individual and normative character to structural systems. Here he threatens to revert to the position of Riegl's *Kunstwollen* whose inadequacies he himself has so acutely criticized, and to assert the priority of the hypostatized abstract category, which exists only within the realm of the inquiry, over the concrete and material reality of individual artist and work, who exist in the world. The applicability of the techniques of structural analysis to the unique and individual, as well as to the general and inclusive phenomenon, though questioned by Kaschnitz, has been indicated by Hetzer's illuminating studies of such highly individual and self-conscious artists as Giotto, Raphael, and Titian. Nevertheless, there is a sense in which Kaschnitz was right to stress the super-individual and unconscious character of the structural system in any period. It derives this character not from any immanence as a "real" historical force, to which individual events are in some way logically subjected, but from the social role of the work of art as an instrument of communication, which confers upon it a public and socially active character. Every work of art has the dual role not only of "expressing"—that is, more accurately, of synthesizing—a total world-view or global state of consciousness, but also of actively transforming the consciousness of the observer, of imposing its structure upon him, and of forming, as part of a collectivity of other works, a "language" of artistic form, which conditions, in terms of its presuppositions and possibilities, the perception of every individual. This language, continually in the process of modification and reshaping by individuals, nevertheless is always the necessary ground upon which such reshaping may occur. One of the most important characteristics of this system is its tacit, largely unconscious nature; it is so "obvious," so all-pervasive, that there is no easily available horizon against which it can be seen as a special phenomenon, deserving of notice or comment. One stands within it, rather than over against it. Thus it is not normally accessible to critical inquiry, or to conscious manipulation. Kaschnitz once termed the structural presuppositions of an age so binding that not even the greatest genius could overstep them. His error is revealed in his choice of metaphor; these presuppositions are not external limits, but modes of action internal to artistic creation; the genius does not "overstep" them, but transforms them from within, consciously or not, but in any case effectively. The structural-analytic method has the unique capacity of illuminating these pervasive and fundamental categories, which condition all directly observable phenomena. The value of such knowledge for the understanding of the way works of art function as communicating devices, influencing as well as reflecting our whole perception of reality, need hardly be pointed out.

Much remains to be done in the field of *Strukturforschung*. Its systematic extension to the problems of individual style is only one such task. The analytical categories immensely deepened and refined by Kaschnitz over those of Riegl, are susceptible of yet greater extension and precision. The great advances made in recent decades in the psychology of perception, and the sharpened awareness of the modes of human existence in the world which perception reflects, largely the work of the school of phenomenological psychology—among others one may mention the names of Maurice Merleau-Ponty, Erwin Straus and Ludwig Binswanger—open the possibility of far more penetrating and flexible categories of structural description. A history of art in terms of the essential meaning and effect of artistic phenomena, their role as instruments of human consciousness, is yet to be written.

That the method of *Strukturforschung,* as sketched out above, coincides in so many respects with that of the *analyse structurale* practiced by Lévi-Strauss ought not to surprise us. They share deep roots in the functionalist, organismic attitudes which have distinguished a broad front of creative twentieth-century thought, and which may perhaps be ultimately traced back to Hegel. A structuralist anthropology and a structuralist art history have much to learn from one another, the latter in regard to the manner in which works of art are conditioned by their social role as means of communication, the former in regard to the way these works, once existing, condition and transform the social environment which evoked them. The *Strukturforschung* of the future, that yet to be built on the existing foundations, has much to learn, in self-critical sharpening of method as well as in heightened awareness of the social texture in which works of art occur, from the achievements and from the example of Claude Lévi-Strauss.

Bibliographical note

A survey and exposition of the *Strukturforschung* movement in archaeology is given in the first chapter of F. Matz, *Geschichte der griechischen Kunst I* (Frankfurt, 1950), without however any extensive discussion of concrete method or philosophical foundations. For these see, in addition to the works of Kaschnitz himself, B. Schweitzer, "Strukturforschung in Archäologie und Vorgeschichte", *Neue Jahrbücher,* 1938, pp. 162 ff.; H. Sedlmayr, "Zu einen strengen Kunstwissenschaft", *Kunstwissenschaftliche Forschungen I,* 1931, pp. 7 ff.

In addition to his important *Mittelmeerische Grundlagen der antiken Kunst* (Frankfurt, 1944) Kaschnitz's contributions to the theory and practice of structural analysis are contained in numerous scattered articles in scholarly journals. Many of the most important of these have been collected as the first two volumes of his *Ausgewählte Schriften*

Jacques Lacan and the structure of the unconscious

Jan Miel

Over thirteen years ago, a conflict which had been developing for some time within the *Société psychanalytique de Paris* erupted into a crisis, a crisis which ended in the resignation from the Society of five of its leading members: Drs. Daniel Lagache, Jacques Lacan, Françoise Dolto, Juliette Favez-Boutonier, and Blanche Reverchon-Jouve. As none of these wished to separate himself from the International Psychoanalytical Association, but only to escape the domination of the hierarchy of the Paris Society, their case was taken up at the 18th International Congress and they were to be considered for membership as an independent French psychoanalytical group, to be called the *Société Française de Psychanalyse*. In spite of the fact that there was precedent for such a split (e.g., in the New York Society) in which both groups were then recognized, the Central Executive ruled that the five French analysts had in effect separated themselves from the International Association by their resignation from the Paris Society; as a result, they were not even allowed to be present at the discussion of their case, which, as was pointed out at the meeting, was "anomalous and unfair."

As to the reasons for this split, the group headed by Lagache and Lacan claimed it was purely a question of personalities. One of the "personalities" involved, the reigning Princess of the Paris Society, Dr. Marie Bonaparte, said on the contrary it was a question of discipline in the matter of

---

(Berlin, 1965), published by the German Archaeological Institute; the third volume is the torso of his great unfinished structural history of ancient Mediterranean art.

training. The two interpretations are perhaps not incompatible: the sort of personality which would insist on "discipline" (in the sense of total submission in a theoretical disagreement) in a supposedly scientific society is bound to create conflict and ultimately rebellion. In any case, "discipline" (or the personalities representing it) carried the day in that 18th Congress; none less than Miss Anna Freud reproached the Lagache-Lacan group with that impardonable sin of "carrying the quarrel . . . into the outer world" (they had in fact published a short circular clarifying their reasons for resigning, primarily for the benefit of the students in training, about half of whom chose to follow the new group); as a result Miss Freud refused to allow them even provisional membership pending an investigation.

A committee was formed for the purpose of investigating the crisis in French psychoanalysis, to report back at the next congress. At the 19th Congress, the President, Dr. Heinz Hartmann, simply announced that the committee had done its work and that the Central Executive had decided to exclude the new group from membership. The reason advanced was that the group did not offer adequate training facilities, a reason which loses some of its point if one recalls that the new *Société Française de Psychanalyse* had only been in existence for three years, while the Paris Society, in all its decades of existence had only just succeeded in establishing a training institute. There was no discussion either at this Congress or at the earlier one of any of the issues involved—even the question on which "discipline" had to be invoked was never openly stated.[1]

Such procedures must inevitably seem to us in the "outer world"—outside the international psychoanalytic Establishment—grotesque and barbarous. They point, however, to one of the fundamental issues dividing the *Société Française de Psychanalyse* from the International Association—if not from all its members. The question involved is nothing less than, Is psychoanalysis a science? And it is his answer to this question

---

[1] The relevant parts of the Reports of the 18th and 19th International Psycho-Analytical Congresses may be read in the *International Journal of Psycho-Analysis*, XXXV (1954), 276-278; and XXXVII (1956), 122.

that will, I think, be seen ultimately to be the most important contribution of Dr. Jacques Lacan, and perhaps the most important contribution since Freud.

When the newly formed group held their own first Congress in Rome in September of 1953, Dr. Lacan's long paper on the "Function and Field of Language and the Word in Psychoanalysis" was quickly hailed as a kind of manifesto of the group and became known familiarly as the "Discourse of Rome."[2] He subsequently undertook to edit a more-or-less annual publication entitled *La Psychanalyse*, the first volume of which, on "Language and the Word," appearing in 1956, attracted the attention of linguists, philosophers, anthropologists, and literary men, as well as those specially interested in psychoanalysis. Subsequent volumes on psychoses, feminine psychology, structuralism, etc. have maintained an extremely high level and Drs. Lacan and Lagache now occupy positions of great prominence in European psychoanalysis, in spite of the fact that their names are still anathema to the International Association, and it is considered in the worst possible taste for members even to allude to them, much less read or quote them.

What then is Dr. Lacan's position on the scientific status of psychoanalysis, and how does it relate to his position vis-à-vis the International Association? Let us look first at the doctrine to which he is opposed, a doctrine he finds all too widely accepted and which he refers to as "neo-Freudian." It consists in regarding Freud as a good doctor who was "lucky enough" (Ernest Jones' phrase[3]) to make certain discoveries of great therapeutic value; however, Freud never really knew what he was doing and, in his attempts to formulate a general theory explaining what he found, involved himself in many inconsistencies or even in such "mystical" flights as the notion of the primordial Father or of the death instinct. Consequently—as this position has it—what must be preserved at all costs are the outward forms of the psychoanalytic interview and the methods of training new analysts, as well as those features of interpretation which are most mechanical and thus

[2] See *La Psychanalyse*, No. 1 (Paris, P.U.F., 1956), 81-166.
[3] In *The Life and Work of Sigmund Freud*, III (New York, 1957), 44.

most easily transmitted; Freud's concern with the posteriority of his doctrine and his establishment of the Central Committee are taken as evidence that he himself accepted this view and wished to preserve an orthodoxy which was essential to the functioning of the system as therapy.

Now one has only to read the correspondence of the period preceding the defection of Rank and Ferenczi to see that the last view is totally erroneous: Freud's attitude was always that their pursuit was scientific and that orthodoxy and conformism were completely out of place.[4] Jacques Lacan, however, goes much farther in what he calls the "return to Freud." He maintains that Freud knew very well what he was doing and that his theoretical formulations, although naturally they will need both revision and expansion, are nevertheless, in spite of the difficulties they present, the only sure guide we have for a truly scientific development of psychoanalysis. For if it is ever to develop beyond a mere shamanism whose power and prestige depend entirely on a rigid set of initiation rites, if psychoanalysts are to become more than the overpaid psychopomps they are on the way to becoming (at least in this country), leading the upper middle classes through their trivial personality crises to a happier "adjustment to modern living"—then surely this development will have to be scientific, achieved through a continual testing of new theories against a background of discoveries already made, and of truths already acquired.

It is easier to invoke scientific method, however, than it is to apply it, especially in a new area, and one involving man's mental life. But surely the basic requirements of any science are that its object be defined and that it have a method of observation and analysis appropriate to that object and capable of discovering its laws. Now the object of psychoanalysis is simply what Freud discovered, namely the unconscious. As to the method appropriate to its study, Freud showed us where to observe it: in dream material and free association, primarily. To find the tools for analyzing this material, we have only to recall—as Dr. Lacan never tires of reminding

---

[4] See, e.g., in Jones, idem, p. 60.

us—that all the material available to the analyst is verbal: what is analyzed in the psychoanalytic interview is not the patient's dreams, but the patient's report of his dreams. We should not be astonished, then, that Freud spends so much time analyzing linguistic associations, puns, slips of the tongue, etc.: linguistic analysis is in fact the method appropriate to the study of the unconscious. At the time of Freud's discovery, however, modern linguistics had not yet been invented (Saussure's lectures were not published until 1916, sixteen years after *The Interpretation of Dreams*), and Freud had to invent his own categories and terminology to describe what he found. But as Dr. Lacan shows, this terminology can be translated directly into the terms and categories of modern structural linguistics, and the correspondence between Freud's terms and system and the structures discovered by modern linguistics is so close and so striking that Dr. Lacan was led inevitably to what is perhaps his most startling conclusion, that *the structure of the unconscious is the structure of language.*

Now the consequences of this principle are first and foremost methodological. Linguistic analysis is thus *the* method appropriate to the scientific study of the unconscious, not just because psychoanalytic material is verbal, but because linguistics can be shown to offer us the best available model to account for the structures and laws of that material. Further, modern linguistic science has developed very rapidly and with its very substantial body of factual and theoretical material, it now offers the one solid basis for the future progress of a field which has been too long fallow, fertilized only by vague biological analogies and an even vaguer adaptational psychology. This does not mean that man is not biological or that we need abandon such a concept as the instinctual drive to understand him. The point is that the drive as it reports to us through the unconscious is no longer the organic mechanism which the biologist can study and account for: it is verbalized, and as a result its structure is entirely different and needs different methods of analysis. In the same way man's relation to society presents only vague and unfruitful parallels with the adaptational life of lower organisms; to account for this relation in detail one needs a structural anthropology—

Lacan's revolution in psychoanalysis has many affinities with the thought of Lévi-Strauss.

But another consequence of the structural approach adopted by Lacan is that our theory of the personality must be revised to account for the peculiar dominance of language and linguistic structures in it. Now one of the main themes of Dr. Lacan's thought over the years has been the ambiguities in the Freudian theory of the ego—the ego as reality-principle in the perception-consciousness system, alongside the destructive and even suicidal force of the ego in the theory of narcissism. In an early paper, he outlined the theory of the importance of the mirror-stage in the early development of the child, that is, the child's discovery of, and complete fascination with its own image in a mirror. This represents, for the child, usually for the first time, the image of itself as a unified controllable body; it is an image which will govern his relations with other children, turning them frequently into games of master and slave, actor and spectator. And here the rejection of reality is obvious: for the reality of one's own sporadically controlled, partially perceived body is substituted the image of a unified, controllable one; for the real recalcitrant individuals in one's peer group, one attempts to substitute an obedient image of oneself. And yet such a stage seems essential to the development of an ego at all.

The development of language shows a similar necessity. The abstractive nature of language, which in fact makes human knowledge possible, amounts to a similar denial of reality. The imposition of single forms or terms on the disparate variety of what we experience is what enables us to know and control our environment, and is essential to intellectual development. Yet this very essential function of language, when it is not part of a human dialogue, and thus subjected to the ordinary laws of human discourse and dialectical thinking, can apply all its powers of displacement, condensation, transfer, to a denial of reality governed entirely by the pleasure principle. Thus is constituted the "forgotten language" of the unconscious, an archaic language lurking beneath our supposedly objective discourse, just as our primal narcissism lurks beneath all our relations to others. Underlying both is an illusion, an illusion of autonomy, objectivity, stability, where there should be a recognition of intersubjectivity and becoming. The psychoanalytic interview, by suppressing normal dialogue—the patient does not talk *to* the analyst, and the analyst does not reply except to point out that the patient usually means something other than what he says—recovers the archaic language and with it the primal relationship expressed in the transference; the two, the linguistic structure and the relational structure, are inseparable, for it is the linguistic structure which renders possible the fixity of the fixation, the repetitiveness of obsession.

In his analyses of the primal narcissism in the structure of the personality, as well as in his effort to understand the unconscious in terms of a larger philosophical framework, Dr. Lacan has been greatly influenced by his extensive knowledge of phenomenological and existential philosophy. For those within that tradition, his writings are filled with insights which have already stimulated new ways of thinking about the person and his relation to meaning. But those addicted to empiricism and logical analysis, to whom the Continental way of philosophizing is both strange and suspect, should not approach his work with a bias—any more than existential thinkers should be put off by his recourse to linguistic analysis and even to combinatorial mathematics; his eclecticism is always founded on what Freud's discovery and his own empirical observations seem to demand. As will be seen from the text which follows, his thought is the very opposite of an obscurantism or mysticism of any variety. It is rather an attempt to bring the obscure and the mysterious—whether they originate in the depths of our illusions and fantasies, or in the height of our aspiration toward meaning and value—into the purview of a thought that is rigorous and in the best sense scientific. And we need, perhaps, to be reminded by Dr. Lacan that the goal of scientific rigor, as also of psychoanalysis, is not to acquaint us with a "reality" which is and must always be unspecifiable and unverifiable, but rather to restore us to that domain to which as human beings and users of language we are condemned and, which we commonly call the truth.

A final word about Jacques Lacan's style. As a friend or doctor to some of the leading artists and poets of this century, and himself an acute critic of literature, Dr. Lacan does not begrudge himself the advantages of a complex literary expression. His style, called Mallarmean by his own colleagues, is distinctive and at times immensely difficult—deliberately so, for reasons that he partly elucidates in the introduction to the following text. In the translation of that text (in fact, one of his most accessible) the choice has been consistently for clarity rather than for an imitation of the precise effect of the original. In some cases a single- (not to say simple-) minded formulation may have replaced what was more accurately presented through a poetic ambiguity; however, in a text which is after all primarily didactic, this seemed the only course to follow. Those who read French will, it is hoped, turn to the original and enjoy its challenge as much as did the translator.

The insistence of the letter in the unconscious

Jacques Lacan

Of Children in Swaddling Clothes
O cities of the sea, I behold in you your citizens, women as well as men tightly bound with stout bonds around their arms and legs by folk who will have no understanding of our speech; and you will only be able to give vent to your griefs and sense of loss of liberty by making tearful complaints, and sighs, and lamentations one to another; for those who bind you will not have understanding of your speech nor will you understand them.
　　　　　　　　　　　　　—Leonardo da Vinci

If the nature of this contribution has been set by the theme of this volume of *La Psychanalyse*, I yet owe to what will be found in it to insert it at a point somewhere between the written and spoken word—it will be halfway between the two.
A written piece is in fact distinguished by a prevalence of

the "text" in the sense which that factor of speech will be seen
to take on in this essay, a factor which makes possible the
kind of tightening up that I like in order to leave the reader
no other way out than the way in, which I prefer to be difficult.
In that sense, then, this will not be a written work.

The priority I accord to the nourishing of my seminars each
time with something new has until now prevented my drawing on such a text, with one exception, not outstanding in the
context of the series, and I refer to it at all only for the general level of its argument.

For the urgency which I now take as a pretext for leaving
aside such an aim only masks the difficulty that, in trying to
maintain this discourse on the level at which I ought in these
writings to present my teaching, I might push it too far from
the spoken word which, with its own measures, differs from
writing and is essential to the instructive effect I am seeking.

That is why I have taken the expedient offered me by the invitation to lecture to the philosophy group of the union of
humanities students[1] to produce an adaptation suitable to my
talk; its necessary generality having to accommodate itself
to the exceptional character of the audience, but its sole object encountering the collusion of their common preparation,
a literary one, to which my title pays homage.

How should we forget in effect that until the end of his life
Freud constantly maintained that such a preparation was the
first requisite in the formation of analysts, and that he designated the eternal *universitas litterarum* as the ideal place for
its institution.[2]

And thus my recourse to the movement of this speech,
feverishly restored, by showing whom I meant it for, marks
even more clearly those for whom it is not meant. I mean that
it is not meant for those who for any reason, psychoanalytic
or other, allow their discipline to parade under a false identity; a fault of habit, but its effect on the mind is such that the
true identity may appear as simply one alibi among others, a
sort of refined reduplication whose implications will not be
missed by the most acute.

---

[1] The lecture took place on 9th May 1957 in the Descartes Amphi-
theatre of the Sorbonne.
[2] *Die Frage der Laienanalyse*, G.W., XIV, pp. 281-283.

So one observes the curious phenomenon of a whole new tack concerning language and symbolization in the *International Journal of Psychoanalysis,* buttressed by many sticky fingers in the pages of Sapir and Jespersen—amateurish exercises so far, but it is even more the tone which is lacking. A certain seriousness is cause for amusement from the standpoint of veracity.

And how could a psychoanalyst of today not realize that his realm of truth is in fact the word, when his whole experience must find in the word alone its instrument, its framework, its material, and even the static of its uncertainties.

I. THE MEANING OF THE LETTER

As our title suggests, beyond what we call "the word," what the psychoanalytic experience discovers in the unconscious is the whole structure of language. Thus from the outset we have alerted informed minds to the extent to which the notion that the unconscious is merely the seat of the instincts will have to be rethought.

But this "letter," how are we to take it here? How indeed but literally.

By "letter" we designate that material support which concrete speech borrows from language.

This simple definition assumes that language not be confused with the diverse psychic and somatic functions which serve it in the individual speaker.

For the primary reason that language and its structure exist prior to the moment at which each individual at a certain point in his mental development makes his entry into it.

Let us note, then, that aphasia, although caused by purely anatomical lesions in the cerebral apparatus which supplies the mental center for these linguistic functions, produces language deficiencies which divide naturally between the two poles of the signifying effect of what we call here "the letter" in the creation of meaning.[3] A point which will be clarified later.

[3] This aspect of aphasia, very suggestive in the direction of an overthrow of the concept of "psychological function," which only obscures every aspect of the question, appears in its proper luminosity in the

The speaking subject, if he seems to be thus a slave of language, is all the more so of a discourse in the universal moment of which he finds himself at birth, even if only by dint of his proper name.

Reference to the "experience of the community" as the substance of this discourse settles nothing. For this experience has as its essential dimension the tradition which the discourse itself founds. This tradition, long before the drama of history gets written into it, creates the elementary structures of culture. And these structures reveal an ordering of possible exchanges which, even unconscious, is inconceivable outside the permutations authorized by language.

With the result that the ethnographic duality of nature and culture is giving way to a ternary conception of the human condition: nature, society, and culture, the last term of which could well be equated to language, or that which essentially distinguishes human society from natural societies.

But we shall not make of this distinction either a point or a point of departure, leaving to its own obscurity the question of the original relation between work and the signifier. We shall be content, for our little jab at the general function of *praxis* in the genesis of history, to point out that the very society which wished to restore, along with the privileges of the producer, the causal hierarchy of the relations between production and the ideological superstructure to their full political rights, has none the less failed to give birth to an esperanto in which the relations of language to socialist realities would have rendered any literary formalism radically impossible.[4]

As for us, we shall have faith only in those assumptions which have already proven their value by virtue of the fact that language through them has attained the status of an object of scientific investigation.

---

purely linguistic analysis of the two major forms of aphasia worked out by one of the leaders of modern linguistics, Roman Jakobson. See the most available of his works, the *Fundamentals of Language,* with Morris Halle (Mouton and Co., 'S-Gravenhage), part II, Chs. 1 to 4.

[4] We may recall that the discussion of the necessity for a new language in the communist society did in fact take place, and Stalin, much to the relief of those depending on his philosophy, cut off the discussion with the decision: language is not a superstructure.

For it is by dint of this fact that linguistics[5] is seen to occupy the key position in this domain, and the reclassification of sciences and regrouping of them around it points up, as is the rule, a revolution in knowledge; only the necessities of communication made us call this volume and this grouping the "human sciences" given the confusion that this term can be made to hide.

To pinpoint the emergence of linguistic science we may say that, as in the case of all sciences in the modern sense, it is contained in the constitutive moment of a formula which is its foundation. This formula is the following:

$$\frac{S}{s}$$

which is read as: the signifier over the signified, "over" corresponding to the line separating the two levels.

This sign should be attributed to Ferdinand de Saussure although it is not found in exactly this form in any of the numerous schemas which none the less express it in the printed version of his lectures of the years 1906-07, 1908-09, and 1910-11, which the piety of a group of his disciples caused to be published under the title, *Cours de linguistique générale,* a work of prime importance for the transmission of a teaching worthy of the name, that is, that one can come to terms with only in its own terms.

That is why it is legitimate for us to give him credit for the formulation S/s by which, in spite of the differences among schools, the beginning of modern linguistics can be recognized.

The thematics of this science is henceforth suspended, in effect, at the primordial placement of the signifier and the signified as being distinct orders separated initially by a barrier resisting signification. And that is what was to make possible an exact study of the relations proper to the signifier, and of the breadth of their function in the birth of the signified.

[5] By "linguistics" we understand the study of existing languages in their structure and in the laws revealed therein; this leaves out any theory of abstract codes sometimes included under the heading of communication theory, as well as the theory, originating in the physical sciences, called information theory, or any semiology more or less hypothetically generalized.

For this primordial distinction goes way beyond the debates on the arbitrariness of the sign which have been elaborated since the earliest reflections of the ancients, and even beyond the impasse which, through the same period, has been encountered in every discussion of the bi-univocal correspondence between the word and the thing, even in the mere act of naming. All this, of course, is quite contrary to the appearances suggested by the importance often imputed to the role of the index finger pointing to an object in the learning process of the infant subject learning his mother tongue, or the use in foreign language teaching of methods sometimes called "concrete."

One cannot and need not go further along this line of thought than to demonstrate that no meaning is sustained by anything other than reference to another meaning;[6] in its extreme form this is tantamount to the proposition that there is no language in existence for which there is any question of its inability to cover the whole field of the signified, it being an effect of its existence as a language that it necessarily answer all needs. Should we try to grasp in the realm of language the constitution of the object, how can we help but notice that the object is to be found only at the level of concept, a very different thing from a simple nominative, and that the thing, to take it at its word reduces to two divergent factors: the cause in which it has taken shelter in the French word *chose*, and the nothing (*rien*) to which it has abandoned its Latin dress (*rem*).

These considerations, however stimulating they may seem to philosophers, turn us aside from the area in which language questions us on its very nature. And one will fail even to keep the question in view as long as one has not got rid of the illusion that the signifier answers to the function of representing the signified, or better, that the signifier has to answer for its existence in the name of any signification whatever.

For even reduced to this latter formulation, the heresy is the same, the heresy that leads logical positivism in search of

---

[6] Cf. the *De Magistro* of Saint Augustine, especially the chapter "De significatione locutionis" which I analysed in my seminar of 23rd June 1954.

the "meaning of meaning" as its object is called in the language its disciples like to wallow in. Whence we can observe that even a text charged with meaning reduces itself, through this sort of analysis, to meaningless bagatelles, all that survives being mathematical formulas which are, of course, meaningless.[7]

To return to our formula S/s: if we could infer nothing from it beyond the notion of the parallelism of its upper and lower terms, each one taken in its globality, it would remain only the enigmatic sign of a total mystery. Which of course is not the case.

In order to grasp its function I shall begin by reproducing the classical, yet faulty illustration by which its usage is normally presented. It is:

TREE

and one can see already how it seems to favor the sort of erroneous interpretation just mentioned.

I replaced this in my lecture with another, which has no greater claim to correctness than that it has been transplanted into that incongruous dimension which the psychoanalyst has not yet altogether renounced because of his quite justified

---

[7] So, Mr. I. A. Richards, author of a work precisely in accord with such an objective, has in another work shown us its application. He took for his purposes a page from Mong-tse (Mencius to the Jesuits) and called the piece, *Mencius on the Mind.* The guarantees of the purity of the experiment are nothing to the luxury of the approaches. And our expert on the traditional Canon which contains the text is found right on the spot in Peking where our demonstration-model mangle has been transported regardless of cost.

But we shall be no less transported, if less expensively, to see a bronze which gives out bell-tones at the slightest contact with true thought, transformed into a rag to wipe the blackboard of the most dismaying British psychologism. And not without eventually being identified with the meninx of the author himself—all that remains of him or his object after having exhausted the meaning of meaning of the latter and the good sense of the former.

feeling that his conformism takes its value entirely from it.
Here is the other diagram:

LADIES   GENTLEMEN

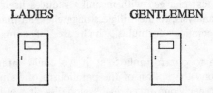

where we see that, without greatly extending the scope of the
signifier concerned in the experiment, that is, by doubling a
noun through the mere juxtaposition of two terms whose
complementary meanings ought apparently to reinforce each
other, a surprise is produced by an unexpected precipitation
of meaning: the image of twin doors symbolizing, through the
solitary confinement offered Western Man for the satisfaction
of his natural needs away from home, the imperative that he
seems to share with the great majority of primitive commu-
nities which submits his public life to the laws of urinary
segregation.

It is not only with the idea of silencing the nominalist debate with a low blow that I use this example, but rather to
show how in fact the signifier intrudes into the signified,
namely in a form which, not being immaterial, raises the very
question of its place in reality. For the blinking gaze of a near-
sighted person would be quite justified in doubting whether
this was indeed the signifier as he peered closely at the little
enamel signs which bore it, a signifier of which the signified
received its final honors from the double and solemn proces-
sion from the upper nave.

But no contrived example can equal the sharpness of the
encounter with a lived truth. And so I am happy to have invented the above since it awoke in the person whose word I
most trust this memory of childhood which having thus hap-
pily come to my knowledge could well be inserted here.

A train arrives at a station. A little boy and a little girl,
brother and sister, are seated in a compartment face to face
next to the window through which the buildings along the
station platform can be seen passing as the train pulls to a stop.

"Look," says the brother, "we're at Ladies!" "Idiot," replies his sister, "can't you see we're at Gentlemen."

Besides the fact that the rails in this story offer a material counterpart to the line in the Saussurian formula (and in a form designed to suggest that its resistance may be other than dialectical), we should add that only someone who didn't have his eyes in front of the holes (it's the appropriate image here) could possibly confuse the place of the signifier and the signified in this story, or not see from what shining center the signifier goes forth to reflect its light into the shadow of incomplete meanings. For this signifier will now carry a purely animal Dissension, meant for the usual oblivion of natural mists, to the unbridled power of ideological Warfare, relentless for families, a torment to the Gods. Ladies and Gentlemen will be henceforth for these children two countries towards which each of their souls will strive on divergent wings, and between which a cessation of hostilities will be the more impossible since they are in truth the same country and neither can compromise on its own superiority without detracting from the glory of the other.

But enough. It begins to sound like the history of France. Which it is more human, as it ought to be, to evoke here than that of England, destined to tumble from the Large to the Small End of Dean Swift's egg.

It remains to be conceived what steps, what corridor, the S of the signifier, visible here in the plurals in which it focuses its welcome beyond the window, must take in order to rest its elbows on the ventilators through which, like warm and cold air, scorn and indignation come hissing out below.

One thing is certain: if the formula S/s with its line is appropriate, access from one to the other cannot in any case have a meaning. For the formula, insofar as it is itself only pure function of the signifier, can reveal only the structure of a signifier in the transfer.

Now the structure of the signifier is, as it is commonly said of language itself, that it be articulated.

This means that no matter where one starts from in order to describe the zones of reciprocal infringement and the areas of expanding inclusiveness of its units, these units are submitted to the double condition of reducing to ultimate distinctive features and of combining according to the laws of a closed order.

These units, one of the decisive discoveries of linguistics, are *phonemes;* but we must not expect to find any *phonetic* constancy in the modulatory variability to which this term applies, but rather the synchronic system of distinguishing connections necessary for the discernment of sounds in a given language. Through this, one sees that an essential element of the word itself was predestined to slide down into the mobile characters which—in a scurry of lower-case Didots or Garamonds—render validly present what we call the "letter," namely the essentially localized structure of the signifier.

With the second property of the signifier, that of combining according to the laws of a closed order, is affirmed the necessity of the topological substratum of which the term I ordinarily use, namely, the signifying chain, gives an approximate idea: rings of a necklace that is a ring in another necklace made of rings.

Such are the conditions of structure which define grammar as the order of constitutive infringements of the signifier up to the level of the unit immediately superior to the sentence, and lexicology as the order of constitutive inclusions of the signifier to the level of the verbal locution.

In examining the limits by which these two exercises in the understanding of linguistic usage are determined, it is easy to see that only the correlations between signifier and signifier supply the standard for all research into meaning, as is indicated in fact by the very notion of "usage" of a taxeme or semanteme which in fact refers to the context just above that of the units concerned.

But it is not because the undertakings of grammar and lexicology are exhausted within certain limits that we must think that beyond those limits meaning reigns supreme. That would be an error.

For the signifier, by its very nature, always anticipates on meaning by unfolding its dimension before it. As is seen at the level of the sentence when it is interrupted before the significant term: "I shall never . . . ," "All the same it is . . . ," "And yet there may be . . ." Such sentences are not without meaning, a meaning all the more oppressive in that it is content to make us wait for it.[8]

But the phenomenon is no different which by the mere recoil of a "but" brings to the light, comely as the Shulamite, honest as the dew, the negress adorned for the wedding and the poor woman ready for the auction-block.[9]

From which we can say that it is in the chain of the signifier that the meaning "insists" but that none of its elements "consists" in the meaning of which it is at the moment capable.

We are forced, then, to accept the notion of an incessant sliding of the signified under the signifier—which F. de Saussure illustrates with an image resembling the wavy lines of the upper and lower Waters in miniatures from manuscripts of Genesis; a double flow in which the guidelines of fine streaks of rain, vertical dotted lines supposedly confining segments of correspondence, seem too slight.

All our experience runs counter to this linearity, which made me speak once, in one of my seminars on psychosis, of something more like spaced upholstery buttons as a schema for taking into account the dominance of the letter in the dramatic transformation which the dialogue can bring about in a subject.[10]

The linearity which F. de Saussure holds to be constitutive of the chain of discourse, in conformity with its emission by a single voice and with its horizontal position in our writing—if this linearity is necessary in fact, it is not sufficient. It applies to the chain of discourse only in the direction in which it is oriented in time, being taken as a signifying factor in all languages in which "Peter hits Paul" reverses its time when the terms are inverted.

---

[8] To which verbal hallucination, when it takes this form, opens a communicating door with the Freudian structure of psychosis—a door until now unnoticed.

[9] The allusions are to the "I am black, but comely . . ." of the *Song of Solomon,* and to the nineteenth-century cliché of the "poor but honest" woman. (Trans.)

[10] We spoke in our seminar of 6th June 1956, of the first scene of *Athalie,* incited by an allusion—tossed off by a high-brow critic in the *New Statesman and Nation*—to the "high whoredom" of Racine's heroines, to renounce reference to the savage dramas of Shakespeare, which have become compulsional in analytic milieux where they play the role of status-symbol for the Philistines.

But one has only to listen to poetry, which perhaps Saussure was not in the habit of doing, to hear a true polyphony emerge, to know in fact that all discourse aligns itself along the several staves of a score.

There is in effect no signifying chain which does not have attached to the punctuation of each of its units a whole articulation of relevant context suspended "vertically" from that point.

Let us take our word "tree" again, this time not as an isolated noun, but at the point of one of these punctuations, and see how it crosses the line of the Saussurian formula.

For even broken down into the double spectre of its vowels and consonants, it can still call up with the robur and the plane tree the meanings it takes on, in the context of our flora, of strength and majesty. Drawing on all the symbolic contexts suggested in the Hebrew of the Bible, it erects on a barren hill the shadow of the cross. Then reduces to the capital Y, the sign of dichotomy which, except for the illustration used by heraldry, would owe nothing to the tree however genealogical we may think it. Circulatory tree, tree of life of the cerebellum, tree of Saturn, tree of Diana, crystals formed in a tree struck by lightning, is it your figure which traces our destiny for us in the tortoise-shell cracked by the fire, or your lightning which causes that slow shift in the axis of being to surge up from an unnamable night into the "Εν Παντα of language:

> No! says the Tree, it says No! in the shower of sparks
> Of its superb head

lines which require the harmonics of the tree just as much as their continuation:

> Which the storm treats as universally
> As it does a blade of grass.[11]

For this modern verse is ordered according to the same law of the parallelism of the signifier which creates the harmony

---

[11] "Non! dit l'Arbre, il dit: Non! dans l'étincellement
    De sa tête superbe
 Que la tempête traite universellement
    Comme elle fait une herbe."
Lines from Valery's "Au Platane" in *Les Charmes*. (Trans.)

governing the primitive Slavic epic or the most refined Chinese poetry.

As is seen in the fact that the tree and the blade of grass are chosen from the same mode of the existent in order for the signs of contradiction—saying "No!" and "treat as"—to affect them, and also so as to bring about, through the categorical contrast of the particularity of "superb" with the "universally" which reduces it, in the condensation of the "head" and the "storm," the indiscernible shower of sparks of the eternal instant.

But this whole signifier can only operate, someone may object, if it is present in the subject. It is this objection that I answer by supposing that it has passed over to the level of the signified.

For what is important is not that the subject know anything whatsoever. (If LADIES and GENTLEMEN were written in a language unknown to the little boy and girl, their quarrel would simply be the more exclusively a quarrel over words, but none the less ready to take on meaning.)

One thing this structure of the signifying chain makes evident is the possibility I have, precisely insofar as I have this language in common with other subjects, that is insofar as it exists as a language, to use it in order to say something quite other than what it says. This function of the word is more worth pointing out than that of "disguising the thought" (more often than not indefinable) of the subject; it is no less than the function of indicating the place of the subject in the search for the truth.

I have only to plant my tree in a locution: climb the tree, indeed illuminate it by playing on it the light of a descriptive context; plant it firm so as not to let myself be trapped in some sort of *communiqué,* however official, and if I know the truth, let it be heard, in spite of all the between-the-lines censures, by the only signifier I know how to create with my acrobatics among the branches of the tree, tantalizing to the point of burlesque, or sensible only to the experienced eye, according to whether I wish to be heard by the mob or the few.

The properly signifying function thus described in language has a name. We learned this name in some grammar of our childhood, on the last page, where the shade to Quintilian, relegated to a phantom chapter of "ultimate considerations on style," seemed in a hurry to get his word in as though threatened with the hook.

It is among the figures of style, or tropes, that we find the word: the name is *metonymy*.

We shall recall only the example given there: thirty sails. For the anxiety we felt over the fact that the word "boat" lurking in the background was only part of the craft employed in this example did less to veil these illustrious sails than did the definition they were supposed to illustrate.

The part taken for the whole, we said to ourselves, and if we take it seriously, we are left with very little idea of the importance of this fleet, which "thirty sails" is precisely supposed to give us: for each boat to have just one sail is in fact the least likely possibility.

By which we see that the connection between boat and sail is nowhere but in the signifier, and that it is in the word-to-word connection that metonymy is based.[12]

We shall designate as metonymy, then, the one slope of the effective field of the signifier in the constitution of meaning.

Let us name the other: it is *metaphor*. Let us find again an illustration; Quillet's dictionary seemed an appropriate place to find a sample which would not seem to be chosen for my own purposes, and for an appropriate dressing I didn't have to go any further than the well known line of Victor Hugo:

> His sheaves were not miserly nor spiteful[13]

[12] We give homage here to the works of Roman Jakobson—to which we owe much of this formulation; works to which a psychoanalyst can constantly refer in order to structure his own experience, and which render superfluous the "personal communications" of which we could boast as much as the next fellow.

Let us thank also, in this context, the author [R. M. Loewenstein] of "Some remarks on the role of speech in psycho-analytic technique" (I.J.P., Nov.-Dec., 1956, XXXVII, 6, p. 467) for taking the trouble to point out that his remarks are "based on" work dating from 1952. This is no doubt the explanation for the fact that he has learned nothing from work done since then, yet which he is not ignorant of, as he cites me as their editor (sic).

[13] "Sa gerbe n'etait pas avare ni haineuse," a line from "Booz endormi." (Trans.)

under which aspect I presented metaphor to my seminar on psychosis.

Let us admit that modern poetry and especially the surrealist school have taken us quite far in this domain by showing that any conjunction of two signifiers would be equally sufficient to constitute a metaphor, except for the additional requirement of the greatest possible disparity of the images signified, needed for the production of the poetic spark, or in other words for there to be metaphoric creation.

It is true this radical position is based on the experiment known as automatic writing which would not have been tried if its pioneers had not been reassured by the Freudian discovery. But it remains a position branded with confusion because the doctrine behind it is false.

The creative spark of the metaphor does not spring from the conjunction of two images, that is of two signifiers equally actualized. It springs from two signifiers one of which has taken the place of the other in the signifying chain, the hidden signifier then remaining present through its (metonymic) relation to the rest of the chain.

One word for another: that is the formula for the metaphor and if you are a poet you will produce for your own delight a continuous stream, a dazzling tissue of metaphors. If the result is the sort of intoxication of the dialogue that Jean Tardieu wrote under this title, that is only because he was giving us a demonstration of the radical superfluousness of all meaning to a perfectly convincing representation of a bourgeois comedy.

It is manifest that in the line of Hugo cited above, not the slightest spark of light springs from the proposition that his sheaves were neither miserly nor spiteful, for the reason that there is no question of the sheaves' having either the merit or demerit of these attributes, since the attributes, as the sheaves, belong to Booz who exercises the former in disposing of the latter and without informing the latter of his sentiments in the case.

If, however, his sheaves do refer us to Booz, and this is indeed the case, it is because they have replaced him in the signifying chain at the very spot where he was to be exalted by the sweeping away of greed and spite. But now Booz himself has been swept away by the sheaves, and hurled into the outer darkness where greed and spite harbor him in the hollow of their negation.

But once *his* sheaves have thus usurped his place, Booz can no longer return there; the slender thread of the little word *his* which binds him to it is only one more obstacle to his return in that it links him to the notion of possession which retains him in the very zone of greed and spite. So *his* generosity, affirmed in the passage, is yet reduced to less than nothing by the munificence of the sheaves which, coming from nature, know not our caution or our casting out, and even in their accumulation remain prodigal by our standards.

But if in this profusion, the giver has disappeared along with his gift, it is only in order to rise again in what surrounds this figure by which he was annihilated. For it is the figure of the burgeoning of fecundity, and this it is which announces the surprise which the poem sings, namely the promise which the old man will receive in a sacred context of his accession to paternity.

So, it is between the signifier in the form of the proper name of a man, and the signifier which metaphorically abolishes him that the poetic spark is produced, and it is in this case all the more effective in realizing the meaning of paternity in that it reproduces the mythic event in terms of which Freud reconstructed the progress, in the individual unconscious, of the mystery of the father.

Modern metaphor has the same structure. So this ejaculation:

Love is a pebble laughing in the sunlight,

recreates love in a dimension that seems to me most tenable in the face of its imminent lapse into the mirage of narcissistic altruism.

We see, then, that metaphor occurs at the precise point at which sense comes out of non-sense, that is, at that frontier which, as Freud discovered, when crossed the other way produces what we generally call "wit" (*Witz*); it is at this frontier that we can glimpse the fact that man tempts his very destiny when he derides the signifier.

But to draw back from that place, what do we find in

metonymy other than the power to bypass the obstacles of social censure? This form which lends itself to the truth under oppression, doesn't it show the very servitude inherent in its presentation?

One may read with profit a book by Leo Strauss, of the land which traditionally offers asylum to those who chose freedom, in which the author gives his reflections on the relation between the art of writing and persecution.[14] By pushing to its limits the sort of connaturality which links that art to that condition, he lets us glimpse a certain something which in this matter imposes its form, in the effect of the truth on desire.

But haven't we felt for some time now that, having followed the path of the letter in search of the truth we call Freudian, we are getting very warm indeed, that it is burning all about us?

Of course, as it is said, the letter killeth while the spirit giveth life. We can't help but agree, having had to pay homage elsewhere to a noble victim of the error of seeking the spirit in the letter; but we should like to know, also, how the spirit could live without the letter. Even so, the claims of the spirit would remain unassailable if the letter had not in fact shown us that it can produce all the effects of truth in man without involving the spirit at all.

It is none other than Freud who had this revelation, and he called his discovery the Unconscious.

II. THE LETTER IN THE UNCONSCIOUS

One out of every three pages in the complete works of Freud is devoted to philological references, one out of every two pages to logical inferences, and everywhere the apprehension of experience is dialectical, with the proportion of linguistic analysis increasing just insofar as the unconscious is directly concerned.

Thus in *The Interpretation of Dreams* every page deals with

---

[14] Leo Strauss, *Persecution and the Art of Writing*, The Free Press, Glencoe, Ill.

what we are calling the letter of the discourse, in its texture, its usage, its immanence in the matter in question. For it is with this work that the work of Freud begins to open the royal road to the unconscious. And Freud gave us notice of this; his confidence at the time of launching this book in the early days of this century[15] only confirms what he continued to proclaim to the end: that his whole message was at stake in this, the whole of his discovery.

The first sentence of the opening chapter announces what for the sake of the exposition could not be postponed: that the dream is a rebus. And Freud goes on to stipulate what I have said from the start, that it must be understood literally. This derives from the persistence in the dream of that same literal (or phonematic) structure through which the signifier in ordinary discourse is articulated and analyzed. So the unnatural images of the boat on the roof, or the man with a comma for a head which are specifically mentioned by Freud, are examples of dream-images which have importance only as signifiers, that is, insofar as they allow us to spell out the "proverb" presented by the rebus of the dream. The structure of language which enables us to read dreams is the very principle of the "meaning of dreams," the *Traumdeutung*.

Freud shows us in every possible way that the image's value as signifier has nothing whatever to do with what it signifies, giving as an example Egyptian hieroglyphics in which it would be sheer buffoonery to pretend that in a given text the frequency of a vulture which is an *aleph*, or of a chick which is a *vau*, and which indicate a form of the verb "to be" or a plural, prove that the text has anything at all to do with these ornithological specimens. Freud finds in this script certain uses of the signifier which are lost in ours, such as the use of determinatives, where a categorical figure is added to the literal figuration of a verbal term; but this is only to show us that even in this script, the so-called "ideogram" is a letter.

But the current confusion on this last term was not needed for there to prevail in the minds of psychoanalysts lacking linguistic training the prejudice in favor of a symbolism by natural analogy, that is of the image as fitted to the instinct.

---

[15] See the correspondence, namely letters 107 and 109.

And to such an extent that, outside of the French school which has been alerted, one must draw the line between reading coffee grounds and reading hieroglyphics, by recalling to its own principles a technique which nothing could possibly justify except the very aim and content of the unconscious.

It must be said that this truth is admitted only with difficulty and that the bad mental habits denounced above enjoy such favor that today's psychoanalyst can be expected to say that he decodes before he will come around to taking the necessary tour with Freud (turn at the statue of Champollion, says the guide) which will make him understand that he deciphers; the distinction is that a cryptogram takes on its full dimension only when it is in a lost language.

Taking the tour is nothing other than continuing in the *Traumdeutung.*

Entstellung, translated as distortion, is what Freud shows to be the general precondition for the functioning of dreams, and it is what we described above, following Saussure, as the sliding of the signified under the signifier which is always active in speech (its action, let us note, is unconscious).

But what we called the two slopes of the incidence of the signifier on the signified are also found here.

The *Verdichtung,* or condensation, is the structure of the superimposition of signifiers which is the field of metaphor, and its very name, condensing in itself the word *Dichtung,* shows how the process is connatural with the mechanism of poetry to the point that it actually envelops its properly traditional function.

In the case of *Verschiebung,* displacement, the German term is closer to the idea of that veering off of meaning that we see in metonymy, and which from its first appearance in Freud is described as the main method by which the unconscious gets around censorship.

What distinguishes these two mechanisms which play such a privileged role in the dream-work (*Traumarbeit*), from their homologous functions in speech? Nothing except a condition imposed on the signifying material by the dream, called *Rücksicht auf Darstellbarkeit,* translated as Considerations of Representability. But this condition constitutes a limitation operating *within* the system of notation; it is a long way from dissolving the system into a figurative semiology on a level with certain phenomena of natural expression. This fact could perhaps shed light on the problems involved in certain modes of pictography which, simply because they have been abandoned by writing systems as imperfect, are not therefore to be considered as mere evolutionary stages. Let us say, then, that the dream is like the parlor-game in which one is put on the spot to cause a group of spectators to guess some known utterance or variant of it by means solely of a silent performance. That the dream uses words makes no difference since for the unconscious they are but one among several elements of the performance. It is exactly the fact that both the game and the dream run up against a lack of taxematic material for the representation of such logical articulations as causality, contradiction, hypothesis, etc., that proves they are both writing systems rather than pantomime. The subtle processes which dreams are seen to use to represent these logical articulations, in a much less artificial way than the game brings to bear, are the object of a special study in Freud in which we see once more confirmed that dream-work follows the laws of the signifier.

The rest of the dream-elaboration is designated as secondary by Freud, the nature of which indicates its value: they are fantasies or day-dreams (*Tagtraum*) to use the term Freud prefers in order to emphasize their function of wish-fulfillment (*Wunscherfüllung*). Given the fact that these fantasies can remain unconscious, their distinctive trait is in this case their meaning. Now concerning these fantasies, Freud tells us that their place in dreams is either to be taken up and used as signifying elements in the message of the dream-thought (*Traumgedanke*), or else to be used in the secondary elaboration just mentioned, that is in a function not to be distinguished from our waking thought (*von unserem wachen Denken nicht zu unterschieden*). No better idea of this function can be got than by comparing it to splotches of color which when applied here and there to a stencil would create for our view in a topical painting the pictures, rather grim in themselves, of the rebus or hieroglyph.

Excuse me if I seem to have to spell out the text of Freud; I do it not only to show how much is to be gained by not cutting or abridging it, but also in order to situate the development of psychoanalysis according to its first guide-lines, which were fundamental and never revoked.

Yet from the beginning there was a general failure to recognize the formative role of the signifier in the status which Freud from the first assigned to the unconscious and in the most precise formal manner. And for a double reason, of which the least obvious, naturally, is that this formalization was not sufficient in itself to bring about a recognition of the insistence of the signifier because the time of the appearance of the *Traumdeutung* was well ahead of the formalizations of linguistics for which one could no doubt show that it paved the way by the sheer weight of its truth.

And the second reason, which is after all only the underside of the first, is that if psychoanalysts were fascinated exclusively by the meanings revealed in the unconscious, that is because the secret attraction of these meanings arises from the dialectic which seems to inhere in them.

I showed in my seminars that it is the necessity of counteracting the continuously accelerating effects of this bias which alone explains the apparent sudden changes, or rather changes of tack, which Freud, through his primary concern to preserve for posterity both his discovery and the fundamental revisions it effected in our other knowledge, felt it necessary to apply to his doctrine.

For, I repeat: in the situation in which he found himself, having nothing which corresponded to the object of his discovery which was at the same level of scientific development —in this situation, at least he never failed to maintain this object on the level of its proper ontological dignity.

The rest was the work of the gods and took such a course that analysis today takes as its basis those imaginary forms which I have just shown to be written on the margin of the text they mutilate—and analysis tries to accommodate its goal according to them, in the interpretation of dreams confusing them with the visionary liberation of the hieroglyphic apiary, and seeking generally the control of the exhaustion of the analysis in a sort of scanning process[16] of these forms whenever they appear, with the idea that, just as they are a sign of the exhaustion of regressions, they are also signs of the remodeling of the "object-relation" which characterizes the subject.

The technique which is based on such positions can be fertile in its diverse results, and under the aegis of therapy, difficult to criticize. But an internal criticism must none the less arise from the flagrant disparity between the mode of operation by which the technique is justified—namely the analytic rule, all the instruments of which, from "free association" on up, depend on the conception of the unconscious of their inventor—and on the other hand the general ignorance which reigns regarding this conception of the unconscious. The most peremptory champions of this technique think themselves freed of any need to reconcile the two by the simplest pirouette: the analytic rule (they say) must be all the more religiously observed since it is only the result of a lucky accident. In other words, Freud never knew what he was doing.

A return to Freud's text shows on the contrary the absolute coherence between his technique and his discovery, and at the same time this coherence allows us to put all his procedures in their proper place.

That is why the rectification of psychoanalysis must inevitably involve a return to the truth of that discovery which, taken in its original moment, is impossible to mistake.

For in the analysis of dreams, Freud intends only to give us the laws of the unconscious in the most general extension. One of the reasons why dreams were most propitious for this demonstration is exactly, Freud tells us, that they reveal the same laws whether in the normal person or in the neurotic.

But in the one case as in the other, the efficacy of the unconscious does not cease in the waking state. The psychoanalytic experience is nothing other than the demonstration that the unconscious leaves none of our actions outside its scope. The presence of the unconscious in the psychological

---

[16] That is the process by which the results of a piece of research are assured through a mechanical exploration of the entire extent of the field of its object.

order, in other words in the relation-functions of the individual, should, however, be more precisely defined: it is not coextensive with that order, for we know that if unconscious motivation is manifest in conscious psychic effects, as well as in unconscious ones, conversely it is only elementary to recall to mind that a large number of psychic effects which are quite legitimately designated as unconscious, in the sense of excluding the characteristic of consciousness, never the less are without any relation whatever to the unconscious in the Freudian sense. So it is only by an abuse of the term that unconscious in that sense is confused with psychic, and that one may thus designate as psychic what is in fact an effect of the unconscious, as on the somatic for instance.

It is a matter, therefore, of defining the locus of this unconscious. I say that it is the very locus defined by the formula S/s. What we have been able to unfold concerning the incidence of the signifier on the signified suggests its transformation into:

$$f(S)\ \frac{1}{s}$$

We have shown the effects not only of the elements of the horizontal signifying chain, but also of its vertical dependencies, divided into two fundamental structures called metonymy and metaphor. We can symbolize them by, first:

$$f(S...S')\ S\sim S\ (-)s$$

that is, the metonymic structure, indicating that it is the connection between signifier and signifier which alone permits the elision in which the signifier inserts the lack of being into the object relation, using the reverberating character of meaning to invest it with the desire aimed at the very lack it supports. The sign—placed between ( ) represents here the retention of the line—which in the original formula marked the irreducibility in which, in the relations between signifier and signified, the resistance of meaning is constituted.[17]

----

[17] The sign $\sim$ here represents congruence.

Secondly,

$$f\left(\frac{S'}{S}\right) S \sim S \ (+)s$$

the metaphoric structure, indicates that it is in the substitution of signifier for signifier that an effect of signification is produced which is creative or poetic, in other words which is the advent of the signification in question.[18] The sign + between ( ) represents here the leap over the line—and the constitutive value of the leap for the emergence of meaning.

This leap is an expression of the condition of passage of the signifier into the signified which I pointed out above, although provisionally confusing it with the place of the subject. It is the function of the subject, thus introduced, which we must now turn to as it is the crucial point of our problem.

Je pense, donc je suis (*cogito ergo sum*) is not merely the formula in which is constituted, along with the historical apogee of reflection on the conditions of knowledge, the link between the transparence of the transcendental subject and his existential affirmation.

Perhaps I am only object and mechanism (and so nothing more than phenomenon), but assuredly insofar as I think so, I am—absolutely. No doubt philosophers have made important corrections on this formulation, notably that in that which thinks (*cogitans*), I can never pose myself as anything but object (*cogitatum*). None the less it remains true that by way of this extreme purification of the transcendental subject, my existential link to its project seems irrefutable, at least in its present form, and that:

> *"cogito ergo sum" ubi cogito, ibi sum,*

overcomes this objection.

Of course this confines me to being there in my being only insofar as I think that I am in my thought; just how far I actually think this concerns only myself and if I say it, interests no one.[19]

---

[18] (S' i.e. prime) designating here the term productive of the signifying effect (or significance); one can see that the term is latent in metonymy, patent in metaphor.

[19] It is quite otherwise if by posing a question such as "Why

To elude this problem on the pretext of its philosophical pretensions is simply to show our inhibition. For the notion of subject is indispensable even to the operation of a science such as strategy (in the modern sense) whose calculations exclude all subjectivism.

It is also to deny oneself access to what we may call the Freudian universe—in the way that we speak of the Copernican universe. It was in fact the so-called Copernican revolution to which Freud himself compared his discovery, emphasizing that it was once again a question of the place man assigns to himself at the center of a universe.

The place that I occupy as the subject of a signifier: is it, in relation to the place I occupy as subject of the signified, concentric or ex—centric?—that is the question.

It is not a question of knowing whether I speak of myself in a way that conforms to what I am, but rather of knowing whether I am the same as that of which I speak. And it is not at all inappropriate to use the word "thought" here. For Freud uses the term to designate the elements involved in the unconscious, that is the signifying mechanisms which we now recognize as being there.

It is none the less true that the philosophical *cogito* is at the center of that mirage which renders modern man so sure of being himself even in his uncertainties about himself, or rather in the mistrust he has learned to erect against the traps of self-love.

Likewise, if I charge nostalgia with being in the service of metonymy and refuse to seek meaning beyond tautology; if in the name of "war is war" and "a penny's a penny" I determine to be only what I am, yet how even here can I eliminate the obvious fact that in that very act I am?

And it is no less true if I take myself to the other, metaphorical pole in my quest for meaning, and if I dedicate myself to becoming what I am, to coming into being, I cannot doubt that even if I lose myself in the process, in that process, I am.

Now it is on these very points where evidence will be sub-

philosophers?" I become more candid than nature, for then I am asking the question which philosophers have been asking themselves for all time and also the one in which they are in fact the most interested.

verted by the empirical, that the trick of the Freudian conversion lies.

This meaningful game between metonymy and metaphor up to and including the active edge which splits my desire between a refusal of meaning or a lack of being and links my fate to the question of my destiny, this game, in all its inexorable subtlety, is played until the match is called, there where I am not because I cannot locate myself there.

That is, what is needed is more than these words with which I disconcerted my audience: I think where I am not, therefore I am where I think not. Words which render sensible to an ear properly attuned with what weasling ambiguity the ring of meaning flees from our grasp along the verbal thread.

What one ought to say is: I am not, wherever I am the plaything of my thought; I think of what I am wherever I don't think I am thinking.

This two-faced mystery is linked to the fact that the truth can be evoked only in that dimension of alibi in which all "realism" in creative works takes its virtue from metonymy; it is likewise linked to this other fact that we accede to meaning only through the double twist of metaphor when we have the unique key: the S and the s of the Saussurian formula are not on the same level, and man only deludes himself when he believes his true place is at their axis, which is nowhere.

Was nowhere, that is, until Freud discovered it; for if what Freud discovered isn't that, it isn't anything.

The content of the unconscious with all its disappointing ambiguities gives us no reality in the subject more consistent than the immediate; its force comes from the truth and in the dimension of being: *Kern unseres Wesen* are Freud's own terms.

The double-triggered mechanism of metaphor is in fact the very mechanism by which the symptom, in the analytic sense, is determined. Between the enigmatic signifier of a sexual trauma and its substitute term in a present signifying chain there passes the spark which fixes in a symptom the meaning inaccessible to the conscious subject in which is its resolution—a symptom which is in effect a metaphor in which flesh or function are taken as signifying elements.

And the enigmas which desire seems to pose for a "natural philosophy"—its frenzy mocking the abyss of the infinite, the secret collusion by which it obscures the pleasure of knowing and of joyful domination, these amount to nothing more than that derangement of the instincts that comes from being caught on the rails—eternally stretching forth towards the desire for something else—of metonymy. Wherefore its "perverse" fixation at the very suspension-point of the signifying chain where the memory-screen freezes and the fascinating image of the fetish petrifies.

There is no other way to conceive the indestructibility of unconscious desire, when there is no natural need which, when prevented from satisfying itself, isn't dissipated even if it means the destruction of the organism itself. It is in a memory, comparable to what they call by that name in our modern thinking-machines (which are in turn based on an electronic realization of the signifying compound), it is in this sort of memory that is found that chain which insists on reproducing itself in the process of transference, and which is the chain of dead desire.

It is the truth of what this desire was in its history which the patient cries out through his symptom, as Christ said that the stones themselves would have cried out if the children of Israel had not lent them their voice.

And that is why only psychoanalysis allows us to differentiate within memory the function of recall. Rooted in the signifier, it resolves the Platonic puzzles of reminiscence through the ascendancy of the historic in man.

One has only to read the "Three Essays on Sexuality" to observe, in spite of the pseudo-biological glosses with which it is decked out for popular consumption, that Freud there derives any accession to the object from the dialectic of the return.

Starting from Hölderlin's νοστος Freud will arrive less than twenty years later at Kierkegaard's repetition; that is, through submitting his thought solely to the humble but inflexible consequences of the talking cure, he was unable ever to escape the living servitudes which led him from the regal principle of the Logos to re-thinking the mortal Empedoclean antinomies.

And how else are we to conceive the recourse of a man of science to a *Deus ex machina* than on that other stage of which he speaks as the dream place, a *Deus ex machina* only less derisory for the fact that it is revealed to the spectator that the machine directs the director? How else can we imagine that a scientist of the nineteenth century, unless we realize that he had to bow before the force of evidence that overwhelmed his prejudices, put more stock in his *Totem and Taboo* than in all his other works, with its obscene and ferocious figure of the primordial father, not to be exhausted in the expiation of Oedipus' blindness, and before which the ethnologists of today bow as before the growth of an authentic myth?

So that imperious proliferation of particular symbolic creations, such as what are called the sexual theories of the child, which supply the motivation down to the smallest detail of neurotic compulsions, these reply to the same necessities as do myths.

Likewise, to speak of the precise point we are treating in my seminars on Freud, little Hans, left in the lurch at the age of five by his symbolic environment, and suddenly forced to face the enigma of his sex and his existence, under the direction of Freud and of his father, Freud's disciple, developed in a mythic form, around the signifying crystal of his phobia, all the permutations possible on a limited number of signifiers.

The operation shows that even on the individual level the solution of the impossible is brought within man's reach by the exhaustion of all possible forms of the impossibilities encountered in solution by recourse to the signifying equation. It is a striking demonstration for the clarifying of this labyrinth of observation which so far has only been used as a source of demolished fragments. We should be struck also with the fact that the coextensivity of the unfolding of the symptom and of its curative resolution shows the true nature of neurosis: whether phobic, hysterical or obsessive, a neurosis is a question which being poses for the subject "from the place where it was before the subject came into the world" (Freud's phrase which he used in explaining the Oedipal complex to little Hans).

The "being" referred to is that which appears in a lightning moment in the void of the verb "to be" and I said that it poses its question for the subject. What does that mean? It does not pose it *before* the subject, since the subject cannot come to the place where it is posed, but it poses it *in place* of the subject, that is, in that place it poses the question *with* the subject, as one poses a problem *with* a pen, or as man in antiquity thought *with* his soul.

It is only in this way that Freud fits the ego into his doctrine. Freud defined the ego by the resistances which are proper to it. They are of an imaginary nature much in the same sense as those adaptational activities which the ethology of animal behavior shows us in courting-pomp or combat. Freud showed their reduction in man to a narcissistic relation, which I elaborated in my essay on the mirror-stage. And he grouped within it the synthesis of the perceptive functions in which the sensori-motor selections are integrated which determine for man what he calls reality.

But this resistance, essential for the solidifying of the inertias of the imaginary order which obstruct the message of the unconscious, is only secondary in relation to the specific resistances of the journey in the signifying order of the truth.

That is the reason why an exhaustion of the mechanisms of defence, which Fenichel the practitioner shows us so well in his studies of technique (while his whole reduction on the theoretical level of neuroses and psychoses to genetic anomalies in libidinal development is pure platitude), manifests itself, without Fenichel's accounting for it or realizing it himself, as simply the underside or reverse aspect of the mechanisms of the unconscious. Periphrasis, hyperbaton, ellipsis, suspension, anticipation, retraction, denial, digression, irony, these are the figures of style (Quintilian's *figurae sententiarum*); as catachresis, litotes, antonomasia, hypotyposis are the tropes, whose terms impose themselves as the most proper for the labelling of these mechanisms. Can one really see these as mere figures of speech when it is the figures themselves which are the active principle of the rhetoric of the discourse which the patient in fact utters?

By the obstinacy with which today's psychoanalysts reduce to a sort of emotional police station the reality of the resistance of which the patient's discourse is only a cover, they have

sunk beneath one of the fundamental truths which Freud re-
discovered through psychoanalysis. One is never happy making way for a new truth, for it always means making our
way into it: the truth demands that we bestir ourselves. We
cannot even manage to get used to the idea most of the time.
We get used to reality. But the truth we repress.

Now it is quite specially necessary to the scientist and the
magician, and even the quack, that he be the only one to
know. The idea that deep in the simplest (and even sick) souls
there is something ready to blossom—perish the thought! but
if someone seems to know as much as the savants about what
we ought to make of it . . . come to our aid, categories of
primitive, prelogical, archaic, or even magical thought, so
easy to impute to others! It is not right that these nibblers
keep us breathless with enigmas which turn out to be only
malicious.

To interpret the unconscious as Freud did, one would have
to be as he was, an encyclopedia of the arts and muses, as
well as an assiduous reader of the *Fliegende Blätter*.[20] And
the task is made no easier by the fact that we are at the mercy
of a thread woven with allusions, quotations, puns, and equivo-
cations. And is that our profession; to be antidotes to trifles?

Yet that is what we must resign ourselves to. The unconscious is neither primordial nor instinctual; what it knows
about the elementary is no more than the elements of the
signifier.

The three books that one might call canonical with regard
to the unconscious—the *Traumdeutung*, the *Psychopathology
of Everyday Life,* and *Wit in its Relation to the Unconscious*
—are but a web of examples whose development is furnished
by the formulas of connection and substitution (though carried to the tenth degree by their particular complexity—the
rundown of them is sometimes given by Freud outside the
text); these are the formulas we give to the signifier in its
transference-function. For in the *Traumdeutung* it is in the
sense of such a function that the term *Ubertragung*, or transference, is introduced, which only later will give its name to the

[20] A German comic newspaper of the late nineteenth and early twentieth centuries. (Trans.)

mainspring of the intersubjective link between analyst and analyzed.

Such diagrams (of the various transfers of the signifier) are not only constitutive of each of the symptoms in a neurosis, but they alone make possible the understanding of the thematic of its course and resolution. The great observations of analyses which Freud gave amply demonstrate this.

To fall back on data that are more limited but more apt to furnish us with the final seal to bind up our proposition, let me cite the article on fetishism of 1927,[21] and the case Freud reports there of a patient who, to achieve sexual satisfaction, needed something shining on the nose (*Glanz auf der Nase*); analysis showed that his early, English-speaking years had seen the displacement of the burning curiosity which he felt for the phallus of his mother, that is for that eminent failure-to-be the privileged signification of which Freud revealed to us, into a *glance at the nose* in the forgotten language of his childhood, rather than a *shine on the nose*.

That a thought makes itself heard in the abyss, that is an abyss open before all thought—and that is what provoked from the outset resistance to psychoanalysis. And not, as is commonly said, the emphasis on man's sexuality. This latter is after all the dominant object in the literature of the ages. And in fact the more recent evolution of psychoanalysis has succeeded by a bit of comical legerdemain in turning it into a quite moral affair, the cradle and trysting-place of attaction and oblativity. The Platonic setting of the soul, blessed and illuminated, rises straight to paradise.

The intolerable scandal in the time before Freudian sexuality was sanctified was that it was so "intellectual." It was precisely in that that it showed itself to be the worthy ally of the terrorists plotting to ruin society.

At a time when psychoanalysts are busy remodeling psychoanalysis into a right-thinking movement whose crowning expression is the sociological poem of the autonomous ego, and by this I mean what will identify, for those who understand me, bad psychoanalysts, this is the term they use to deprecate all technical or theoretical research which carries

[21] *Fetischismus*, G.W., XIV, p. 311.

forward the Freudian experience along its authentic lines:
intellectualization is the word—execrable to all those who,
living in fear of being tried and found wanting by the wine of
truth, spit on the bread of men, although their slaver can no
longer have any effect other than that of leavening.

III. BEING, THE LETTER AND THE OTHER

Is what thinks in my place then another I? Does Freud's discovery represent the confirmation on the psychological level
of Manicheism?[22]

In fact there is no confusion on this point: what Freud's re-
searches led us to is not a few more or less curious cases of
split personality. Even at the heroic epoch we were talking
about, when, like the animals in fairy stories, sexually talked,
the demonic atmosphere that such an orientation might have
given rise to never materialized.[23]

The end which Freud's discovery proposes for man was
defined by him at the apex of his thought in these moving
terms: *Wo es war, soll Ich werden.* I must come to the place
where that (id) was.

The goal is one of reintegration and harmony, I could even
say of reconciliation (*Versöhnung*).

But if we ignore the self's radical ex—centricity to itself
with which man is confronted, in other words, the truth discovered by Freud, we shall falsify both the order and methods
of psychoanalytic mediation; we shall make of it nothing more
than the compromise operation which it has effectively become, namely just what the letter as well as the spirit of
Freud's work most repudiates. For since he constantly invoked
the notion of compromise as the main support of all the mis-
eries which analysis is meant to help, we can say that any recourse to compromise, explicit or implicit, will necessarily

---

[22] One of my Colleagues went so far in this direction as to wonder
if the Id of the last phase wasn't in fact the "bad Ego."

[23] Note, none the less, the tone with which one spoke in that period
of the "elfin pranks" of the unconscious; a work of Silberer's is called,
Der Zufall und die Koboldstreiche des Unbewussten—completely anach-
ronistic in the context of our present soul-managers.

disorient psychoanalytic action and plunge it into darkness.

Neither does it suffice, moreover, to associate oneself with the moralistic tartufferies of our times or to be forever spouting something about the "total personality" in order to have said anything articulate about the possibility of mediation.

The radical heteronomy which Freud's discovery shows gaping within man can never again be covered over without whatever is used to hide it being fundamentally dishonest.

Then who is this other to whom I am more attached than to myself, since, at the heart of my assent to my own identity it is still he who wags me?

Its presence can only be understood at a second degree of otherness which puts it in the position of mediating between me and the double of myself, as it were with my neighbor.

If I have said elsewhere that the unconscious is the discourse of the Other (with a capital O), I meant by that to indicate the beyond in which the recognition of desire is bound up with the desire of recognition.

In other words this other is the Other which my lie invokes as a gage of the truth in which it thrives.

By which we can also see that the dimension of truth emerges only with the appearance of language.

Prior to this point, we can recognize in psychological relations which can be easily isolated in the observation of animal behavior the existence of subjects, not on account of any projective mirage, the phantoms of which a certain type of psychologist delights in hacking to pieces, but simply on account of the manifest presence of intersubjectivity. In the animal hidden in his lookout, in the well-laid trap of certain others, in the feint by which an apparent straggler leads a bird of prey away from a fugitive band, we see something more emerge than in the fascinating display of mating or combat ritual. Yet there is nothing even there which transcends the function of decoy in the service of a need, nor which affirms a presence in that Beyond where we think we can question the designs of Nature.

For there even to be a question (and we know that it is one Freud himself posed in *Beyond the Pleasure Principle*), there must be language.

For I can decoy my adversary by means of a movement contrary to my actual plan of battle, and this movement will have its deceiving effect only insofar as I produce it in reality and for my adversary.

But in the propositions with which I open peace negotiations with him, what my negotiations propose to him is situated in a third place which is neither my words nor my interlocutor.

This place is none other than the area of signifying convention, of the sort revealed in the comedy of the sad plaint of the Jew to his crony: "Why do you tell me you are going to Cracow so I'll believe you are going to Lvov, when you are really going to Cracow?"

Of course the troop-movement I just spoke of could be understood in the conventional context of game-strategy where it is in function of a rule that I deceive my adversary, but in that case my success is evaluated within the connotation of betrayal, that is, in relation to the Other who is the guarantee of Good Faith.

Here the problems are of an order the basic heteronomy of which is completely misunderstood if it is reduced to an "awareness of the other" by whatever name we call it. For the "existence of the other" having once upon a time reached the ears of the Midas of psychoanalysis through the partition which separates him from the Privy Council of phenomenology, the news is now bruited through the reeds: "Midas, King Midas is the other of his patient. He himself has said it."

What sort of breakthrough is that? The other, what other?

The young André Gide, defying the landlady to whom his mother had confided him to treat him as a responsible being, opening with a key (false only in that it opened all locks of the same make) the lock which this lady took to be a worthy signifier of her educational intentions, and doing it with ostentation in her sight—what "other" was he aiming at? She who was supposed to intervene and to whom he would then say: "Do you think my obedience can be secured with a ridiculous lock?" But by remaining out of sight and holding her peace until that evening in order, after primly greeting his return, to lecture him like a child, she showed him not just another with the face of anger, but another André Gide who is no longer sure, either then or later in thinking back on it, of just what he really meant to do—whose own truth has been changed by the doubt thrown on his good faith.

Perhaps it would be worth our while pausing a moment over this dominion of confusion which is none other than that in which the whole human opera-buffa plays itself out, in order to understand the ways in which analysis can proceed not just to restore an order but to found the conditions for the possibility of its restoration.

Kern unseres Wesen, the nucleus of our being, but it is not so much that Freud commands us to seek it as so many others before him have with the empty adage "Know thyself"—as to reconsider the ways which lead to it, and which he shows us.

Or rather that which he proposes for us to attain is not that which can be the object of knowledge, but that (doesn't he tell us as much?) which creates our being and about which he teaches us that we bear witness to it as much and more in our whims, our aberrations, our phobias and fetishes, as in our vaguely civilized personalities.

Folly, you are no longer the object of the ambiguous praise with which the sage decorated the impregnable burrow of his terror; and if after all he finds himself tolerably at home there, it is only because the supreme agent forever at work digging its galleries and labyrinths is none other than reason, the very Logos which he serves.

So how do you imagine that a scholar with so little talent for the *"engagements"* which solicited him in his age (as they do in all ages), that a scholar such as Erasmus held such an eminent place in the revolution of a Reformation in which man has much of a stake in each man as in all men?

The answer is that the slightest alteration in the relation between man and the signifier, in this case in the procedures of exegesis, changes the whole course of history by modifying the lines which anchor his being.

It is in precisely this way that Freudianism, however misunderstood it has been, and confused the consequences, to anyone capable of perceiving the changes we have lived through in our own lives, is seen to have founded an intangible but radical revolution. No need to collect witnesses to the fact:[24] everything involving not just the human sciences, but the destiny of man, politics, metaphysics, literature, art, advertising, propaganda, and through these even the economy, everything has been affected.

Is all this anything more than the unharmonized effects of an immense truth in which Freud traced for us a clear path? What must be said, however, is that any technique which bases its claim on the mere psychological categorization of its object is not following this path, and this is the case of psychoanalysis today except insofar as we return to the Freudian discovery.

Likewise the vulgarity of the concepts by which it recommends itself to us, the embroidery of Freudery which is no longer anything but decoration, as well as the bad repute in which it seems to prosper, all bear witness to its fundamental denial of its founder.

Freud, by his discovery, brought within the circle of science the boundary between being and the object which seemed before to mark its outer limit.

That this is the symptom and the prelude of a reexamination of the situation of man in the existent such as has been assumed up to the present by all our postulates of knowledge —don't be content, I beg of you, to write this off as another case of Heideggerianism, even prefixed by a neo- which adds nothing to the trashcan style in which currently, by the use of his ready-made mental jetsam, one excuses oneself from any real thought.

When I speak of Heidegger, or rather when I translate him, I at least make the effort to leave the word he proffers us its sovereign significance.

If I speak of being and the letter, if I distinguish the other and the Other, it is only because Freud shows me that they

---

[24] To pick the most recent in date, Francois Mauriac, in the *Figaro Litteraire* of May 25, excuses himself for not "narrating his life." If no one these days can undertake to do that with the old enthusiasm, the reason is that, "a half century since, Freud, whatever we think of him" has already passed that way. And after being briefly tempted by the old saw that this is only the "history of our body," Mauriac returns to the truth that his sensitivity as a writer makes him face: to write the history of oneself is to write the confession of the deepest part of our neighbors' souls as well.

are the terms to which must be referred the effects of resistance and transfer against which, in the twenty years I have engaged in what we all call after him the impossible practice of psychoanalysis, I have done unequal battle. And it is also because I must help others not to lose their way there.

It is to prevent the field of which they are the inheritors from becoming barren, and for that reason to make it understood that if the symptom is a metaphor, it is not a metaphor to say so, no more than to say that man's desire is a metonymy. For the symptom *is* a metaphor whether one likes it or not, as desire *is* a metonymy for all that men mock the idea.

Finally, if I am to rouse you to indignation that, after so many centuries of religious hypocrisy and philosophical bravado, nothing valid has yet been articulated on what links metaphor to the question of being and metonymy to its lack, there must be an object there to answer to that indignation both as its provocator and its victim: it is humanistic man and the credit, affirmed beyond reparation, which he has drawn on his intentions.

T.t.y.m.u.p.t. 14-26 May, 1957.

Structuralism: the Anglo-American adventure

Geoffrey Hartman

Structuralism is a complex and many-faceted intellectual movement: born in Russia and Switzerland, confirmed in Prague, sowing a wild and fertile seed in France, but respecting the separation of disciplines and keeping to linguistics in America. It is not suited for monogamy, however; and is about to form a dangerous alliance with literary criticism. In France that alliance has already begotten a vast and sophisticated offspring. If, as Claude Lévi-Strauss demonstrated, the new method for studying language could yield a "Structural Anthropology," it should also be transferable to the study of literature. Having made the term "social sciences" respectable, structuralism becomes more ambitious and holds out the hope that even literary criticism might be counted one day among the *sciences humaines*.

New movements win out over old by their purity, or simplicity—by removing a burden of unnecessary assumptions and freeing the energy released for a more integral purpose. It is easy to predict that structuralism will have an era, a genuine and lasting influence. The purity of the structural method results from the central place accorded to the idea of mediation. We usually think of mediation as give-and-take, barter, interpretation, dialogue, or ritual. Its basic formula is *do ut des,* or the converse. A whole group of related notions, such as parity, equity, balance of power, and compensation, also enter. The structuralist, inspired by the Saussurian principle that language has a systematic (synchronic) as well as historical (diachronic) form, tries to gain a conspectus of all these relations or institutions—of which speech is indeed the paradigm case. Aristotle defined soul as the form of forms: he seeks the relation of relations. If we take Mauss' essay on gifts and Lévi-Strauss' on kinship as the classic examples, structural theory comprises the following theses. 1. That societies are systems, and that there is a totality of these systems which makes the structure of the societal visible; 2. That to clarify this structure is to clarify the form of "mediation," where mediation is always a total social phenomenon, and always inter-subjective, i.e., an I-Thou and not I-it relation, a relation of persons or personae, even when the thing mediated seems to have the "it" character of property, money, the past, etc.[1] 3. That there is always a *contrat social* (see 1

---

[1] Cf. M. Mauss on gifts with E. Cassirer on language: "What they [the Polynesians] exchange is not exclusively goods and wealth, real and personal property, and things of economic value. They exchange rather courtesies, entertainments, ritual, military assistance, women, children, dances and feasts; and fairs in which the market is but one

above) whether or not the participants are conscious of it; indeed they cannot be fully conscious of it, since it is so complex, concrete, and comprehensive, with an almost Kafkaesque extension. The structure of society is therefore latent rather than manifest.

Thus structuralism is a "unified field" theory. Its subject is not this or that culture (a corpus of texts, a geographically or historically delimited area) but the very process of mediation, and how rites, values, meanings, and all such *recurrent currencies* relate to it. But to turn now to the study of literature. The structuralist asks: what is the status of words in society? Is literature to be compared to ritual, or does it mediate in a distinctively different way? At the most general level: are not social systems best defined by analogy to language systems? With respect to the special role of literature, we have case studies and brilliant general hints, but no one with the scope of a Lévi-Strauss. De Saussure, for instance, in unpublished notebooks recently brought to light, suggests that certain types of religious poetry are created out of a primal or cultic Name which is covertly (anagrammatically) "distributed." Grammar, language, and poetry might then be looked at as a purposive *sparagmos,* as a second mode and second power of naming.[2] We could think of literature as a hoard of sacred or magical words which the poet, as secular

---

element and the circulation of wealth but one part of a wide and enduring contract" (*The Gift*). "In speech and art the individuals not only share what they already possess; it is only by virtue of this sharing process . . . that individuals have attained what they possess. This can be observed in any living and meaningful conversation. It is never simply a question of imparting information, but of statement and response. It is only in this twofold process that true thought emerges. Plato has said that 'questioning and answering each other in discourse' is our only access to the world of the 'idea.' In question and answer 'I' and 'you' must be distinguished, not only that they may understand each other, but even if each is ever to know himself. Here both factors are in continual interplay. The thought of one partner is kindled by that of another. And by virtue of this interaction each constructs for himself a 'shared world' of meaning within the medium of language" (*The Logic of the Humanities*). "They will give each other a hundred new names, and take them away again, as quietly as one takes off an earring" (Rilke). "Lass die Sprache dir sein, was der Körper den Liebenden. Er nur/Ist's, der die Wesen trennt und der die Wesen vereint" (Schiller).

[2] "Les anagrammes de Ferdinand de Saussure," Textes présentés par Jean Starobinski, *Mercure de France* (Fevrier, 1964).

priest, makes available. This is pure speculation. In the absence of a more definitive essay on literary mediation, it is best to be content with the brief eulogy of a famous rabbi by his disciple: "He changed my gold into silver coins . . ." *La monnaie de l'absolu;* words reveal the individual talent, and make it negotiable.

It may still seem, however, as if structuralism were a foreign import, especially in literary studies. This is because Anglo-American tradition is endemically suspicious of systematization. We remember Dr. Johnson on Bishop Hurd. "Hurd, sir, is one of a set of men who account for everything systematically;" and he proposes "scarlet breeches" as a worthy topic for the Bishop's interest in origins. Now Richard Hurd, Bishop of Worcester, author of *Letters on Chivalry and Romance* (1762), is one of our first structure-minded critics. He justified the peculiarities of Gothic Romance (Spenser's *Fairie Queene*) by grounding it in the manners and rituals of an earlier age. He is not as yet the perfect structuralist, for his interest is strongly antiquarian. But there is an important *English* tradition of structural analysis which emerges here as part of a movement to put native sources on a par with the Classics. The interest in native poetry goes hand in hand with a body of criticism seeking to justify that poetry's eccentric, non-classical form; and the idea that art is to be seen in its relation to social institutions (which became a nineteenth century cliché) helps this end.

The idea of a formal relation between literature and social institutions does not in itself define a structural approach. It may even obscure it if "relation" implies the priority of the societal and the purely mimetic or documentary status of art.[3] A naive sociological assumption of this kind is not removed till the beginning of the present century. Then the renewed study of oral tradition reveals the archetypal rather than archaic, and universal rather than local character of conven-

---

[3] There is, however, a "structuralisme génétique" of Marxist inspiration, based on the theory that art reflects, in its structure rather than content, the collective vision of certain social groups, "whose consciousness tends toward a total vision of man." Lucien Goldmann identifies these groups with the "classes" of orthodox Marxism. A problem here is the casuistry needed to distinguish between structure and content, as well as, on occasion, between structure and form.

tion. W. P. Ker's investigations of Epic and Romance, E. K. Chamber's research into the origins of Medieval Drama, and F. B. Gummere's theories on the Ballad showed that all literature was governed by similar conventions. At least all literature with a source in oral tradition; and the strength of these scholars lay in uncovering that source. But this meant that the formal features of Romance could no longer be explained, as in Hurd, by the institutions of an Age of Chivalry, since they are found in literature from the beginning. It cleared the way for a new kind of criticism which could view literature as an institution with its own laws or structural principles, yet relate these laws to both local traditions and to the societal as such. Any interpretation that can respect these aims is rightly called structural.

Consider C. L. Barber's *Shakespeare's Festive Comedy* (1959). It is surely inadequate to think of it only as "myth-criticism." Subtitled, "A Study of Dramatic Form and its relation to Social Custom," its affinity to Hurd is apparent. The eccentricities of Shakespearean comedy are attached to a "saturnalian pattern" whose ritual origin F. M. Cornford had described, but which came to Shakespeare through such native holiday customs as the May Games and the convention of the Lord of Misrule. Like Sartre or Lucien Goldmann, Barber is interested in the local mediations by which a social structure comes to the artist. Yet his perspective reaches beyond Elizabethan England. The saturnalian pattern, present both in Greek and Shakespearean Comedy, expresses a problematic human need which must last as long as society is society—hierarchic, repressive, in conflict with itself. Malinowski would have said that it resolves a social tension.

The reason why studies like Barber's are not recognized for what they are, is that they remain obstinately naive in point of theory and shy away from explicit social criticism. The opposite is true of Kenneth Burke, but his theorizing is so thick and unpurified that its influence can only gradually filter into literary studies. Francis Fergusson's *Idea of a Theater,* on the other hand, is exemplary in its combination of theoretical and practical criticism. It is only fair to acknowledge, however, that in Anglo-American practice a brilliant method is often accompanied by an undeveloped theory. Barber holds no less than three variant views concerning the relation of social to artistic structure: that social forms are translated into artistic, that it is peculiarly significant that *Shakespeare* manages to translate social forms into artistic, and that the social is not so much prior to art as it is a mixed form created by the conflict of ludic and legal—a form, therefore, in which art participates constitutively. But to transcend antiquarianism—to become genuinely critical—needs a firm idea of the role of art in the light of which the particular work can be judged.

Literary theory has been striving for exactly this: a firm and adequate conception of the role of art in human life. The modern increase in literary criticism suggests, in fact, that art is now subjected to greater expectations than ever. Since the early part of this century, and already since the Romantic period, we have turned to art in order to sustain our diminishing sense of "the common nature" of man.[4] There is no need to discuss in detail why the individual should feel a loss in his sense of communal identity, and why he should now turn to art for a saving hypothesis. It is enough to point out that Bergson, writing at the time of crisis, views art as an instinctive defense against social disintegration. Also during this time myth-criticism arises, encouraged by new evidence concerning the communal or ritual origin of art. Our first modern and inspired structuralists are Jane Harrison in *Themis* (1912), F. M. Cornford in *The Origins of Attic Comedy* (1914), and a great breed of classicists and orientalists indebted to Frazer (Gilbert Murray, Jessie Weston, T. H. Gaster, G. R. Lévy).

Part of the crisis, clearly, is that the classics have lost their power to be models for communal behavior. What follows is an upsurge of individualism but also a deepening insight into the nature of model-making. The realization is gradually won that society is always based on some form of social lie or vital myth; indeed that myths, however barbarous in content, serve

---

[4] See chapter 1 in Maud Bodkins, *Archetypal Patterns in Poetry* (1934), and the conclusion of F. B. Gummere's *The Beginnings of Poetry* (1901).

the same purpose in their society as the classics in ours. Borrowing a term from biology, one can say that all myths are analogous, that they show a correspondence of function if not of structure. But this recognition, which still allows myth to be criticized for its primitive content (Frazer stops here), is followed by the recognition that myths may also be homologous, or of the same structure. The first recognition can lead to the view that each society has its own classics, which are mortal, or gradually purified; but the second disparages a naive historicism of this kind. Since all models productive of social cohesion are basically of one structure, the reason they become obsolete must lie in a modification of that structure. The literary cliché and popular stereotype exemplify disabling change of this kind. By the same token, however, the dead convention can be restructured and revived, as it is in all authentic art. We recover its nature by an act of historical or artistic sympathy—in short, by some sort of hermeneutic engagement. "Le symbole donne à penser" (Paul Ricoeur). When Nietzsche sees Dionysus behind Apollo, when Jane Harrison sees the Daimones behind the Olympians, when Yeats talks of "grounding mythology in the earth," they not only revive an ancient model, but reveal something of the structure of every myth. The recognition that myths are homologous entails a theory of the life-cycle of myth.

In the final analysis, then, structuralism is based on two important and related discoveries. The first, that myths are models productive of social cohesion, grants myth and art an exemplary role in society. The second, that all such models are myths, homologous in structure as well as analogous in function, enables structuralism to become a science of all social-systemic behavior. This *nova scienza,* however, is always faced with explaining the difference between the manifest content of myths and their latent "structural" identity. Here two developments play a crucial role: one is psychoanalysis, with its technique for uncovering latent meanings; the other is structural linguistics, with its discovery that meaning resides not in the sounds themselves but rather in their combination at a phonemic (latent) level. A structural interpretation of literature may utilize categories which appear abstract because they are the equivalents to phonemes and their laws of combination.[5]

Such interpretation, however, must never become so formalistic as to forget its origin. The aim of myth-criticism from Jane Harrison to Northrop Frye, and of anthropology from Durkheim to Lévi-Strauss, is to save the "common nature" of man—despite fragmentation, specialization, and ideological wars. Structuralism cannot follow this aim unless it exerts a genuine historical consciousness vis-à-vis itself. To learn with Lévi-Strauss that primitive thought is as logical as our own leads to a *humanizing* recognition, one that both comforts and disconcerts. We turn now to examine the progress of structuralism in England and America, choosing a few central figures but inevitably neglecting others of importance.

The refinement which allowed myth-criticism to become a form of literary criticism had almost no connection with the rise of structural linguistics.[6] It came about as a natural development of the basic theory. The latter, adjusted to the study of literature, and extended from archaic society to all cultures, converted archeology into anthropology. Gilbert Murray is less advanced in this than Northrop Frye, but the direction is already apparent. Murray, F. M. Cornford and Jane Harrison are contemporaries; and Murray had contributed an important "Excursus on the Ritual Forms pre-

[5] There remains, however, an unresolved conflict between the "depth-analysis" of linguists and of Freudians. Psychoanalytic technique represents the latent entities as "symbols" or "archetypes," i.e., they are, if anything, overdetermined, and the consciousness of the individual is a context that limits or objectifies their meaning. The entities of structural linguistics, however, are underdetermined or "arbitrary" without an a priori, systematic and intersubjective context that generates meaning like a "Kantian" unconscious.

[6] A rival theory of linguistics does, however, influence Anglo-American criticism. It is set forth in C. K. Ogden and I. A. Richards, *The Meaning of Meaning* (1923), to which Malinowski contributes a supplement on "The Problem of Meaning in Primitive Languages." Malinowski stresses what he calls the *context of situation* (Ogden and Richards' "sign-situation") in addition to the *linguistic context*. A problem common to this theory and structuralism is the role of the meta-verbal (context of situation, social reality, sacred mime, *praxis* as distinguished from *lexis*) in a verbal system. A recent attempt to resolve the "referential-contextual" dichotomy is Murray Krieger's *A Window to Criticism* (Princeton, 1964).

served in Greek Tragedy" to Harrison's *Themis*. He expands Aristotle's description of the plot-structure of tragedy, treating it as reflection of the ritual acts of hypothetical *sacer ludus*. Aristotle's anagnorisis and peripety are expanded as agon, pathos, threnos, theophany, etc. A few years later, in a famous lecture on "Hamlet and Orestes" (1914), Murray established the similarities between the Hamlet and Orestes stories; and not finding a direct historical explanation for them falls back on something like the Jungian theory of a collective unconscious. According to this theory a primal pattern is inscribed on the memory of man and acts as an a priori determinant of his experience. This pattern not only reflects our racial history but remains vital to it, vital to our continued *communal* life. It is the communal or social whose locus is being widened; we are clearly in the midst of a general effort to save "the common nature," to revalue the claim of "tradition" vis-à-vis the "individual talent." (Jane Harrison, strongly conscious of Durkheim and Bergson, called her book *Themis* because of her conviction that god-making and society-making were deeply related.) But though Murray realized that collective representations are the structural principles of literature, he was unable to dissociate poetics from the historical study of ritual and religion.

The progress of structuralism centers in good part on this dissociation. Aristotle had achieved it almost as a matter of course. But the *Poetics* remains a limited field theory: it deals with only one culture in its maturity. Eliot, however, says in his first essay that "The historical sense compels a man to write not merely with his own generation in his bones, but with a feeling that the whole of the literature of Europe from Homer, and within it the whole of the literature of his own country has a simultaneous existence and composes a simultaneous order." These circumstances compel a wider, even universal field of vision, and lead us beyond special historical redemptions of the past and toward archetypal rather than archaic principles of structure. Northrop Frye, a new Aristotle, says in the opening chapter of the *Anatomy of Criticism* (1957) that his book will annotate that sentence of Eliot's.

Though Frye's theory is unified only for literature, it has larger implicit ambitions and is concerned with the "fables of identity" latent in all cultural or symbolic forms. The difference between his work and earlier myth-criticism can be illustrated by inventing a new subtitle for the *Anatomy*. In 1903 Durkheim and Mauss published one of their most famous essays, "De quelques formes primitives de classification: contribution à l'étude des representations collectives." This could be adapted to Frye's *Anatomy* by means of few changes: "De quelques formes générales de classification littéraire: contribution à l'étude des archétypes." Yet Frye's work is misunderstood if its classifications are taken too rigidly. Culture aims to do away with classes, as Matthew Arnold says; we are all spiritual Marxists. The *Anatomy* is a carnival rather than a scholastic Summa: its multiplication of terms and phases has a promiscuous aim, that of unification. The millennial hope which makes of Frye our most energetic critic is that the arts are one, that even science is a sister-art with its mythical matrix and social purpose, and that literature reveals this unity best.

Close to half a century, however, separates Frye's work from Murray's. Before we enter more deeply into our *terminus ad quem* an intermediate figure should be mentioned. This is G. Wilson Knight, whose *Miracle and Myth* (1929) and *Wheel of Fire* (1930) were radical steps forward in Shakespeare interpretation. They anticipate Frye and enunciate clearly certain structuralist tenets. The strangest of these is a distinction between "criticism" and "interpretation." Criticism is "a judgment of vision;" interpretation "a reconstruction of vision." But Knight insists on a distinction he admits is impractical only to introduce a new concept of holism. The greater the artist, says Knight, the more purely interpretive our judgment; we must accept the artist's vision in its entirety. In practice this means that we should consider Shakespeare's plays as a totality and a "Progress:" a visionary whole, a complex of characterization (Knight calls it "personification" to diminish the idea of external reference), atmospheric suggestion and continuities of theme. "Each incident," writes Knight, "each turn of thought, each suggestive symbol . . . radiates inwards from the play's circumference to the burning central core without knowledge of which we shall miss their relevance and necessity: they relate primarily, not directly to each other, nor to the normal appearances of human life, but to this central reality alone." Many years later, when *The Wheel of Fire* was reissued (1949), Knight saw that his method had an analogy in physics, and that he had replaced "character" and all such "rigid particles" by a *field* theory. His hero is not "an isolated 'character' rigidly conceived, but in direct and living relation to his own dramatic environment . . . it is precisely such a 'relationship' that lies regularly behind Shakespeare's use of symbolism as distinct from persons."

It is hard to think of a more important development for modern criticism than this change from particle to field theory. True, there had been an organicist postulate of this kind, at least since Coleridge; but now the naive dichotomy of mechanical versus organic is broken down, and the word "organicism" is seen to stand for the fact that the whole is greater than its parts, and that the whole is a system. A dream, a plant, a work of art, a machine, are all systems; the common factor being that they separate, ecologically, what is "outside" from what is "inside," and so impose, within limits, their form on whatever passes into them.

Knight, unfortunately, having modified the biological metaphor, introduces one of his own. "A Shakespearian tragedy is set spatially as well as temporally in the mind. By this I mean that there are throughout the play a set of correspondences which relate to each other independently of the time-sequence which is the story." We know what experience he is describing: the greater a work of art, the greater our sense of something that conditions every element in it. Is that something an *arche*, or a *telos*? The concept of spatial form, like structuralism itself, evades that question. By reducing time to mere sequence of events, and making it, as it were, a dimension of space, Knight is able to cross from the single work to the corpus of the artist and from that to all literature as "correspondent." His concept of spatial form is thus related to what Frye will call "total form"—the synoptic vision of all works of art as composing a simultaneous order.

But Frye carries Knight's position a step further. He argues that whatever literary structure is in itself, it must be spatial *to the critic*. Interpretation, to grasp the work as a complete and simultaneous pattern, must ignore its movement in time. The spatial is now a form that enables the understanding of art and makes criticism possible as a progressive science. This Kantian turn in the philosophy of literary structure is remarkable, but its explanation lies less in Kant than in technology. For the concept of total form is unimaginable while the artifact is still attached to sacred place or sacred time. As long as the work of art participates in its place of origin as a kind of *genius loci* it cannot enter that ideal museum—the "museum without walls"—foreseen by Eliot. Technology must first deliver art from *originality* by allowing its universal duplication and distribution. Only then can art yield its aura, and become a secular property. The "spatial" relation of critic to art thus reflects a change in the "temporal" relation of the work of art to its source in ritual or sacred history.

Frye's criticism can be seen as an attempt to value positively the influence of technology on culture, and especially on the appreciation of art. The quality of art is not his subject, but the quality of our attitude towards it, which alone can be improved. He claims, as we saw, to be writing about the structure of literary recognition, and not about the work of literature "in itself." To be transitively understood, to be understood in such a way that it can play its role in society, the work must be placed among other works, and finally among that ideal order of existing monuments which Eliot mentioned. "You cannot value the artist alone; you must set him for contrast and comparison among the dead. I mean this as a principle of esthetic, not merely historical, criticism." Technology breaks the exclusiveness of canon or cult: Frye is anything but a formalist in this respect.

Still, these optimistic Magi of the North, Frye and McLuhan, surprise me. A generation after Eliot, and in the full swing of the technological revolution, they do not seem to be afflicted by the darker insights of Ortega y Gasset, Erich Auerbach, Walter Benjamin and Günter Anders. Nor by the instinctive and general feeling that too much criticism, too much appreciation, is, if anything, dangerous to the unmediated element in art. As Keats knew: "The creative must create itself." The loss of "originality," already mentioned, and which has prompted critics like Gaston Bachelard, Georges

Poulet and Maurice Blanchot to emphasize anew poetry's "valeur d'origine," cannot be seen only as a gain for the consumer.

We approach here a critique of Frye. His archetypes are defined primarily as *communicable* symbols. They are neo-Kantian forms that serve to objectify our experience of art. Unlike the archetypes of Jung, which have too much content, and may therefore overwhelm consciousness, those of Frye have as little content as wave-lengths.[7] But media are not mediations: their structure is quite different. Whereas mediation is always precarious, media have the fixity of Kant's synthetic a priori. "The medium is the message," as one slogan puts it. The term *archetype*, however, like *principle*, is in etymological tension with the meaning Frye imposes. Both words suggest a "valeur d'origine," and our distance from it. Whether we think of Plato or Jung, archetype infers a radical discontinuity between firsts and seconds, between original and copies. Mediation is, as it were, a "third" which allows us to return to an origin, to recover, if only at moments, some link between second and first. Technology's Midas-touch, however, has turned all things into duplicates; and media, as distinguished from mediations, prevent the possibility of transcendence.

Now myth, ritual and art are clearly mediations rather than media. They presuppose a discontinuity, a separation from the *presence* they seek. Theophany, epiphany, parousia, are formal concepts defining that presence. The actors become gods, the word becomes flesh, the figure is fulfilled. Ritual seeks this "fulness of Time" by a rediscovery of the origin. Ritual is The Way Back.[8] Organic form is already, therefore, a more difficult concept to apply to art, for the organic seems always in touch with the origin, instead of having to seek it by one fateful method. In nature there is no Single Way except what leads to death; and as long as the organism can modify itself, that is, change its ways, it avoids death.

---

[7] In theory only; as a practicing critic, Frye vacillates fruitfully between the positions distinguished in note 6. His archetypes are underdetermined as principles of structure and overdetermined as poetic symbols.

[8] Cf. Mircea Eliade, *Myth and Reality* (1956; English, 1963).

Seed becomes petal, petal blossom, blossom fruit, fruit seed. As to spatial form (field theory), that seems to deny the very idea of origin, to the point where nothing is "here and now" yet everything "there."[9] Spatial form emphasizes the co-presence of all creative human acts, as if they were *gesta* of a single culture. "The four *mythoi* that we are dealing with," says Frye "may . . . be seen as four aspects of a central unifying myth. *Agon* or a sequence of marvellous adventures is the basis or archetypal theme of romance, *pathos* or catastrophe, the archetypal theme of tragedy; *sparagmos,* or the sense that heroism and effective action are absent, the archetypal theme of irony and satire; and *anagnorisis,* or recognition of a newborn society, the archetypal theme of comedy" (*Anatomy of Criticism,* p. 192). Frye's "total form" is a strange and problematic equivalent to the Presence evoked by ritual and myth.

But we never, of course, encounter *historically* Frye's total or unifying myth. No more than we meet our own anatomy. It remains the potential vision of a potential Albion. Hence it is said that Frye is a gnostic, who prefers myth to the scandal of a historical revelation. But Frye actually neglects myth rather than history: he omits a vital *structural* aspect of mythic thought. A myth mediates a discontinuity—winter, death, paradise lost, "temps perdu;" and its very movement, the narrative, is a series of bridges over a gulf. Myth participates in what Van Gennep has called a rite of passage; and since *literary* rites have at least one character in common, that they are words, or more exactly timely words, we infer that the discontinuity is temporal (like winter) and logological (like Moses's stutter).

The difference between Frye's theory of literature and a true theory can be stated most simply as the difference between two particular myths: that of Ceres and Proserpina and that of Orpheus and Eurydice. The former is Frye's fa-

---

[9] As, for example, in the copy of an original. The significance of spatial form has been variously explored by Joseph Frank, "Spatial Form in Modern Literature" (1945), Georges Poulet, *La Distance Interieure* (1952), *Les Metamorphoses du Cercle* (1961), and *Exploration in Communication,* eds. E. Carpenter and M. McLuhan (Boston 1960). But terms are deceptive: Lévi-Strauss, in the "Ouverture" to *Le Cru et Le Cuit* (1964) sees musical form as the proper analogue to the structure of myths.

vorite, but both contain identical elements. There is the quest, the descent into the underworld, the theme of death and revival. The persons in the one are gods, in the other humans; which indicates, for Frye, the difference between myth proper and Romance. This is the right distinction to make, for poetry, or the sympathetic powers of the human voice, enter the latter story far more strongly. The quest of Ceres, to be sure, is already associated with images or acts of the voice, with crying, lamenting, beseeching, and within or behind these the sense of sudden transition, the sense of being swallowed, of going from light, "the fair field of Enna," to darkness, or "gloomy Dis." All this is there, although it is not used by Frye. But the story of Orpheus, more tragic than myth, and less associated with a natural cycle, centers on poetry itself, on the mediation of the human voice. Orpheus is much closer to the figure of a mediation that failed, of a presence not brought back, of "mortal power frozen at its source." The difference between the two myths is also that between Frye and Maurice Blanchot, and represents one of the great divides separating Anglo-American and European criticism.

Yet Frye's theory is not so much faulty as incomplete. For he does, to some extent, respect the nexus of myth with discontinuity. By means of Blake's concept of imaginative states, which holds that we cannot rise directly from innocence to perfection, he introduces a dialectical principle and modulates from one (seasonal) mythos to another. This factor, however, is not truly dialectical: it does not reveal at what point the mediation failed. It is more like a natural law of the order "what goes up must come down." In fact, the seasonal cycle and the dying god archetype are used to affirm that poetry seeks the typical and recurring:

> The sequence of seasons, times of day, periods of life and death, have helped to provide for literature the combination of movement and order, of change and regularity, that is needed in all the arts. Hence the importance in poetic symbolism of the mythical figure known as the dying god, whether Adonis or Proserpina or their innumerable allotropic forms, who represent the cycle of nature.

> (*Fables of Identity,* p. 58)

What we need is a theory of recurrence (repetition) that includes a theory of discontinuity. Rites center on a periodic discontinuity in the mediatory process, but what corresponds in art to this "seasonal" awareness? This is the question badly resolved by Frye's important work; and even Lévi-Strauss, who comes closest to an answer, does not succeed in defining the true *agon*.

Lévi-Strauss proposes that myths are logical techniques to resolve the basic antinomies in thought or social existence. The Oedipus myth, for example, expresses the inability of a culture to reconcile the belief in man's autochthony with the knowledge that he is born of man and woman. Barely stated, this may not seem convincing; and I must refer the sceptic to Lévi-Strauss's key essay on "The Structural Study of Myth." But even without that fuller exposition, we can see that myth, for Lévi-Strauss, is fundamentally conservative, that it tries to respect an older theory (in the Oedipus story a cosmological belief) in the face of a knowledge irreconcilable with it. It might therefore be better to call myth a hermeneutic rather than logical technique; but this is not the place to quarrel over terms.

One should point out, however, that to call myth a logical tool ("outil logique") reflects more than the Gallic *faible* for Reason; it shows Lévi-Strauss is in the functionalist tradition. He holds that human thought is bound to run into perplexities serious enough to obstruct the progress of the mind or even of society. In this he is not different from Freud, Malinowski or Wittgenstein. Language, social structure and mental life are systems that must be cleared of blockages, pseudo-problems, or scleroses. The function of myth is to allow man to keep on functioning; and the originality of Lévi-Strauss is to show that myths resolve their antinomies not by some special logic but by the universal and common logic we use for any problem. The antinomies may change, but the logical forms remain constant.

How do these logical forms deal with the antinomy they are to resolve? Here structuralism becomes technical, and may resort to mathematical language. But I gather the following: the original problem is made to expand its context until it is brought into association with other problems which are moral and social, rather than metaphysical—in short, for which a socially structured solution exists. The Oedipus myth establishes the following linkage according to Lévi-Strauss: "The overrating of blood relations is to the underrating of blood relations as the attempt to escape autochthony is to the impossibility of succeeding in it." Social life validates the cosmological belief; and we notice again that nothing is actually dissolved or eliminated, but rather conserved by being put into this larger and specifically social context of relations.

I hope this somewhat slanted summary has suggested certain of my doubts. Do we need the dignification of an appeal to logic or mathematics? Does Lévi-Strauss say more than that certain existential paradoxes, or ontological discomforts, which might indeed perplex and even destroy the untutored mind—the paradox of love, for example, phrased memorably both by Augustine and Yeats, "For love has built his mansion in/The place of excrement"—must be integrated into life and society? In other words, that they need mediation? What myths do, then, is to provide that mediation, not so much by their apparent content, which is often a naive and jumbled story, but by a latent meaning for which a degree of initiation or at least historical sympathy is required.

Now initiation is itself an integrative and socializing procedure, so that the difference between manifest and latent meaning, if not carried too far, would itself be functional. But let us leave this possibility aside. If we wish to respect surfaces as well as depths, and so to trust our immediate impression of myths, would we not have to say that what is most obvious in them is the instability of the story-line, or of the "mediator" found for a particular problem? Is not the structure of myths, and especially of folklore, precisely that of the American movie cartoon, where, as soon as one impossible problem is resolved by the ingenuity of the hero, another supervenes? The labors of Loopy de Loop or of Jerry the Mouse are not unlike those of Hercules, or of the young boy in this Bororo legend, which serves as one of Lévi-Strauss's "myths of reference" in *Le Cru et Le Cuit* (I abridge considerably):

Once in ancient times, when the women went to gather

palms for the male initiation rites, a boy followed his
mother and raped her. The boy's father finds out and decides to take revenge. He sends his son three times to
the kingdom of the souls, asking him to bring back various musical instruments. The boy succeeds each time
with the help of his grandmother and three animals.
Furious, the father invites his son to go parrot catching.
Since parrots build their nest high in mountain sides, the
boy has to climb up a long pole to reach them. As soon
as he is up, the father takes the pole away, and the boy,
dangling in the air, holds on in the nick of time with a
magic stick provided by his grandmother. By using a liana
he gets to the top of the mountain, where he survives by
killing lizards. He eats some of them, and tucks the
others in his belt. But they rot and start asphyxiating
him. Vultures come and eat the lizards, and wake the
boy up when they start eating him too. Being sated,
however, they save him by conveying him in their beaks
down the mountain . . . (p. 43-45)

The instability of established social relations is most remarkable here. If the story reveals a "structure" it is clearly that of
the *unreliable mediator,* those vultures for instance, which by
eating the lizards save the boy from asphyxiation, but then
start eating him too. (I find this an especially appealing instance of black humor.) We easily perceive how tenuous the
thread of the tale is, as tenuous as existence itself. It is almost
as if the narrative line were the life-line. Thus we find a direct
structural equivalent to that "periodic discontinuity in the
mediatory process" previously mentioned.

Lévi-Strauss does nothing to explain the simplest, most
formal characteristic of myths or stories: their tendency to
run on, and their repetitiveness. Or rather, he simplifies this
characteristic of repetition by saying its function is to make
the structure of the myth apparent. But repetition is itself the
structure we are interested in; and here we have Kierkegaard,
Hegel, and Freud behind us. Lévi-Strauss does realize that
some story-extension of time is necessary, but only, according
to him, to allow the social integration of a basically anti-
social dilemma. By this he omits the link of repetition with
miming, with strong religious or emotional participation, and
also with a compulsive element which Freud emphasized in

the phrase "repetition-compulsion." Repetition, in other words, is a venture, an incarnation, an assault: anything but a "logical" operation. Teleological or even soteriological would be better terms.

And so we realize our aim: a theory of repetition that would include a theory of discontinuity. Story-extension of time suggests that time is not the reliable mediator Kant thought it was. The mind cannot know or resolve itself except by a temporal run, but we are unsure how much time we have, or whether we will be allowed, morally, any number of runs. We are always in the situation of Sheherezade whose life depends on telling a different story each night, and so, in a very real sense, on "making time." Perhaps language is also more precarious than we have the power to acknowledge. Perhaps the very existence of literary as distinguished from non-literary discourse shows that we "make language" as we make time. Yet language too is raised by structuralism to the dignity of a Kantian form or a priori mediation. Here Ernst Cassirer and I. A. Richards have been equally influential. Their optimistic view of the symbolic or therapeutic powers of language makes it a medium and a method rather than a mediation to be renewed by the vulnerable genius of each single poet. "Genius," says Blake, "dies with its Possessor, and does not rise again until Another is born." Everything turns on the individual, on his saving power of address, though with it he calls into being something greater—a society, a world.

A theory of literature should be able to distinguish between literary and non-literary discourse, but it should also tell us the difference between literature and other forms of symbolic action, such as ritual. The difference between, in particular, ritual and literature, is defined neatly by the school of Frazer as one between source and derivation: ritual is prior, and myth is the middle term between the *dromenon* of ritual (the sacred mime, the thing acted in distinction to the thing said) and literature. But structuralism discounts the genetic or historical assumptions of Frazer. As Frye puts it: "The *Golden Bough* . . . reconstructs an archetypal ritual from which the structural and generic principles of drama may be *logically*, not chronologically, derived. To the critic, the archetypal ritual is hypothesis, not history."[10] This is methodologically sound, but does not help us to state how art differs from myth or ritual.

What *can* help us? I think we must first accept something like Frazer's hypothesis, but explore it in a phenomenological rather than logical (à la Frye) way. When Georges Poulet determines the "beginning" position of a poet's consciousness, or when the analyst seeks to discover the primal scene expressed obliquely and repetitively in a writer's work, he respects the structure of art even if he cannot prove the historical, or more-than-imaginary, reality of this *first event*. Even the formalist, who has renounced depth-analysis, cannot deny that art evokes the sense of something hidden which teases the mind like Keats' "Bride of Quietness." This hermeneutic character of art is quite apparent and always contains a hint of the muteness of the things to be interpreted. Thus the plot of *Hamlet* is set going by a "spectacle," an apparition that demands to be deciphered (it is "a questionable shape"); while in the play itself we have Hamlet's "mime" to catch the conscience of the king. The mime is the *dromenon* of sacred drama in vestigial form; but is there a literary work without the quality of a charade? Poetry has often been defined as "a speaking picture."

Art, in short, discovers something that corresponds on the level of society or history to the movement from esoteric to exoteric and from sacred to secular. Perhaps we can differentiate art from ritual by determining how it structures this movement. It is of the most utmost importance to overcome naive antinomies of sacred and secular. They prevail not only in historiography but also in personal and even national psychoses. Anthropology has helped to overcome them by showing that the sacred is not a class of special things but rather a special class of things. Every kind of content can be found in this class of the sacred; what differentiates one society from another, or one historical stage from another, is the change in what is classified as sacred and what as profane. But art seems generically and ambiguously involved

[10] "The Language of Poetry," in *Explorations in Communication*, eds. E. Carpenter and M. McLuhan. Cf. *Anatomy of Criticism*, pp. 108-110.

with sacred and profane. Its relation to myth and romance has persisted; it is always "inauthentic" vis-à-vis the purity of ritual *and* vis-à-vis a thorough-going realism. This generic impurity is the best clue to its nature.

A Kafka parable may help us to define more closely art's mixed essence:

> Leopards break into the temple and drink the sacrificial chalices dry; this occurs repeatedly, again and again: finally it can be reckoned on beforehand and becomes part of the ceremony.

Profanation enters the inner sanctum, and becomes part of the holy. From a purist or ritual point of view there is contamination. The sense that the holy is contaminated is one of the views that emerges from Kafka's work as a whole. Not the death of God, but his impurity. Yet as soon as we read the story as a parable, which refers beyond the special case of ritual to life as such, a new meaning emerges. Does not every society, every relationship, every system have its necessary and permitted profanations? We think of the Greek satyr play, the Roman Saturnalia, and the "holy profanation" of the body in the daily institution of marriage. Is not art itself an institution of this kind?

To begin with words *as* words. They can be viewed as on the side of profanation. The ineffable is expressed; they are intrinsically a movement from esoteric to exoteric, or beyond solipsism. But there are solipsistic societies as well as solipsistic individuals. If words "expose" the private dream, they also "expose" public illusions—the solipsistic on the level of society is the sacred, and literature is a kind of loyal (though not always legal) opposition which opens the sacred to scrutiny, and so at once profanes and purifies it. But it is less a matter of destroying than of demystifying whatever is held to be sacred. Philosophies that consider secularization as a fall from some holy age and golden clime are infected by the very mentality which art criticizes from within. The secular is the sacred integrated, rather than degraded or displaced.

In some writers we feel the trespass of words directly. Henry James comes immediately to mind. Myth is not only the open form of ritual, the "leaf-fring'd legend" which "haunts about" an "unravish'd" event; myth is a necessary and precarious profanation of a "sacred secret." And so is literature: but now speech itself becomes vulnerable and open to violation. Poetry moves us toward a new sense of the profaned word. The history of literature, in its broadest aspect, appears to be a continual breach of levels of style (high style being profaned, low style elevated), or a history of metaphorical transference (sacred attributes being secularized, and vice-versa).[11] Thus literature and myth are not mere accretions to a central mystery but involved in its very nature. They *penetrate* and become part of the structure of the sacred event, as in Kafka's parable. Great art is always flanked by its dark sisters, blasphemy and pornography. What Yeats says cannot be bettered, and I conclude with it. The soul must become "its own betrayer, its own deliverer, the mirror turn lamp." Without an exemplary trespass of this kind there would be no self-transcendence, no heroism, no myth, no literature—indeed no regeneration.

[11] This emerges not only from the synoptic work of Erich Auerbach, Northrop Frye, M. H. Abrams, André Malraux and others, but also from the simple if important criterion of stylistics (popularized by the Russian formalists) that in literary as distinguished from normative discourse language is "deformed," "estranged," "rebarbarized." The poet subjects language to an "organized violence." Yet, as Mukarosky pointed out, it is the essence of the esthetic norm to be broken. Cf. the brilliant and neglected article of Walker Percy, "Metaphor as Mistake," *Sewanee Review*, LXVI (1958), 79-99.

Structures of exchange in *Cinna*

Jacques Ehrmann

At the exact center of Corneille's *Cinna* (III, iii), we find Cinna soliloquizing. He is undecided as to whether he should continue to plot against Auguste in order to win Emilie's love or remain faithful to a ruler who not only has just given him permission to marry Emilie but also intends to give him a share of the power which Auguste now finds tiresome. I would like to paraphrase the three parts of his soliloquy as a prelude to examining more closely the second part which is at the center of this particular center. Cinna is questioning himself:

1. How, he asks, shall I label the act which I am about to commit (the murder of Auguste) except as a "weakness"? I am doing it only in order to please a woman (Emilie) who has brought me to this weakness. What should my decision be? (v. 865-874).

2. Every solid reason which I latch on to (that I am sacrificing myself for love, revenging myself, performing a glorious and liberating act) does not seem sufficiently strong to justify an act which is no less than treason against the emperor who "has overwhelmed me with honors," "laden me with goods." No, I cannot commit this crime (v. 875-893).

3. Still, I have an obligation to Emilie and so cannot withdraw: "On you Emilie, falls the decision about what I must do" (v. 893-905). But perhaps there is a chance that I can make her change her mind (v. 893-905).

Let us take a closer look at the second part of this scene:

> Qu'une âme généreuse a de peine à faillir!
> Quelque *fruit* que par là j'espère de cueillir,
> Les douceurs de l'amour, celles de la vengeance,
> La gloire d'affranchir le lieu de ma naissance,
> N'ont point assez d'appas pour flatter ma raison,
> S'il les faut *acquérir* par une trahison,
> S'il faut percer le flanc d'un prince magnanime
> Qui du peu que je suis fait une telle estime,
> Qui me *comble* d'honneurs, qui m'*accable* de biens,
> Qui ne *prend* pour régner de conseils que les miens.
>   (v. 875-884)

> *Périsse* mon amour, périsse mon espoir,
> Plutôt que de ma main parte un crime si noir!
> Quoi? ne m'*offre*-t-il pas tout ce que je souhaite,
> Et qu'au *prix* de son sang ma passion *achète*?

Pour jouir de ses *dons* faut-il l'assassiner?
Et faut-il lui *ravir* ce qu'il me veut *donner*?
(v. 887-892)

The italic words establish with adequate clarity the nature of
the relations which exist between the three main characters—
Emilie, Cinna, and Auguste. These relations are based on a
certain conception of exchange, so much so that it is not exaggerated to say that they are almost "economic" by nature. I
intend to follow this theme with each of the partners in the
exchange and, in the process, show the play's organization, its
internal arrangement, and the structures which make it coherent.

I should point out straight off that the malaise experienced
by Cinna is an outgrowth of his hesitation between two systems of exchange: the one proposed by Emilie and the one
which the emperor proposes. In his relations with Emilie,
Cinna cannot cull benefits (Emilie herself, Rome's freedom,
glory) except by *acquiring* them at the *price* of treason since
the man he must assassinate in order to win Emilie is the same
Auguste who *overwhelms* him with honors and *ladens* him
with goods. In terms of Emilie's system, the exchange is set
up on the following links:

gather—acquire—overwhelm.

In his relations with Auguste, Cinna prefers to see his love
perish rather than betray his emperor who is ready to *offer*
him what he, Cinna, is about to *buy*—Emilie, Rome's freedom
—by bringing about the death of the giver; such an action
amounts in a way to *pillaging* the goods he is about to *be
given*. In this second system (v. 887-893), the exchange is set
up on the following links:

perish—offer—buy—prize—pillage—(—give, idem offer)

To understand the meaning of each of these acts and of each
of the systems of exchange, we need only consider their double nature: to gather is to take, but it is also to receive freely;
to acquire is at once to take and pay for what one has taken;
to overwhelm is, for one person, to give and, for the other,
to receive freely. A network of identities (=) or equations

and of contraries (+) is thus set up. The first system looks schematically like this:

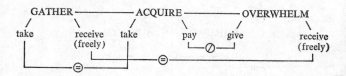

The second system looks like this:

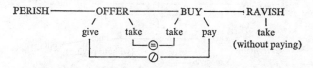

In the latter scheme we see that: 1) *to offer* and *to buy* are symmetrical; 2) *to perish* is the equivalent of *to lose:* "May my love perish . . ." Cinna cries out, indicating that he prefers to lose Emilie rather than betray Auguste; 3) to pillage and to lose (to perish) are also symmetrical because both have the common property of being indivisible. Since they are verbs with only one meaning—and describe one-way actions—they cut the exchange off abruptly; but they are also opposites since, in the case of *to pillage,* the subject profits from his action; in the case of *to lose* he finds himself stripped of a possession.

Finally, if we set up the first system as a kind of mirror to the second, we notice the symmetry of the acts which compose them and which thereby serve to set off the difficulty in which Cinna finds himself. (See page 162.)

This is a double symmetry which can be considered either along the vertical axis set up by Cinna (A A') or else along the horizontal axis which passes from acquire to buy (B B'). There is, as we have already seen, only one point where the symmetry breaks down: with *pillage,* a word with a one-way meaning. Here the imbalance of the system shows itself and here, too, is the beginning of Cinna's disarray. For, as Cinna now sees, to kill Auguste is an act with no counterpart and therefore an act with no justification. *To pillage* the life of

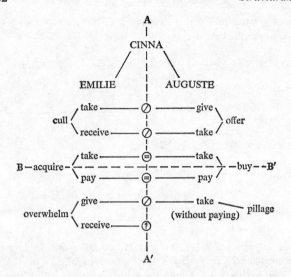

Auguste is *to take, without payment,* the life of the individual who, as the other axis shows, is overwhelming his murderer with goods and honors. The only possible outcome, as Cinna indicated in the third part of his soliloquy, would be *to give back* what one intends to pillage. But how can Cinna give back that which, because of the fealty he has pledged to Emilie, he no longer possesses (v. 897-900):

> C'est à vous à régler ce qu'il faut que je fasse;
> C'est à vous, Emilie, à lui donner sa grâce;
> Vos seules volontés président à son sort,
> Et tiennent en mes mains et sa vie et sa mort.

The decision is no longer his because he is now no more than the hand which carries out Emilie's wishes. This leads to the important theme of the hand, the gift's agent, about which I shall have more to say presently.

The problem of exchange is complicated by the problem of the person. To give, to offer, to acquire, etc., are not adequate to give a proper account of the whole act. In order to give proper meaning to acts, we must also know who is giving what to whom. Cinna puts it this way (v. 250-254):

Demain j'attends la haine ou la ferveur des hommes,
Le nom de parricide ou de libérateur,
César celui de prince ou d'un usurpateur.
Du succès qu'on obtient contre la tyrannie
Dépend ou notre gloire ou notre ignominie . . .

There are two alternatives. The identity of the individual who
deals death to another, like the identity of the individual who
is murdered, will depend on the success or failure of the plot.
If the plot succeeds, Cinna will be the Liberator; if he fails,
he will be a parricide. If the plot succeeds, Auguste will be
the tyrant; if it fails, he will be the ruler.

Reciprocally, the nature of the gift will be dependent on
the person of the giver or the receiver. Schematically, it works
out this way:

Cinna brings death to Auguste
Cinna brings freedom to Rome
Cinna receives love from Emilie
Cinna receives fame from Rome

Everything would be for the best if this schematization coin-
cided with reality. But we must ask whether Auguste is still
the tyrant whose portrait Cinna traced, first to the conspirators
and, later, to Emilie (v. 163-243). Or is he the just monarch
of the portrait which the same Cinna traces in the presence of
Auguste himself (v. 405-442)? Reality has changed once
Auguste informs Cinna of his intention to give Cinna both
the empire and Emilie. The equation made between the death
of Auguste and the freedom of Rome is false once Cinna becomes the first to recognize that Auguste is no longer a tyrant
and once he is the first to profit from the transformation
which has taken place in the emperor.

Since the identity of the recipient involves that of the giver,
the giver's act boomerangs. And so we have the contradictory
situation in which Cinna finds himself—"basely working towards a noble goal" (v. 852). The contradiction is manifest
in his anguish and indecision. As a result, his soliloquy is the
pause between two decisions and corresponds to the character's need to evaluate the possibilities of the exchange, to
weigh the probable gain and loss which will result from his
commitment.

The other soliloquies in the play show similar characteristics. That is particularly true with Emilie's at the opening of
the play; in that soliloquy she is trying to "get things straight,"
to think over the conditions of the gamble and the stakes involved (v. 6-8):

> Durant quelques moments souffrez que je respire,
> Et que je considère, en l'état où je suis,
> Et ce que je *hasarde,* et ce que je *poursuis.*

What she is after is the death of her father's murderer, Auguste: "A thousand deaths are his due for the murder he has
done." In other words, no price can be set on the death of a
father. What she is endangering is the life of Cinna, the man
she loves: "I risk your blood in asking you for his." In other
words, she is gambling Cinna's life with Auguste as the stakes:
"If, in revenging myself, I lose you, then I have no revenge"
(v. 36).

> Et l'on doit mettre au rang des plus cuisants malheurs
> La mort d'un ennemi qui *coûte* tant de pleurs.
> Mais peut-on en verser alors qu'on venge un père?
> Est-il *perte* à ce *prix* qui ne semble légère?
> Et quand son assassin tombe sous notre effort,
> Doit-on considérer ce que *coûte* sa mort?
>
> (v. 39-44)

This turnabout leads to a very Cornelian situation: love must
be fame's servant and, in so being, increase fame's reserves.
It isn't much different from getting better dividends through
shrewd investment of capital (v. 48-52):

> Amour, sers mon devoir, et ne le combats plus:
> Lui céder, c'est ta gloire, et le vaincre, ta honte:
> Montre-toi généreux, souffrant qu'il te surmonte;
> Plus tu lui *donneras,* plus il te va *donner,*
> Et ne triomphera que pour te couronner.

But she has made up her mind. Once her confidente appears,
Emilie can convey her decision in categorical terms (v.
53-56):

> Je l'ai juré, Fulvie, et je le jure encore,
> Quoique j'aime Cinna, quoique mon coeur l'adore,
> S'il veut me *posséder,* Auguste doit *périr:*
> Sa tête est le seul *prix* dont il peut m'*acquérir.*

The last verse is an amplification of the preceding, almost a translation of Emilie's thought into the economic language of the exchange. The roles she accepts can be seen in this kind of breakdown; 1) Emilie sells herself to Cinna for the price of Auguste; 2) Emilie buys Auguste from Cinna with herself as the prize. We should notice that the "price" and the "prize" are barter, not abstract or monetary. This gives them their double meaning. If the price which Cinna must pay in order to *obtain* Emilie is Auguste, the prize (the reward) that he will obtain for the murder of Auguste will be Emilie since, at that point, he will be able to "possess" her. Emilie's roles are thus reversible and contradictory since she is at once the buyer and the seller, the object sold and the purchase price.

The fact that the prices are fixed "as barter" does not make them any more stable. Quite the contrary. As Fluvie knows when she questions the price that Emilie is demanding from Cinna. The prize is Auguste, the emperor who distributes benefices and favors, the emperor who, like Emilie, gives prizes. And these prizes, these rewards, are awards from which Emilie herself will profit—as Fluvie reminds her (v. 63-64):

> Auguste chaque jour, à force de bienfaits,
> Semble assez réparer les maux qu'il vous a faits . . .

Emilie answers this argument (v. 69-74; 78-84):

> Toute cette faveur ne me *rend* pas mon père;
> Et de quelque façon que l'on me considère,
> Abondante en *richesse,* ou puissante en *crédit,*
> Je demeure toujours la fille d'un proscrit.
> Les *bienfaits* ne font pas toujours ce que tu penses;
> D'un main odieuse ils tiennent lieu d'offenses . . .
> Je suis ce que j'étois, et je puis davantage,
> Et des mêmes *présents* qu'il verse dans mes mains
> J'*achète* contre lui les esprits des Romains;
> Je *recevrois* de lui la place de Livie
> Comme un moyen plus sûr d'attenter à sa vie.
> Pour qui venge son père il n'est point de forfaits,
> Et c'est *vendre* son sang que se *rendre* aux *bienfaits.*

Though Auguste may have changed, Emilie has stayed the same in spite of the gifts which have been tendered her. Why?

Because all the material benefits, or even the prestige which
Auguste might grant to Emilie, would not be enough to compensate for the death which he has "given" to her father or,
seen from another angle, the life he has "taken" from him.
No price, as we have seen, can be set on a father's life. Furthermore, the issue goes beyond the question of a father's
death to touch on the question of every death and every life
which no material offer can redeem. Emilie knows this: All
the riches offered by Auguste, and transmitted to the conspirators, cannot make the plot succeed unless she gives herself
almost as the booty which the leader of the plot will receive in
exchange for the life of Auguste that she is demanding. Emilie
is also aware of the importance of her person in the economy
of vengeance and the coup d'état since she gambles with it
in speaking to Cinna (v. 1035-1036):

> Mille autres à l'envi *recevroient* cette *loi*,
> S'ils pouvoient m'*acquérir* à même *prix* que toi.

In addition she is fully aware that, whatever his power, Auguste cannot *give* her to anyone. Whatever goods he may control, Auguste does not yet possess mastery over hearts (v.
939-944). Since persons and goods are situated on two different planes, they constitute incomparable, un-exchangeable
gifts-in-kind. The person in Corneille's universe may be de-
structible; he cannot be trafficked in. Emilie begins her
soliloquy by saying that "all these favors do not bring my father back to me," and concludes by picking up the same idea
again (v. 83-84):

> Pour qui venge son père il n'est point de forfaits,
> Et c'est *vendre* son sang que se rendre aux bienfaits.

If personal revenge has the prime place in Emilie's mind, it
is reinforced and confirmed by the spirit of public vengeance
(v. 107-112):

> Joignons à la douceur de venger nos parents,
> La gloire qu'on remporte à punir les tyrans,
> Et faisons publier par toute l'Italie:
> "La liberté de Rome est l'oeuvre d'Emilie;
> On a touché son âme, et son coeur s'est épris;
> Mais elle n'a donné son amour qu'à ce *prix*."

"Emilie's interest" comes before "that of the Romans," for the fame that will be the *dividend* of her act is purely egocentric, "interested," even though, in appearance at least, it goes against her own (amorous) *interest*—as Fluvie tries to make her understand (v. 113-114):

> Votre amour à ce *prix* n'est qu'un présent *funeste*
> Qui porte à votre amant sa *perte* manifeste.

It is unquestionably a somber gift, not only because in giving herself to Cinna, Emilie is at the same time handing him over to death but also because she is taking him away from herself by her own will. After wavering for a moment, she gets hold of herself (v. 133-134):

> Quoi qu'il en soit, qu'Auguste ou que Cinna périsse,
> Aux mânes paternels, je *dois* ce sacrifice.

Emilie's primary interest is the same as her family's. Within the terms of this interest—at least as far as she can see—one life is worth another. At this level of the exchange, lives become interchangeable:

> Auguste: Cinna : : Emilie's father

What is important to Emilie is that there be a sacrifice of some kind; that there be some destruction equivalent to the destruction of her father.

Emilie's intransigence is not understandable unless we recognize that she does not claim the sacrifice as an individual but rather as a moral person, as the representative of her blood, her family, her household gods.[1] By sacrificing Au-

---

[1] There are certain resemblances visible between this and the system of *potlatch* analyzed by Marcel Mauss in his now classic "Essai sur le don" (*Sociologie et Anthropologie*, P.U.F., 1950). In the potlatch—a form of gift exchange which is at once freely willed and performed under constraint, gratuitous and yet done with a purpose, that is practised in Polynesia, Melanesia, and elsewhere—individuals do not find themselves in confrontation as individuals so much as in their capacity as representatives of the "mind of their ancestors." With them, as with Corneille's characters, it is a question of honor. "This," Mauss writes, "is noble commerce, full of politeness and generosity; in any case, whenever it is done in some other spirit, with an eye to immediate gain, it is the object of clearly manifested scorn" (p. 201-202). Elsewhere, Mauss writes: "Polynesian *mana* itself symbolizes not only the magical force

guste—and, if necessary, Cinna—to these demands she expects to earn an abundance of honor. The sacrifice, therefore, is positive for her. Auguste, for his part, is obeying a similar principle when he offers the empire and Emilie to Cinna. He, too, is counting on emerging from his sacrifice and gift as a greater man.

We have seen that Cinna has nothing to counterbalance these exercises in prestige—at least he can set up no alternative which will add to his prestige. If he *offers* Auguste to Emilie, he will betray Auguste and, in the bargain, *lose* his honor which amounts to no more nor less than *losing* himself; if he agrees to receive the empire and Emilie from Auguste's hands, he will also lose. As a result, neither the gift nor the sacrifice makes any sense unless they offer the promise, as a counterpart to the loss the sacrificing individual undergoes, of an immaterial gain in fame and honor which alone give the individual his amplitude and genuine identity. When applied to the three main characters this dialectic between sacrifice (or gift) and identity unveils the architecture and the rhythm of the play. Each character possesses a "special space" which is properly his and to which he brings a particular mood. Emilie's special space corresponds to the beginning of the play where her mood is aggressive and set on conquest. Cinna's special space is at the play's center when the mood is one of questioning and doubt. Auguste's special space corresponds to the denouement of the play; generosity and assurance are its dominant qualities.

As the play opens, Emilie declares, after some hesitation, that she is ready to sacrifice Auguste (or Cinna) to the de-

of each being but also his honor; some of the best translations of this word would be: authority, richness" (p. 203). As can be seen, the economy of relationships as it appears in Corneille is partially based, as in the potlatch, on a system of "generous" gifts which is at once free and obligatory. But the honor of the characters—like the *mana* Mauss speaks of—is also involved in this exchange; it is stronger than the individuals who practise it and without it they could not properly be said to exist. Though I do not wish to push the comparison any further, I hope that these few similarities will have allowed us to get a surer hold on the economic elements which are an essential part of the Corneilian individual's constitution.

mands of her household gods. Cinna also agrees with enthusiasm (I, iii) to sacrifice a tyrant to Rome and to Emilie, a tyrant who never hesitated to affirm his own power through countless sacrifices. But what will come to pass if the tyrant, at the height of his power (v. 357-359), worn out by ambition which no longer has any object (v. 365), instead of *taking* decides to *give*, instead of sacrificing others sacrifices himself? (v. 624-627)

> Je consens à me *perdre* afin de la [Rome] sauver.
> Pour ma tranquillité mon coeur en vain soupire:
> Cinna, par vos conseils je retiendrai l'empire;
> Mais je le retiendrai pour vous en *faire part.*

Not satisfied with leaving his empire to Cinna, he offers "as a bonus," Emilie, the woman Cinna loves (v. 637; 643-645):

> Pour épouse, Cinna, je vous *donne* Emilie: . . .
> Voyez-la de ma part, tâchez de la *gagner:*
> Vous n'êtes point pour elle un homme à dédaigner;
> De l'*offre* de vos voeux elle sera ravie.

The splendor of this double gift is enough to astonish the potential assassin, enough to make him do a literal turnabout. The murder which was supposed to free Rome from a tyrant and allow Cinna to marry Emilie no longer has a strict object once Auguste is no longer a tyrant and offers Emilie to Cinna.

The middle of the play, which I used as my point of departure—believing that we can only untie knots where we find them—corresponds to that balanced moment where *the meaning of the exchange changed.* The moment is one of paralysis, of breakdown, of *meaninglessness,* all of which prevent Cinna, the prisoner of two betrayals and two false understandings, from acting. His indecision in the third scene of Act III continues through the following scenes and even into Act IV. It affects Auguste as much as it does Cinna.

By starting with Cinna's case, we can see how this confusion about the person of the giver and the object given provokes this identity crisis. This is especially visible if we read Cinna's dialogue with Emilie which comes immediately after the soliloquy of scene iii. Here we see the degree to which gift and identity have become (or should become) synonymous, as I suggested at the outset (v. 911-916):

> *Cinna:* Le désavouerez-vous, et du *don* qu'il me fait
> Voudriez-vous retarder le bienheureux effet?
> *Emilie:* L'effet est en ta *main.*
> *Cinna:* Mais plutôt en la *vôtre.*
> *Emilie:* Je suis toujours moi-même, et mon coeur n'est
> point autre:
> Me *donner* à Cinna, c'est ne lui *donner* rien,
> C'est seulement lui faire un *présent* de son *bien.*

Emilie alone knows who she is because she alone knows what she is giving. Cinna has no similar certainty anymore. He realizes that Emilie's present does not correspond to the identification, the equation, Emilie-Cinna (v. 915) which she claims to be establishing: "But think at what price you are giving me your soul," he exclaims. To which Emilie replies, not without reason, by setting up a distinction with regard to the nature of the gift (v. 936-939; 943):

> Et ton esprit crédule ose s'imaginer
> Qu'Auguste, pouvant tout, peut aussi me *donner.*
> Tu me veux de *sa main* plutôt que de la *mienne;*
> Mais ne crois pas qu'ainsi jamais je *t'appartienne:* . . .
> Mais le coeur d'Emilie est hors de son pouvoir.

Further on she says (v. 957-960):

> et tu veux que moi-même
> Je retienne *ta main!* qu'il vive, et que je l'aime!
> Que je sois le *butin* de qui l'ose l'*épargner,*
> Et le *prix* du conseil qui le force à régner!

To consent to this, I might add, would be to lose possession of oneself and to agree to being treated as an object, as booty pillaged by the conqueror. This explains Emilie's anger and her rejection of her lover's offers of service once she has informed him that others would have been happy to do what he has refused (v. 1034-1038):

> Et si pour me *gagner* il faut trahir ton maître,
> Mille autres à l'envi *recevroient* cette loi,
> S'ils pouvoient m'*acquérir* à même *prix* que toi.

Mais n'appréhende pas qu'un autre ainsi m'*obtienne*.
Vis pour ton cher tyran, tandis que je meure *tienne* . . .

Immediately after, she claims she is ready to kill Auguste with her own hands and sacrifice herself through this deed.

In bypassing the possibility of an intermediary, she places the responsibility of her death on her lover and produces, quite literally, a short circuit which is likely to burn out the network of the exchange. Faced with this, Cinna begins indulging in a similar kind of blackmail (v. 1055-1066). The sacrifice, since it has no counterpart, amounts to a genuine suicide: it is founded on an unreciprocated gift and is thus a pure loss. The short circuit, the break in the exchange, is thus not only a means whereby the individual denies himself, but also a way of denying the society in which he is one of the necessary links.[2] Auguste gives clear expression to the social meaning of suicide. When Euphorbe informs him of the supposed suicide of Maxime (v. 1113-1114), Auguste answers (v. 1115-1117):

Sous ce pressant remords il a trop succombé,
Et s'est à mes bontés lui-même *dérobé;*
Il n'est crime envers moi qu'un repentir n'efface.

By removing himself from life, Maxime has deprived and cheated the emperor of the possibility of pardoning him and consequently of redeeming him.

Yet Auguste himself is tempted by suicide which he envisages as one of the possible solutions of the conspiracy which is being formed against him and about which he has learned. By taking his own life, he expects to be able to anticipate a similar design on Cinna's part and in so doing to deprive him of whatever fame might come to him from the assassination (v. 1170-1176):

Meurs et *dérobe*-lui la gloire de ta chute . . .
Meurs, puisque c'est un mal que tu ne peux guérir;
Meurs enfin, puisqu'il faut ou tout *perdre,* ou mourir.

---

[2] For a discussion of the social value attributed to suicide in the literature of the first half of the seventeenth century, see my *Un Paradis désespéré* . . . , P.U.F., 1962.

The alternative is simple: either the conspirators are doomed or he is. In either case there will be a sacrifice, a dead loss. Still, this is only one of the alternatives which Auguste envisages in his soliloquy (IV, ii). The lack of resolution which he evinces is the same as that shown by Cinna in his soliloquy. It is inspired by similar reasons which have to do with the ties that bind gift and identity together. If Auguste is forced to question his identity once again, it is because he has observed how the exchange has become impossible once the circulation of gifts is blocked. The question is no longer one of giving the empire to Cinna since Cinna's design is to take it from him by taking his life. He no longer knows either in whom he can confide his own interests nor to whom he can confide the empire (v. 1121-1124):

> Ciel, à qui voulez-vous désormais que je fie
> Les secrets de mon âme et le soin de ma vie?
> Reprenez le pouvoir que vous m'avez commis,
> Si donnant des sujets il ôte les amis.

Asking heaven to accept the empire's burdens is a fairly frivolous way of giving up one's own responsibilities and of removing the problem of power from the political arena in order to place it in a very personal realm, or even in the care of eternity.

After this first movement—which reveals how far Auguste has yet to go—Auguste considers several solutions. In the first he adopts the conspirators' viewpoint and attempts to see the reasons behind their actions through their eyes. He reviews the history of bloodshed for which he was responsible while acquiring the empire and concludes that faithless blood will be infidelity's price.[3] Meditating on the conspirators' fraud, he stumbles across his own: for this blood, far from giving him the empire *in exchange,* is something he has *taken* from those who opposed him. Having made others *pay* for a good he possesses, he should in turn *pay* by giving his blood at this point in his life in order to *give* the empire *back.* The situation

[3] This is the argument which Livie will answer later in maintaining that state crimes cannot be compared to individual crimes (v. 1609-1610).

once again is symmetrical, albeit in a thoroughly negative
way—the way of exchanges which are established on the
reciprocity of a contradiction. On the one hand, it is a question
of *taking* the blood of others in order to *purchase* the empire.
On the other, it is a question of *giving* his blood in order to
pay for the empire.

To this kind of solution, Auguste opposes another: destroy
Cinna who seeks to destroy the empire in the person of its
leader. But such a solution is no more possible than the other.
Cinna's attempt cannot be compared to his predecessors', for
they had sought to overturn a tyrant and Auguste was obliged
to suppress them in order to affirm his power. Now that he
has this power, Auguste is no longer a tyrant—and Cinna
knows it. Thus an attack on Auguste's life is no more nor less
than an attack on the "state's good fortune." What bothers
Auguste is that punishment meted out to Cinna risks becoming a return to tyranny and thereby risks justifying a posteriori
Cinna's attempt and those which may come in its aftermath.
Auguste realizes that the loss of Cinna would be a dead loss
because, as a result of it, he would fall back to the *status quo
ante:* tyranny.

All the emperor's envisaged solutions—recourse to heaven,
compliance in his own assassination, punishment for Cinna,
suicide—are defective. Why? Because each of them, as I have
tried to show, rests on a suppression which has no counterpart, on an annulment, since Auguste either steals or steals
away. In other words, no one of the solutions is possible because all of them contradict all the rules governing the circuit
of exchange.

At the end of his soliloquy Auguste has found no solution;
his questions and exclamations are evidence of his indecision
(v. 1187-1192):

> O Romains, ô vengeance, ô pouvoir absolu
> Qui fuit en même temps ce qu'il se propose!
> D'un prince malheureux ordonnez quelque chose.
> Qui des deux dois-je suivre, et duquel m'éloigner?
> Ou laissez-moi périr, ou laissez-moi régner.

In the following scene Livie makes a proposal which would
allow Auguste to open the circuit once again: "Pardoning

him can add to your renown" (v. 1214). It seems that there is still something else which Auguste can acquire; his empire and his fame are not yet at an end since, to his present possessions, Auguste can add something.

Still, Auguste's fatigue leads him to answer Livie's arguments with a desire to go away, to give up (v. 1237-1240):

> *Livie:* Quoi? vous voulez *quitter le fruit* de tant de
>   peines?
> *Auguste:* Quoi? vous voulez *garder* l'objet de tant de
>   haines?
> *Livie:* Seigneur, vous emporter à cette extrémité,
>   C'est plutôt désespoir que génerosité.

Her head still clear, Livie points out that it is just this generosity (the *clémence* of the play's subtitle) which corresponds to self-possession. "This," she tells him, "is how one governs himself." But Auguste does not *possess* himself precisely because he is letting himself go. He therefore is not ready to *give*, to be clement for once, not where goods are involved, but where a life is at stake.

Before discussing how Auguste finally achieves self-possession and at the same time manifests his clemency, we should return to the beginning of the crisis—a crisis which is concerned simultaneously with power and identity.

At the beginning of the second act, Auguste asks his two close counselors, Cinna and Maxime, if he should hold on to his power or give it up. In possession of everything, Auguste remains unsatisfied. He knows that this dissatisfaction is the result of desire's tendency to want what it does not yet possess. Since he already possesses everything, the only thing left to possess is himself (v. 365-370):

> L'ambition déplaît quand elle est assouvie,
> D'une contraire ardeur son ardeur est suivie;
> Et comme notre esprit, jusqu'au dernier soupir,
> Toujours vers quelque objet pousse quelque désir,
> Il se ramène en soi, n'ayant plus où se prendre,
> Et monté sur le faîte, il aspire à descendre.

Yet who is he? A tyrant cut from the same cruel cloth as Sylla and possessed of the hope that simply by giving up all

power he will die peacefully? Or, like Caesar, a just sovereign
risking assassination by the Roman senate? A circle emerges
from such questions, for each question interminably sends
him back to the following: What do I possess? And do I possess myself? How have I gained my possessions? What do I
possess? etc . . . Such questioning produces indecision in
Auguste and leads him to do what precisely is impossible
for one in his position: he asks his advisors to make up his
mind for him (v. 393-396):

> Voilà, mes chers amis, ce qui me met en peine.
> Vous, qui me tenez lieu d'Agrippe et de Mécène,
> Pour résoudre ce point avec eux débattu,
> *Prenez* sur mon esprit le *pouvoir* qu'ils ont eu.

Cinna and Maxime reply in turn, Cinna urging Auguste to remain at the helm for the following reasons (v. 413-416):

> On ne *renonce* point aux grandeurs légitimes;
> On *garde* sans remords ce qu'on *acquiert* sans crimes;
> Et plus le *bien* qu'on *quitte* est noble, grand, exquis,
> Plus qui l'ose *quitter* le juge *mal acquis.*

On the basis of such arguments, Auguste is not a tyrant. His
armed conquest of Rome was legitimate. If he disavows this,
he disavows Caesar and, in so doing, identifies himself with
Sylla (v. 424-432):

Pour être usurpateurs [les conquérants] ne sont pas des tyrans
Quand ils ont sous leurs lois asservis des provinces,
Gouvernant justement, ils s'en font juste princes:
C'est ce qui fit César; il vous faut aujourd'hui
Condamner sa mémoire, ou faire comme lui.
Si le pouvoir suprême est blâmé par Auguste,
César fut un tyran, et son trépas fut juste,
Et vous devez aux Dieux compte de tout le sang
Dont vous l'avez vengé pour monter à son rang.

It is clear that this proposal anticipates those which Auguste
will himself put forward in his fourth act soliloquy. Cinna
pursues his point by offering an apologia of monarchy: the
prince is the "rightful possessor" of the kingdom and the sole
dispenser of goods and honors (v. 505). The monarch, as a
result, falls under the sign of the gift in contrast to the "popu-

lar state" (the republic) which Cinna denounces by placing it
under the venal sign of sale or theft: "Honors are sold . . .
authority given up." And again: "Since they have little concern with the goods they control, they reap a rich harvest from
the public field" (v. 517-518). As far as Cinna is concerned,
returning Rome to freedom in order to give Rome her freedom back amounts to little more than returning Rome to the
very disorder from which Auguste rescued the city; the profit
which Rome has taken from Auguste's rise to power will be
annulled; it is very much like a suicide on the political level,
for the result of the exchange is *a dead loss* (v. 607-616):

> Considérez le *prix* que vous avez *coûté*:
> Non pas qu'elle vous croie avoir trop *acheté*;
> Des maux qu'elle a soufferts elle est trop bien *payée*;
> Mais une juste peur tient son âme effrayée;
> Si jaloux de son heur, et las de commander,
> Vous lui *rendez* un *bien* qu'elle ne peut *garder*,
> S'il lui faut à ce *prix* en *acheter* un autre,
> Si vous ne préférez son *intérêt* au vôtre,
> Si ce funeste *don* la met au désespoir,
> Je n'ose dire ici ce que j'ose prévoir.

For his part, but from a different position, Maxime reinforces
Cinna's arguments in support of the legitimacy of the power
Auguste holds (v. 445-446):

> Et qu'au *prix* de son sang, au péril de sa tête,
> Il a fait de l'Etat une juste conquête . . .

He draws quite contrary conclusions, however (v. 451-458):

> Rome est à vous, Seigneur, l'empire est votre *bien*;
> Chacun en liberté peut disposer du sien:
> Il le peut à son choix *garder*, ou s'en *défaire*;
> Vous seul ne pourriez pas ce que peut le vulgaire,
> Et seriez devenu, pour avoir tout dompté,
> Esclave des grandeurs où vous êtes monté!
> *Possédez*-les, seigneur, sans qu'elles vous *possèdent*.
> Loin de vous captiver, souffrez qu'elles vous *cèdent* . . .

In a curious and paradoxical way, Maxime shows himself
to be much more perceptive than Cinna, much closer to the

deepest preoccupations of Auguste. He is trying to disassociate power from the possession of goods. In his mind the capacity to bestow goods is a proof that a man is not enslaved and therefore is a proof that a man is in possession of himself. If Auguste gives the empire away, he will give away infinitely more than he will have received; he will thus—as in the potlatch—emerge from the test greater than ever (v. 469-472):

> Je veux bien avouer qu'une action si belle
> *Donne* à Rome bien plus que vous ne tenez d'elle;
> Mais commet-on un crime indigne de pardon,
> Quand la reconnoissance est au-dessus du *don?*

But the circuit of the exchange does not stop there. Auguste's gift is not entirely gratuitous since, in giving the empire away, Auguste will earn fame (v. 475-476):

> Et vous serez fameux chez la posterité,
> Moins pour l'avoir conquis que pour l'avoir quitté.

What is especially striking is that this argument, applied here to the empire, is the same as the one which later in the play, will allow Auguste to pardon the conspirators. Maxime already appears as Auguste's conscience which the emperor is not yet ready to heed. Unable to fulfil the first condition set up by Maxime—the possession of oneself—he can only at this point adopt a bastard solution (v. 626-627):

> Cinna, par vos conseils je *retiendrai* l'empire;
> Mais je le retiendrai pour vous en *faire part.*

Then, in a moment of irony, wanting to thank his counselors for their "disinterested" advice, he offers a reward to each: Cinna will have Emilie; Maxime will become governor of Sicily. Quite clearly, he deceives himself in the attribution of these gifts. Would it not have been more sensible for him to give a person to the individual who had advised himself to possess himself as a person, and political power to the individual who had spoken to him in terms of political power as the first step in preparing him for the succession?

The error stems, as I have already suggested, from the fact that Auguste, unable to possess himself, confuses the giving of power and gifts with the giving of persons. When Auguste leaves, Cinna and Maxime comment on his gesture (v. 691-694):

> Cinna: Et tout ce que la gloire a de vrais partisans
>   Le hait trop puissamment pour aimer ses
>   *présents.*
> Maxime: Donc pour vous Emilie est un objet de haine?
> Cinna: La *recevoir* de lui me seroit une gêne.

(Cinna, incidentally, will change his mind later.) He finishes with this categorical statement (v. 698-700):

> Je veux . . .
> L'épouser sur sa cendre, et qu'après notre effort
> Les *présents* du tyran soient le prix de sa mort.

In the very dense formulation of the last verse, Cinna confirms the dual and contradictory function of Emilie in the economy of the play: between Auguste and Cinna, Emilie is at once "present" and "prize." Only later will Cinna become conscious of this contradiction.

Maxime, for his part, has discovered that he has been "taken in" by Cinna:

> Et c'est pour l'acquérir qu'il nous fait conspirer. (v. 712)
> Je pense servir Rome, et je sers mon rival. (v. 720)
> Cependant par mes mains je vois qu'il me l'enlève. (v. 725)

Suddenly Maxime realizes that he has become the mediator of his own loss, at least to the extent that he helps his friend achieve what he himself wants: Emilie. The disturbance which he feels does not seem to be shared by Euphorbe, his freeman, who without any hesitation proposes a solution more in Maxime's interests (v. 730-734):

> L'issue en est aisée: agissez pour vous-même;
> D'un dessein qui vous *perd* rompez le coup fatal;
> *Gagnez* une maîtresse, accusant un rival.
> Auguste, à qui par là vous *sauverez* la vie,
> Ne vous pourra jamais *refuser* Emilie.

Thus, rather than help in giving Emilie to Cinna, he has only to give her to himself. How? Simply by giving Cinna to Auguste who, in turn, will give Emilie to Maxime. In moving

from the first to the second situation, we notice a further
interchange: the recipient of the gift is being transformed
into the gift to be given.

Situation	Giver	Gift	Recipient & Giver	Gift	Recipient
	Phase I			Phase II	
1	Maxime	Emilie	Cinna	Auguste	Emilie
2	Maxime	Cinna	Auguste	Emilie	Maxime

If we now compare the nature of the "gifts," we notice that
the two situations present a perfect symmetry. In the first situation Maxime, in giving Emilie to Cinna, gives him a positive gift (+), and Cinna, in giving Auguste to Emilie, brings
about an elimination (−); in the second situation, Maxime
eliminates Cinna (−) by giving him to Auguste who offers a
positive gift to Maxime by giving him Emilie (+):

	Givers	Gifts	Recipients
Situation 1	Maxime ⟶	Emilie (+) ⟶	Cinna
	Cinna ⟶	Auguste (−) ⟶	Emilie
Situation 2	Maxime ⟶	Cinna (−) ⟶	Auguste
	Auguste ⟶	Emilie (+) ⟶	Maxime

If we look only at the column which lists the gifts, the symmetry is perfect and we can thus rightfully wonder why
Maxime experiences his scruples and sudden embarrassment.
For Euphorbe, the problem is simple: where is there any
wrong in betraying a traitor? No one, he says, is a criminal
when he punishes a crime (v. 742). Maxime, enthusiastically,
answers: "A crime which will give Rome her freedom" (v.
743). Such a reply proves that Maxime is capable of distinguishing between a political crime and a crime of passion,
which he places on another level. He has the right to give

Cinna since Cinna has used political means in order to obtain personal ends. This is precisely what Maxime does not wish to do, for he wants to make a clean distinction between political conscience and personal conscience (v. 769-777):

> Nous disputons en vain, et ce n'est que folie
> De vouloir par sa *perte acquérir* Emilie:
> Ce n'est pas le moyen de plaire à ses beaux yeux
> Que de *priver* du jour ce qu'elle aime le mieux.
> Pour moi j'estime peu qu'Auguste me la *donne:*
> Je veux *gagner* son coeur plutôt que sa personne,
> Et ne fais point d'état de sa *possession,*
> Si je n'ai point de part à son affection.
> Puis-je la mériter par une triple offense?

To moral arguments of this kind Euphorbe opposes tactical fine points which are his contribution to Maxime's loss. We shall see why presently. For now, what we should notice is that Maxime's moral viewpoint is paradoxically loftier than Cinna's and certainly loftier than Emilie's. Cinna is beginning to feel remorse but, unwittingly, Maxime reproaches him for this (v. 838-841; 847-848):

> Et formez vos remords d'une plus juste cause,
> De vos lâches conseils, qui seuls ont arrêté
> Le bonheur renaissant de notre liberté.
> C'est vous seul aujourd'hui qui nous l'avez ôtée . . .
> Mais entendez crier Rome à votre côté:
> "*Rends*-mois, rends-moi, Cinna, ce que tu m'as ôté . . ."

By appointing himself as the spokesman of the Roman people, Maxime accuses his friend of having frustrated Rome's freedom, of having stolen it from her by pleading with Auguste to remain in power. He accuses him of misappropriating power. It matters little that, in his answer to this accusation, Cinna repeats his promise to assassinate Auguste (v. 854); his action is now being undertaken for another reason and cannot have the same value since it is inspired by personal interest.

Unfortunately, it is precisely the fault Maxime denounces in Cinna which Maxime himself, in a moment of aberration, will commit by revealing the plot to Auguste and in proposing

to Emilie that she flee with him. For her the suggestion is
both impossible and unthinkable since it proposes a shameful
way of leaving the Game; it is even a kind of caricature of suicide. Emilie refuses because she sees that Maxime is trying to
pass himself off as another Cinna (v. 1346-1348):

> Ouvrez enfin les yeux, et connoissez Maxime:
> C'est un autre Cinna qu'en lui vous regardez;
> Le ciel vous *rend* en lui l'amant que vous *perdez* . . .

But, as I have already said, one being cannot be replaced by
another. Maxime, too, is brought to grief trying to do just
that. It had to be this way: the most lucid individual, the person most capable of distinguishing personal motives from
political motives becomes the person who eventually makes
the most radical confusion between them. Maxime becomes
the traitor. Maxime becomes literally the one who gives—who
gives his prince, his friend, the woman he loves. It is perverse
and catastrophic conduct par excellence because these gifts,
having no counterpart, are gratuitous gifts and therefore will
never be allowed by social morality (v. 1401-1406):

> Un même jour t'a vu, par une fausse adresse,
> Trahir ton souverain, ton ami, ta maîtresse,
> Sans que de tant de droits en un jour violés,
> Sans que de deux amants au tyran immolés,
> Il te reste aucun *fruit* que la honte et la rage
> Qu'un remords inutile allume en ton courage.

The *gratuitous* gift is a dead loss for society; it is a dead loss
for the individual, too. Not only is the operation profitless,
but it is also and quite literally, of an inestimable cost to the
individual since it robs him of life and renown: "Il m'en
coûte la vie, il m'en *coûte* la gloire" (v. 1417).

This is not Auguste's reaction to the situation. Having
promised the greatest punishments for Emilie and Cinna, he
greets Maxime in these words (v. 1667-1669):

> Ne parlons de crime après ton repentir,
> Après que du péril tu m'as su garantir:
> C'est à toi que je *dois* et le jour et l'empire.

But Maxime explains straightaway that his motives, far from
being political, have to do only with passion. He ends his

speech by accusing himself once again of treason and proposing suicide (v. 1689-1692):

> J'ai trahi mon ami, ma maîtresse, mon maître,
> Ma gloire, mon pays, par l'avis de ce traître,
> Et croirai toutefois mon bonheur infini,
> Si je puis m'en punir après l'avoir puni.

By speaking in this way, Maxime delivers a final blow to Auguste who now knows that he can count on no one. Betrayed
by Cinna, betrayed by Emilie, he now is betrayed by Maxime,
by the very person towards whom he had hoped, in a last
and futile effort, to be *indebted* for something. Auguste had
believed that he possessed everything, persons as well as goods,
and the goods were naught without the persons. Suddenly, he
finds that he has been thoroughly dispossessed. Yet it is because he no longer possesses (the confidence of) anyone that
Auguste can look forward to possessing the only thing which
remains to him, the only thing he has not yet possessed: himself. His aboutface, his conversion must come to pass; it leads
to the triumph which shimmers through his celebrated declaration: "I am the master of myself as I am of the world"
(v. 1696).

The whole process leads to an equation: By giving others,
Maxime has lost himself; by losing others, Auguste has found
himself. Once he is in possession of himself, only he can save
everything, recover everything to his advantage. He does this
especially for those who have lost themselves. But he saves
them not in order to have them in his care—which would be
the same as subjugating them as though they were his goods
—but rather in order to *give them back to themselves* (v.
1701-1710):

> Soyons amis, Cinna, c'est moi qui t'en convie:
> Comme à mon ennemi je t'ai *donné* la vie,
> Et malgré la fureur de ton lâche destin,
> Je te la *donne* encore comme à mon assassin.
> Commençons un combat qui montre par l'issue
> Qui l'aura mieux de nous ou *donnée* ou *reçue.*
> Tu trahis mes bienfaits, je les veux *redoubler;*
> Je t'en avais *comblé,* je t'en veux *accabler:*
> Avec cette beauté que je t'avais *donnée,*
> *Reçois* le consulat pour la prochaine année.

To Emilie, he says (v. 1714):

> Te *rendant* un époux, je te *rends* plus qu'un père.

As Auguste was converted, so Emilie and Cinna find themselves converted—but because of and through Auguste.

Only Maxime remains to be saved. Auguste sets himself to this task by asking Cinna and Emilie to help him with it (v. 1734-1738):

> Et tous deux avec moi faites grâce à Maxime:
> Il nous a trahis tous; mais ce qu'il a commis
> Vous *conserve* innocents, et me *rend* mes amis.
> (*A Maxime*)
> *Reprends* auprès de moi ta place accoutumée;
> Rentre dans ton *crédit* et dans ta renommée.

I have said that Maxime's conduct was catastrophic both for the individual and for society. And that is so, since in giving all the world away, he lost everything. Still, there now seems to be evidence that the wholly negative function of the traitor has a positive counterpart, at least to the extent that the hero needs the traitor in order to become a hero. Without Maxime, Octave could not become Auguste.

The circuit of gift-giving has not yet run its course. Once Auguste has given each person back to himself, each person can, in turn, give himself *freely* to Auguste and be prepared to sacrifice his life for the person who has restored that life. This is exactly what Cinna recognizes, and he speaks of it almost in accounting terms (v. 1749-1752):

> Puisse le grand moteur des belles destinées
> Pour *prolonger* vos jours, *retrancher* nos annés;
> Et moi, par un bonheur dont chacun soit jaloux,
> *Perdre* pour vous cent fois ce que je *tiens* de vous!

Moreover, in spite of—or more justly *because of* this sublimated accounting system, an accounting system rooted in voluntary sacrifice—we now move in a realm of pure *generosity*.

This concept of "generosity"—the glorious gift of a self which is in possession of itself—which is so vital to our understanding of Corneille and his contemporaries, is suddenly

illuminated. We see plainly that gift and identity are inseparable and interchangeable. On their balance and fusion depends the fullness of the individual, the harmony of society—
both and each being perfectly integrated.

One more observation must be made. Once each of these
characters has given a demonstration of his generosity, the
only act which remains for Auguste is to thank the gods by
announcing that he will double the sacrifice he had intended
to offer in their honor (v. 1777-1778):

> Qu'on redouble demain les heureux sacrifices
> Que nous leur offrirons sous de meilleurs auspices.

It is not the result of chance that the emperor's last gift is
destined not for men but rather for the gods. That fact un-
derscores and confirms the religious nature of power to which
I have made several allusions in these last pages. As God's
representative on earth, the sovereign possesses everything.
He provides the drive for the exchange; he is the center from
which all things set forth and to which they return.

The Auguste we see at the end,[4] betrayed but triumphing

---

[4] I am making a deliberate distinction; the Auguste we encounter at
the end is quite different from the Auguste we meet at the beginning of
the play. There is, after all, a world of difference between a man who is
seeking to abandon his power and one who grants pardon to his intended assassin.

There is a greater relationship between the two words, abandon and
pardon, than might meet the eye at a casual glance. Etymologically the
two words have an identical and contradictory meaning. The verb *abandon* comes from the Old French *mettre a bandon* which meant "to
put under someone else's ban, i.e. to relinquish oneself to another's
authority" (O.E.D.). To abandon, then, is to divest oneself of a properly
possessed power. By another token, to pardon is to excuse from a debt.
We see an example of this in an Old French text where it is written:
"Quant Rolles vit qu'ele ot tele amour viers son segnor, si li *pardonna*
la moitie de sa raencon." Thus, to pardon is also to strip oneself of
something; but, in contradistinction to abandon, it is to do so in a way
which leads to rendering something which the other does not yet possess
(since he is to receive it from me) and which therefore clearly belongs to me. From the juridical and economic point of view, the process
of pardoning is thus much more complex than the process of abandon-
ing, for it implies a dual debt, a debt which can only be paid by currency which, while immaterial, is none the less essential to every society
to the extent that such currency is the very basis of "credit." It is a
matter of the recognition which brings glory and honor to the person
who is its object. Pardon, by the very complexity of the ties which it

over betrayal by accepting it, can be considered the political equivalent of Christ, the Redeemer. In forgiving all, he redeems all and allows for the conversion both of those who were opposed to him (v. 1715-1716) and those who, like Cinna, are now ready to sacrifice themselves for him. Finally, Livie's prophecy, which incorporates a heavenly revelation and which limns the immortal glory of Auguste, legitimates the comparison to Christ and allows us to believe that Corneille intended, probably indirectly, to be the apologist of the divine right of kings. This religious and political orientation of Cinna supplies the natural transition to the play which was to follow: *Polyeucte*.[5]

RETROSPECTION

This essay does not pretend to offer a total explanation of *Cinna* and I have not meant to give any such impression.

The method I have adopted, and the perspectives which that method opens on the play, do not contradict certain earlier approaches. On the contrary, in at least one instance, they serve to complement and buttress; for, it seems to me, that my interpretation and Serge Doubrovsky's converge (*Corneille et la dialectique du héros,* Paris, 1963). I have been pleased to note this in re-reading, after I had finished my essay, the chapter of his book devoted to this play. The reader may decide. Doubrovsky, writing of Emilie, says, though he does not linger on the point: "The rivalry is transformed into bargaining with her as the merchandise" (p. 191); of Cinna he writes: "love's slavery leads Cinna to swindling" (p. 193); and of Auguste "Auguste's problem has to do with possession" (p. 193). It seems therefore that the dialectic of the hero and the politics of the exchange are complementary in character.

---

binds, tends to tighten up the social fabric—which is what we are seeing at the end of *Cinna*—whereas any process of abandonment slackens them. The anthropological ramifications of these remarks brings us back to Marcel Mauss' "Essai sur le don."

[5] See Michel Beaujour, *"Polyeucte et la monarchie de droit divin,"* *The French Review,* April 1963.

Since the present essay takes as its points of departure the concepts of gift, exchange, and prize, juxtaposing them to the idea of the potlatch, a reader might be tempted to believe that my intention has been to delineate either an economy or an anthropology of literature as others have sought to establish a sociology, a psychoanalysis, or a history of literature. That would be a mistaken conception. Far from wanting to impose an alien language on the work, I have sought to base my analysis primarily on the metaphors found in the text. It was those metaphors, repeated insistently in the text, which formed the theme that struck me as the most prominent and also the most promising for any comment on the play—not that I put forward any claim to having exhausted its meaning.

By pursuing this thematic organization to its reasonable conclusion, using certain techniques borrowed from Lévi-Strauss and adapted to literary analysis, I have been able to show the internal structures of the work and, in so doing, comment on the behavior of the characters and the general organization of the play from a literary point of view.

Furthermore, as I have indicated in my conclusion, this theme, along with its structures, is related to a reality (economic, religious, political, and even magical) which, while external to the work, none the less provides its historical and anthropological basis. Thus, while my appraisal remains primarily literary, it becomes anthropological to the extent that it goes beyond literature and touches on social facts and mental attitudes of an extraliterary nature.

One would, of course, have to see if and how this method and these analyses can be applied to other works of Corneille and possibly to the whole of his work. On a broader scope, one would have to hunt out the themes of the exchange and the gift which are the most frequent and the most characteristic images found in the literary language of this whole era.

In this connection, it is well to draw attention to the fact that a critic who enlarged his investigation to include all the works, or the major works, of an era would see his goal metamorphosed. At that point, with the goal changed, the nature of his study would change. Instead of being literary, it would be either sociological or anthropological. The question is then raised of knowing at what moment the analysis of literary structures ceases to isolate the esthetic or literary aspects of an object and moves on to isolate its anthropological and sociological aspects.

I would like to add a final remark which carries me one step further away from the present essay but which also justifies the essay by projecting it against an even more general context. I have said that I was not interested in looking upon literature as a form of economics. But that doesn't necessarily mean that the phenomenon of literature should be seen as unlike the phenomenon of economics. Using this perspective, it would be as much a question, with the one, of understanding the system established for the exchange of services, merchandise, and women which form the network of communications in ancient and modern collectivities as it would be, for the other, a question of understanding the system of word and image exchange in literary or artistic communication. The latter system of exchange is, in effect, readily comparable to the former: literary language, like the language of the other arts, has a metaphorical function in relation to everyday language, the language of reality, just as money has a metaphorical function in relation to the merchandise it is intended to represent.

Literary language is a guidepost to everyday language either by providing its "value" (as classical and tragic language do) or in questioning its value (as modern language and the language of comedy do). A not illegitimate deduction could be made from this, namely that all literature constitutes an economics of language, that literature is language's economy. The laws of this economy vary. What formulates them is rhetoric. Every rhetorical structure is therefore an economic system (and could be a juridical, linguistic, or other system) which determines literary communication.

Still, the discovery of the ensemble of these laws for a given work would not exhaust the meanings of that work since the work does not remain vital, contemporary, and thereby, communicable unless each generation, each period finds a new meaning in it. And that meaning in some way escapes from the rules, either implicit or explicit, which governed at the moment of its creation and which its structures manifest.

How then is it possible not to see in literature, and in art in general, the exemplary and metaphorical mode of all other forms of communication which, each in its own way, attempt to reduce and to overcome the non-meaning of the world? How can we avoid thinking that literature and art are communication par excellence since this residue of meaning which constitutes their essence represents and actualizes infinitely that nugget—or that edge—of meaninglessness which brings about the necessity of all communication?

Translated by Joseph H. McMahon

The original French version of this article will appear in the November 1966 issue of *Les Temps Modernes*, devoted to Structuralism.

Describing poetic structures: Two approaches to Baudelaire's *les Chats*

Michael Riffaterre

Poetry is language, but it produces effects that language in everyday speech does not consistently produce; a reasonable assumption is that the linguistic analysis of a poem should turn up specific features, and that there is a causal relationship between the presence of these features in the text and our empirical feeling that we have before us a poem. The act of communication—the sending of a message from speaker to addressee—is conditioned by the need it fills: the verbal structure of the message depends upon which factor of communication is focused on. In everyday language, used for practical purposes, the focus is usually upon the situational context, the mental or physical reality referred to; sometimes the focus is upon the code used in transmitting the message, that is, upon language itself, if there seems to be some block in the addressee's understanding, and so forth. In the case of verbal art, the focus is upon the message as an end in itself, not just as a means, upon its form as a permanent, unchangeable monument, forever independent of external conditions. The naked eye attributes this enduring, attention-getting quality to a higher unity and more intricate texture: the poem follows more rules (e.g. meter, lexical restrictions, etc.) and displays more conspicuous interrelationships between its constitutive elements than do casual utterances.

For these features Roman Jakobson has proposed a general formula. Selection and combination are the two basic ordering principles of speech. Selection is based upon equivalence (metaphoric relationship), either similarity or dissimilarity; the speaker designates his topic (subject) by choosing one among various available synonyms and then says what he has to say about it (predicate) by another selection from another set of interchangeable words (paradigm). The combining of these words, that is, their contiguity, produces a sentence. Jakobson defines a poetic structure as one characterized by the projection of the principle of equivalence from the axis of selection to the axis of combination.[1] For instance, words are combined into rhythmic, alliterative, and rhymic sequences because of their equivalence in sound, and this inevitably establishes semantic equations between these words; their respective meanings are consequently perceived as related by similarity (hence a metaphor or simile) or dissimilarity (hence an antithesis).

Which is to say that the recurrence of equivalent forms, *parallelism,* is the basic relationship underlying poetry. Of course, since language is a system made up of several levels superimposed one on top of the other (phonetic, phonological, syntactical, semantic, etc.), parallelism manifests itself on any level: so then, a poem is a verbal sequence wherein the same relations between constituents are repeated at various levels and the same story is told in several ways at the same time and at several times in the same way. This can be usefully restated in structural terms once we have called to mind basic

[1] "Linguistics and Poetics," *Style in Language,* ed. T. A. Sebeok (New York: 1960), esp. pp. 358 ss.

definitions: a structure is a system made up of several elements, none of which can undergo a change without effecting changes in all the other elements; thus the system is what mathematicians call an invariant; transformations within it produce a group of models of the same type (that is, mechanically interconvertible shapes), or variants. The invariant, of course, is an abstraction arrived at by defining what remains intact in the face of these conversions; therefore we are able to observe a structure only in the shape of one or another variant. We are now ready to agree with Cl. Lévi-Strauss that a poem is a structure containing within itself its variants ordered on the vertical axis of the different linguistic levels. It is thus possible to describe the poem in isolation, so that we need not explain its singularity by dragging in hard-to-define concepts like non-grammaticalness or departure from the norm. Comparison of variants, prerequisite to analysis, is accomplished by simply scanning the text at its various linguistic levels one after the other.

Such is the approach tried out by Jakobson and Lévi-Strauss on "Les Chats," a sonnet of Baudelaire's, and with extraordinary thoroughness.[2] They modestly declare that they are interested only in describing what the poem is made of. Never the less they do draw conclusions as to the meaning of the poem and try to relate it to the esthetics and even the psyche of the poet, purlieu of literary scholars. This raises a question: how are we to pass from description to judgment—that is, from a study of the text to a study of its effect upon the reader? The sonnet is a good occasion for such discussion, for critics generally downgrade the poem (*Fleurs du Mal*, LXVI), a product of Baudelaire's early period (1847), and find it less Baudelairean than most of the others. But the poet did not feel that way about it: he thought it good enough to publish in the feuilleton of a friend, in hopes of drumming up some interest; then he selected it for a preview of his abortive *Limbes* (1851); finally, he thought it worth keeping in the editions of the *Fleurs* that he was able to prepare himself. If structuralism can help determine who is right here, we shall

[2] Jakobson (Roman), Lévi-Strauss (Claude) *"Les Chats* de Charles Baudelaire," *L'Homme,* 2 (1962), 5-21.

have tested its practical workability in matters of literary criticism.

Far more important, however, is the question as to whether unmodified structural linguistics is relevant at all to the analysis of poetry. The authors' method is based on the assumption that any structural system they are able to define in the poem is necessarily a poetic structure. Can we not suppose, on the contrary, that the poem may contain certain structures that play no part in its function and effect as a literary work of art, and that there may be no way for structural linguistics to distinguish between these unmarked structures and those that are literarily active? Conversely, there may well be strictly poetic structures that cannot be recognized as such by an analysis not geared to the specificity of poetic language.

Les Chats

1 Les amoureux fervents et les savants austères
2 Aiment également, dans leur mûre saison,
3 Les chats puissants et doux, orgueil de la maison,
4 Qui comme eux sont frileux et comme eux sédantaires.

5 Amis de la science et de la volupté,
6 Ils cherchent le silence et l'horreur des ténèbres;
7 L'Erèbe les eût pris pour ses coursiers funèbres,
8 S'ils pouvaient au servage incliner leur fierté.

9 Ils prennent en songeant les nobles attitudes
10 Des grands sphinx allongés au fond des solitudes,
11 Qui semblent s'endormir dans un rêve sans fin;

12 Leurs reins féconds sont pleins d'étincelles magiques,
13 Et des parcelles d'or, ainsi qu'un sable fin,
14 Etoilent vaguement leurs prunelles mystiques.

Jakobson and Lévi-Strauss submit the text to scannings of its meter, sound texture, grammar, and meaning; they are thus able to collect several sets of the equivalent signs that actualize the sonnet's structure. Let me describe briefly the systems thus obtained, with a sampling of the variants comparatively studied in order to establish these systems. My aim here is only to show how the authors' analysis is carried through. The most significant of their arguments omitted here will be taken up in my discussion of the validity of their approach.

Jakobson and Lévi-Strauss recognize the following complementary or intersecting structures:

1) a *tripartite division* into: *quatrain I,* which represents the cats as passive creatures, observed by outsiders, lovers and scholars; *quatrain II,* where the cats are active but, again, seen as such from the outside, by the powers of darkness; the latter, also seen from outside, are active: they have designs on the cats and are frustrated by the independence of the little beasts; *sestet,* which gives us an inside view of the cat life-style: their attitude may be passive, but they assume that attitude actively. Thus is the active-passive opposition reconciled, or perhaps nullified, and the circle of the sonnet closes.

This tripartite structure is defined by two equivalent models: one grammatical, formed by three complex "sentences" delimited by periods, and further defined by an arithmetic progression in the number of their independent clauses and personal verbal forms (as distinct from forms in the infinitive or participle); one metric (the rhyme systems unify the tercets into a sestet while separating it from the quatrains). These two models are further bound together by the relationship between rhyme and categories: every feminine rhyme coincides with a plural ending, every masculine one with a singular.

2) a *bipartite division* that opposes the octet and the sestet. In the *octet* the cats are seen from an outside observer's point of view and are imprisoned within time and space ([2]*saison* and [3]*maison,* which rhyme and meaning make equivalent). In the *sestet* both viewpoint and space-time limits drop away: the desert bursts the house wide open; the eternity of [11]*dans un rêve sans fin* annuls [2]*dans leur mûre saison:* in this case the equivalence is an antinomy and is formally established by the parallelism of the *dans* constructions, the only two in the poem). This overall opposition combines with two secondary ones: *quatrain I tercet I* ([3]*maison:* [10]*solitudes* :: [2]*saison:* [11]*sans fin*) and *quatrain II tercet II* (cats in darkness vs. cats radiating light).

To take only one of these secondary oppositions: in *quatrain II tercet II,* on the one hand, [12]*Leurs reins féconds sont pleins* is synonymous with [5]*Amis . . . de la volupté* (p. 16), and one of the subjects in the quatrain and three subjects in the tercet all alike designate inanimate things; on the other hand, the antinomy of darkness and light is backed up by corresponding sets of equatable items: [7]*Erèbe* and [6]*ténèbres* echo each other in meaning and in sound, as do [12]*étin-CELLES,* [13]*parCELLES d'or* and [14]*prunELLES.*

3) a *chiasma-like division* linking quatrain I and tercet II, where the cats function as objects ([3]*chats,* [12,14]*Leurs*) and, on the other hand, quatrain II and tercet I, where they are subjects. The *quatrain I-tercet II coupling,* to which I shall limit this summary, contains the following formal equivalences: both stanzas have more adjectives than the internal strophes; the first and last verbs are both modified by rhyming adverbs ([2]*aiment également;* [14]*étoilent vaguement*); these are the only two stanzas made up of sentences with two subjects for one verb and one object, each subject and object being modified by one adjective, etc. A semantic relationship underlies these formal features: in *quatrain I* a metonymic relationship between the animals and their worshippers (i.e. cats and people live in the same house) generates a metaphoric similarity ([4]*comme eux* twice repeated); the same thing in *tercet II,* where a synecdochic (*pars pro toto*) description of the cats, using different parts of their body, permits their metaphoric identification with the cosmos, or so say the two analysts.

These three systems fit one inside the other and together make of the sonnet a "closed" structure, but they coexist with a *fourth system* that makes the poem an open-ended structure which develops dynamically from the first line to the last: two equal *sestets* (1. 1-6 and 9-14), separated by a *distich.* Of the four structures, this last is the one most at variance with the stanza and rhyme architecture that defines the sonnet as a genre: the aberrant distich presents features that do not occur anywhere else, against a background of features that occur only elsewhere in the poem, some of them related to those of the distich by antonymy (every single subject-verb group is plural except for [7]*L'Erèbe les eût pris;* against the rule followed throughout the rest of the poem, [7]*funèbres-*[8]*fierté* alliterate, etc.). Now Jakobson and Lévi-Strauss regard this distich as a transition: the pseudo-sestet describes objectively a factual situation of the real world; two opposite human categories, sensual and intellectual, are reconciled through their identification with the animal endowed with the diametric traits of both types of men; these traits in turn explain the cats' love for silence and darkness—a predilection that exposes them to temptation. Erebus threatens to confine them to their animal nature by taming them; we are relieved to see him fail. This episode, translated in terms of parallelism, should be seen not just as another antonymy but as "l'unique équivalence rejetée" (p. 14).

Never the less, this rejection has its positive effect: an equivalence with the sphinx can substitute for it. The sphinx, with a human head on an animal body, transposes into myth the identification between real cats and people. Also, the monsters' motionless daydreaming and the cats' sedentariness (likewise characteristic of the human types they symbolize) are synonymous; and the way the cats ape the sphinxes is a new equivalence stated simultaneously at the grammatical level, in the narrative (it is [9]*en songeant* that they look like the [10]*sphinx allongés*), at the morphological level (*allongés* and *songeant* are the only participles in the text) and at the sound level the two verbs are related by paronomasia. The second *sestet* is devoted to the deepening mystery of this *miracle des chats* (p. 15). Tercet I still sustains the ambiguity: it is difficult to decide whether cats and sphinxes are linked merely to magnify the image of the cats stylistically, or whether we have here the description of actual similarity, the racial bond between the household sphinx and the desert cat. In tercet II, however, substitution of parts of his body for the whole cat dissolves the beast into particles of matter, and the final identification associates these particles with desert sands and transmutes them into stars: the fusion of cats and cosmos has been accomplished. This apotheosis to infinity does not exclude a circular structure from the text. The authors believe there is a parallelism between tercet II and line 1, the myth being seen as a variant on a universal scale of the "constricting" union, inward-turning, when the lover folds his love into his arms, and of the expansive union, outward-turning, when the scholar takes the universe in his embrace; similarly, cats either interiorize the universe, or else they spread themselves out beyond the bounds of time and space (p. 20).

From all the foregoing, we can at least draw the conclusion that these mutually combinatory and complementary structures interplay in a way unique. The poem is like a microcosm, with its own system of references and analogies. We have an absolutely convincing demonstration of the extraordinary concatenation of correspondences that holds together the parts of speech.

THE IRRELEVANCE OF GRAMMAR

But there is no telling which of these systems of correspondences contribute to the poetry of the text. And there is much to be said about the systems that do not.

The divisions proposed explain a good deal of the tension between symmetrical and asymmetrical rhymes and the grammar arrangements upon which the composition of the sonnet rests. The first division is beyond criticism; the second is well substantiated, since it hinges on an articulation (the octet-sestet boundary) which corresponds to a change so sharp that it prompted postulation of the fourth division. Divisions three and four, especially the last, make use of constituents that cannot possibly be perceived by the reader; these constituents must therefore remain alien to the poetic structure, which is supposed to emphasize the form of the message, to make it more "visible," more compelling.

Equivalences established on the basis of purely syntactic similarities would seem particularly dubious—for instance, the parallelism pointed to between the relative clauses of lines 4 and 11: this last allegedly draws the "contour of an imaginary quatrain, a make-believe homologue of the first quatrain" (p. 13). At most, this might be conceivable if the clauses appeared against an empty or uniform context; not in an actual sonnet, whose continual variation of verbal shapes makes a marked contrast necessary in order to impose perception. Even there, the parallelism from one line to another can be superseded by a stronger relation within one of the two lines involved. This happens in the case of the equation urged by Jakobson and Lévi-Strauss between [4]*Qui comme eux sont frileux* and [12]*Leurs reins féconds sont pleins,* on account of their syntactic parallelism and their internal rhymes. In context the difference outweighs the similarities: an internal rhyme like [5]*science*-[6]*silence* is obvious, and so is *eux-frileux*, because identical stresses "confirm" them; but a natural reading of line 12 will have to take into account the tight unity of *leurs reins féconds*, which demands a pause after *féconds*, the normal caesura disappearing almost because *pleins* cannot be severed from *d'étincelles; pleins* is enclitic, which practically cancels out the rhyme. Suppose we read without regard for meaning or grammar: the rhyme resuscitates, but any responsion to the rhyme in line 4 still appears purely theoretical, for *comme eux sont frileux* is homologous only to *comme eux sédentaires* and is not free to connect elsewhere. For the significant rhyme system, the one that organizes the rhythm and "illustrates" the meaning, is the homophony under equal stress of *comme eux* repeated twice. The *frileux* rhyme is a secondary modulation: it "makes believe" that the line ends at the caesura,[8] thus getting the rhythm off to a fresh start and making the "unexpected" repetition all the more striking; the fact that it rhymes with *comme eux* lays emphasis upon *sédentaires* by contrast—a second *comme eux* led the reader's subconscious sense of balance to expect a second rhyme, and the expectation is beautifully frustrated. We did find a parallelism anyway, but the remoter one has lost the contest, and this suffices to make homologue-collecting an unreliable tool. Extensive similarities at one level are no proof of correspondence: a parallelism is seen between quatrain I and tercet II, based upon the equivalence of two subjects ([1]*Les amoureux fervents, les savants austères*/[13]*des parcelles d'or, un sable fin*), one verb with rhyming adverb ([2]*Aiment également*/[14]*Etoilent vaguement*), one adjective-noun object ([3]*Les chats puissants et doux*/[14]*leurs prunelles mystiques*) in identical sequence (p. 9). But, in any verse structure, I do not see how two variants can be equivalent if the positions of their components are not homologous: meter lends significance to the space occupied by the sentence. The relation of object to verb in line 14 is not the same as in quatrain I, since the

---

[8] This structural role of the break is well documented: Malherbe condemned internal rhymes precisely because they had such effects.

quatrain keeps them apart with parentheses and enjambement, whereas the tercet unites them. Hence inevitably a difference in emphasis and a shift in respective positions within the line. Furthermore, the equation of the subjects is all askew: the components are alike, and we could link *amoureux fervents* vertically with *parcelles d'or* or diagonally with *sable fin;* but the systems they enter are not comparable, for *sable fin* does not stand in the same relation to *parcelles d'or* as *savants* does to *amoureux.* These last two are opposite equals, and their contiguity expresses their polarity; but the contiguity of *parcelles* and *sable* simply repeats twice the same meaning, *ainsi que* indicating a metaphorical relation. *Ainsi que* and *et* may have the same virtual function in language and be classified alike: but not here, where they are neither synonymous nor antonymous. The parallelism suggested by grammar remains virtual because it has no homologue in the meter or in the semantic system.

No segmentation can be pertinent that yields, indifferently, units which *are* part of the poetic structure, and neutral ones that are not. The weak point of the method is indeed the categories used. There is a revealing instance where Jakobson and Lévi-Strauss take literally the technical meaning of *feminine* as used in metrics and grammar and endow the formal feminine categories with esthetic and even ethical values. They are trying to prove a sexual ambiguity in the poem, the motif of the androgyne, and they find some evidence in the "paradoxical choice of feminine substantives as masculine rhymes" (p. 21). True, the gender of French nouns does orient the associations they trigger: this kind of effect is conceivable with words that signify concrete objects or even abstract concepts, as long as they can be humanized or personified—for example, [5]*volupté*, which is more female than *plaisir* would be. It hardly holds, however, in the case of purely technical terminology, where *masculine* means merely "ending on a fully pronounced syllable" and *feminine* merely "ending on an unstressed syllable" (especially where one need not even be aware of these conventions in order to perceive an alternance). By stretching this to the limit, we may discover cases where the feminine rhyme does evoke some such associations because it coincides with the specific feminine gender ending; it is altogether unlikely with masculine rhymes, which do not offer any similar concurrence. Only technicians would think of it (they have thought of it); metalinguistic rationalization of this sort betrays how easily the wariest of analysts slips into a belief in the intrinsic explanatory worth of purely descriptive terms.

The two critics obviously assume that the definition of categories used to collect data is also valid to explain their function in the poetic structure—that linguistic oppositions, for example, automatically entail stylistic differences. The role of liquid phonemes in the sonnet's sound texture, for example, is declared to be significant: quatrain II is certainly characterized by noticeable variations, since this is a stanza where the phonetic dominance shifts from nasal vowels (only 3) to liquid consonants (24); extreme variations cannot fail of their effect. There is, however, a linguistic opposition between /l/ and /r/, particularly marked in French, and this is frequently exploited in poetry in a manner consistent with the phonetic nature of the opposing features. A slight regression of /r/ before /l/ in the tercets is interpreted as "eloquently accompanying the passage from the empirical feline to his mythic transfigurations" (p. 12). But no one is likely to believe that there is any significance in a difference as imperceptible as that between fourteen /l/ and eleven /r/, especially when tercet II, with /l/ enjoying a majority of two, begins with a /r/ cluster (*Leurs reins*) which will surely catch the eye and ear sooner than an inequality attenuated by distribution along the lines. If we look only for sharp changes, then the drop in the number of liquids from quatrain II to tercet I affects both contenders equally, /l/ ending on top by one point; the one smashing victory of /l/ over /r/—three to nothing—occurs in line 5 *before* the transfiguration; in quatrain II, which is also the only place where brutal variations can be found, the liquids go hand in hand for the whole stanza, rejoicing at the peak of their power. Since liquids as a group do appear significant, the authors assume that every essential linguistic feature of the group must also be significant. The fact is, however, that it does not work out that way: the liquids are significant only as a group; their oppositions, *within* the group, though they are actualized and play their part in the linguistic structure, are not actualized in the style.

Conversely, the analytical categories applied can pull together under one label phenomena which are in fact totally different from one another in the poetic structure. A case in point is the plural. Jakobson and Lévi-Strauss rightly note its high frequency and its concurrence with important elements. Because a single grammatical category is applicable to every line of the poem, they see it as a key to the understanding of the sonnet; they quote a pronouncement of the poet that seems to give symbolic meaning to the plural: *Multitude, solitude: termes égaux et convertibles par le poète actif et fécond.* Better still, the authors see this mutual "convertibility" symbolized in [10]*solitudes,* where "solitude" as the word itself and "multitude" as the morpheme *-s* enjoy togetherness. This argument recalls their confusion of femaleness and feminine gender; they seem to assume that there is always a basic relationship between actual plurality (and what it symbolizes in Baudelaire's eyes) and plural morphemes. Needless to say, there are many exceptions to that general rule—and what is more, one of them occurs right here: [6]*ténèbres* is a conventional, meaningless plural; let us skip it, and also its rhyme companion [7]*funèbres.* We should probably discount all descriptive plurals, since they are dictated by nature and not the poet's choice: *mystiques* would drop out, cats having two *prunelles,* and also *reins.* We can keep *chats* and their human counterparts: collective singulars being available for groups, the plural may well have meaning. But *solitudes,* the pretext for this philosophical foray, will have to go: it is no paradox at all, just a hyperbole, a cliché where *solitudes* means "desert"—an emphatic plural stemming from the Latin. Baudelaire's quotation may apply elsewhere, certainly not here, and no interpretation of the sonnet can be drawn from it. The authors' mistake is understandable. In their search for a plural structure, they needed a unifying factor. The text yielded no sign that the data could be related, yet their common label demanded that they be so related. Faced with this dilemma, the authors must have gladly seized upon the coincidence between *solitudes* and Baudelaire's aphorism: the poet's mental obsession provided just the invariant required. Had all plural

forms not been brought under the one label, there would have
been no compulsion to find, at all costs, an equivalence value
for every plural form.

But among these data lumped together because of their
morphological similarity, there is a group of plurals set apart
from the others because of their distribution: that is the plural
feminine rhymes. These do form a stylistic structure, because
their -*s* endings make the rhyme "richer" for the eye by increasing the number of its repeated components. In [1,4]*austères-
sédentaires,* for instance, the *s* reinforces the visual similarity
and offsets the spelling vagaries that spoil the transcription
of /ɛ/. The way in which the -*s* is related to and functions
in the rhyme system has nothing to do with its simultaneous
function in the singular-plural opposition, where it carries a
meaning: in the rhyme it works only as an eye-catcher. The
interrelations of the -*s* rhymes within the conventional rhyme
system are what gives them significance. Poetic convention
demands, first, that the rhymes of the sonnet should form an
invariable pattern alternating feminine and masculine rhymes;
second, that this invariant alternation be combined with sound
variants within each alternating series. The visual and aural
implementation of the variant is constantly reinforced and
constantly compels attention, thus strongly individualizing
each stanza; this depends entirely upon the poet's creative
fancy. The implementation of the invariant, on the contrary,
is normally limited to the compulsory masculine-feminine
alternation. By adding -*s* to the -*e,* Baudelaire personalizes,
so to speak, what was an automatism, reemphasizes the opposition for the eye. A second constant element in the system
of the sonnet as a whole gives more weight to the unifying
factor in the rhymes, which more effectively countervails
the centrifugal tendencies of each stanza to form an independent unit. Every line affected by this addition is thereby
made to look longer, and the fact that such a line ends the
sonnet contributes to its unity by emphasizing the final item
and therefore the reader's consciousness of a terminal accord;
since the word thus underlined happens to be *mystiques,* the
combination of meaning and visual emphasis, accompanying
it like an upbeat, make the end of the poem a point of departure for reverie and wonder. Jakobson and Lévi-Strauss

point out that the feminine rhyme is orally actualized, despite the total disappearance of the unstressed end syllable in modern pronunciation, by the presence of a postvocalic sounded consonant in the rhyming syllable, and they remark, indeed, that this coincides with plural morphemes (pp. 7, 11); but they see the plural as a parallel to the postvocalic consonant, that is, reinforcing each rhyme pair, separately, since that consonant varies and therefore structures only the stanza in which it occurs (/r, br, d, k/). In fact, the invariable -*s* creates a frame that tightens the whole sonnet. This structure would not be overlooked if the term chosen did not also cover forms that are grammatically identical but stylistically foreign to these -*s* rhymes; [1]*amoureux,* [3]*doux,* [10]*sphinx* would not further obscure the operation of the -*s* ending; grammatical equivalence would not be equated with stylistic equivalence.

What I have just said should not be construed as a rejection of the principle of equivalence: similarity in dissimilarity, dissimilarity in similarity, are apparent at all levels. But it seems evident that its pertinence cannot be shown by using grammatical terminology, or any preconceived, aprioristic frame. R. Jakobson chose grammar units to make this exegesis and many others because grammar is the natural geometry of language which superimposes abstract, relational systems upon the concrete, lexical material: hence grammar furnishes the analyst with ready-made structural units. All parts of speech, in fact, may function in parallelism and contrasts; the importance of pronouns, long neglected by style analysts—pronouns are, precisely, typical relational units—comes out clearly in the first division of the poem. Jakobson seems to think that any reiteration and contrast of a grammatical concept makes it a poetic device, that the interrelationship of meter, morphological classes and syntactic construction actualizes the structure and creates the poetic effect.[4] There is no doubt that a linguistic actualization does take place, but the question remains: are the linguistic and poetic actualizations coextensive?

The sonnet is rebuilt by the two critics into a "superpoem,"

---

[4] R. Jakobson, "Poetry of Grammar and Grammar of Poetry" (in Russian), *Poetics, Poetyka* (Warsaw: 1961), pp. 398 ss, esp. 403, 408-9.

inaccessible to the normal reader, and yet the structures described do not explain what establishes contact between poetry and reader. No grammatical analysis of a poem can give us more than the grammar of the poem.

THE POEM AS RESPONSE

The literary scholar, especially of the humanist stripe, has always assumed that grammar failed because it was incomplete, that the narrow, rigorous methods of the *esprit de géométrie* could never catch the subtle, indefinable *je ne sais quoi* that poetry is supposed to be made of. In fact the opposite is true: the linguist sees all the data, and that is precisely the reason he was prone, especially in pre-structuralist times, to define a poetic utterance as abnormal, as language plus something else. The whole idea of structure, of course, is that within the body of the text all parts are bound together and that stylistically neutral components and active ones are interrelated in the same way as the marked and unmarked poles of any opposition. Our only solution is to observe and rearrange the data from a different angle. A proper consideration of the nature of the poetic phenomenon will give us the vantage point required.

First of all, the poetic phenomenon, being linguistic, is not simply the message, the poem, but the whole act of communication. This is a very special act, however, for the speaker —the poet—is not present; any attempt to bring him back only produces interference, because what we know of him we know from history, it is knowledge external to the message, or else we have found it out by rationalizing and distorting the message. The message and the addressee—the reader— are indeed the only factors involved in this communication whose presence is necessary. As for the other factors—language (code), non-verbal context, means of keeping open the channel—, the appropriate language of reference is selected from the message, the context is reconstituted from the message, contact is assured by the control the message has over the reader's attention, and depends upon the degree of that control. These special duties, and the esthetic emphasis characteristic of poetry demand that the message possess features corresponding to those functions. The characteristic common to such devices must be that they are designed to draw responses from the reader—despite any wanderings of his attention, despite the evolution of the code, despite the changes in esthetic fashion.

The pertinent segmentation of the poem must therefore be based on these responses: they pinpoint in the verbal sequence the location of the devices that trigger them. Since literary criticism aims at informing and improving such responses, we seem to have a vicious circle. It is only apparent, however, for what is blurred in a response is its content, the subjective interpretation of that response, which depends on elements exterior to the act of communication. The response itself testifies objectively to the actuality of a contact. Thus two precautions absolutely must be taken: 1) empty the response of its content; I can then use all forms of reaction to the text—idiosyncrasy-oriented responses (positive or negative according to the reader's culture, era, esthetics, personality) and goal-oriented responses (those of the reader with non-literary intent, who may be using the poem as a historical document, for purposes of linguistic analysis, etc.: such a reader will rationalize his responses to fit into his sphere of interest and its technical terminology); 2) multiply the response, to guard against physical interference with contact, such as the reader's fatigue or the evolving of the language since the time the poem was encoded.

This tool of analysis, this "superreader" in no way distorts the special act of communication under study: It simply explores that act more thoroughly by performing it over and over again. It has the enormous advantage of following exactly the normal reading process, of perceiving the poem as its linguistic shape dictates, along the sentence, starting at the beginning (whereas many critics use the end to comment on the start, and so destroy suspense; or else they use diagrams that modify the balance of the text's natural emphasis system —the chiasma-like division in the Jakobson and Lévi-Strauss analysis, or what they call diagonal or vertical correspondences); it has the advantage of screening pertinent structures and only pertinent structures. My "superreader" for "Les Chats" is composed of: to a limited extent, Baudelaire (correction of line 8, placing the sonnet in the ensemble of the collection); Gautier (his long paraphrase of the sonnet, in his preface to the third edition of the *Fleurs*), and Laforgue (some echoes in *Sanglot de la Terre,* "La Première Nuit"); the translations of W. Fowlie, F. L. Freedman and F. Duke; as many critics as I could find, the more useful being those whose reason for picking out a line had nothing to do with the sonnet; Jakobson and Lévi-Strauss for those points in the text where they deviate from their method (when they are being faithful, their analysis scans everything with even hand and is therefore misleading); Larousse's *Dictionnaire du XIXème Siècle* for the entries which quote the sonnet; philological or textbook footnotes; informants such as students of mine and other souls whom fate has thrown my way.

Each point of the text that holds up the superreader is tentatively considered a component of the poetic structure. Experience indicates that such units are always pointed out by a number of informants who usually give divergent rationalizations. These units consist of lexical elements of the sentence interrelated by their contrasting characteristics. They also appear to be linked to one another by relations of opposition. The contrasts they create is what forces them upon the reader's attention; these contrasts result from their unpredictability within the context. This unpredictability is made possible by the fact that at every point in a sentence, the grammatical restrictions limiting the choice of the next word permit a certain degree of predictability. Predictability increases as the number of levels involved and the number of restrictions increase, which happens with any kind of recurrence, like parallelism in general and meter in particular—and where predictability increases, so does the effect of an unpredicted element.

Units of this kind and the systems they constitute form the basis of the following analysis.

ANALYSIS

Title: The definite article and the plural lead us to expect a precise and concrete description: against such a backdrop, the spiritualization of the cats will be more arresting. Structurally the title focuses our expectations upon the first recurrence of *chats* in the text, which helps to unify the poem: every pronoun henceforth refers back unequivocally to that word, the only noun thus singled out.

Quatrain I: Coming as it does right after the terse title, the contrasting first line gives an even greater sense of plenitude. Twice the slot left empty next to *chats* is filled up with an adjective; this fullness of the nominal group is emphasized by the parallel word order—a symmetry reinforced on another level by the stresses and by the fact that phrases and hemistichs are coterminal. Of course the internal rhyme *fervents-savants* contributes to unification of the line: the similarity between the rhyme fellows (underlined, perhaps, by the contrast of their grammatical dissimilarity) makes up for the caesura and culminates the intonational curve. The enjambement stresses *aiment,* of course, at grammar level because the reader will compensate for the metric and rhythmic stop by an increased awareness of the grammatical relationship between verb and subjects. But at prosody level it also stresses the end of the line, where the meaning seems to be suspended for a fleeting moment. Thus the line as a whole looks almost like a subtitle, an anticipatory comment on the deep relatedness of *chats, amoureux* and *savants* (this impression will be confirmed every time we come across a pair of nominal phrases; for nowhere in the text is the model Noun-Adjective so symmetrically actualized).

Now this serves to stress the link between the two phrases bound by *et,* as would an equation. Yet scholars and lovers are diametrical opposites, as far apart as Venus Urania and carnal Aphrodite. Here is an archetypal representation of mankind: imagination links lovers and scholars as two kinds of men who can be defined by their opposition. The scholar stricken in his scholarness, despoiled of his wisdom, the ruined scholar is the scholar in love; the contradiction is as absurd or moving as that of another stereotype, the amorous grey-beard. From Aristotle on all fours, bridled, saddled, and mounted by his courtesan, to Professor Delteil besotted by the conflict between love and lexicography in the *Contes d'été* (1852) of Champfleury, Baudelaire's bosom companion, lover and scholar dwell incompatible within the same individual. It is not by chance that Balzac regards chastity as one of the fundamental traits of the man of science; and it is not by chance that in his erotic "Lesbos" Baudelaire resorts to an antithesis between the lascivious spectacle provided by the reprobates, and Plato's *oeil austère* indignantly upon it.

Now this opposition is part of a whole psychological structure, the archetypal representation of mankind divided into various classes of men. Yet the opposition is still further strengthened by the fact that its two poles are hyperbolic statements. *Amoureux* and *fervents* are like synonyms repeating each other, since love and fervor are often associated, and *ferveur* is a frequent metonymy for *amour*; *fervent* makes explicit an already obvious quality and implication of the noun and thereby stresses the noun; *fervent* works as would an *épithète de nature* in classical style, the adjective invariably linked to a given noun. *Austère* (or its synonyms) plays the same role in modifying *savant*: it conveys the mood of the meditative scholar as he is conceived in the popular imagination: Hugo's *Mages* are *les sévères artistes . . . Les savants, les inventeurs tristes, les puiseurs d'ombre* (*Contemplations* 3.30.383. 391-4). Thus *fervent* is to *amoureux* and *austères* to *savants* what "noble" is to "lord" or "unsolved" is to "mystery." Scholars and lovers are the standard exemplars of each genus, which means that their relation to each other is also exemplary, and their polarity more widely distanced. Add to this the fact that *fervent* is etymologically related to fire (in "Le Léthé," the lover's fervor fans the fiery pain of unrequited love); *austère* can be associated with cold (e.g. the "austere coldness" of the monastery, in "Le Mauvais Moine").

This context makes for the striking contrast of *aiment également . . . Les chats puissants et doux;* this oneness of feeling, this consensus so unexpected, contrasts the two mu-

tually opposing subjects, an effect increased by *également*.
The impact of *également* is further stressed on the semantic
level because it superimposes a synonymity upon the antonymy
of the first line; it is stressed at the same time by the disjunction, since the verb demands an object which is not yet forthcoming; and the disjunction actualizes the caesura—so that
in oral reading the meter will give strong support.

The importance of the adverb has another effect: it is a
first hint that lovers and scholars have much in common and
that the very qualities that mark their separateness also join
them. A possible analogy can now be perceived—the analogy
that permits Baudelaire to declare that Beauty's lovers *Con-
sumeront leurs jours en d'austères études . . .* ("La Beauté"),
the analogy that makes passion a common metaphor for the
pursuit of knowledge. As we read along, the importance of
également grows, since its meaning is confirmed by two more
resumptions of the theme that there is a profound similarity
between cats, lovers and scholars—but from the viewpoint of
the cats (lines 4 and 5): scholars and lovers love cats, cats
love science and love.

A similar flashback effect (the word being reinforced by
repeating the title) helps to contrast [3]*les chats* with what precedes; the contrast consists in the distance separating the subjects from the object on the plane of reality: this choice among
possibilities offered by the connotations of *chat* is oriented,
on the verbal plane, by the disjunction as a suspensive or de-
laying device, and by the disjunction as meaning, since it leads
the reader to expect a mature attachment to a commensurate
object, not a mere fondness, almost childish, for pets.

Whatever the orientation, the emphasis is undergirded by
[3]*puissants et doux*. The dual adjectival group itself is set off by
the contrast with its homologues, the adjectives in the first
line (their positions are identical, their meanings equally
positive, but the ratio one to two) and by the inner contrast
that makes *doux* an odd combination with *puissants*. This last
contrast is so strong that it has become a cliché—about which
more will be said later. The expressiveness of the opposition
created by *orgueil* is brought out by its contiguity to the pair
of adjectives, whose meaning it reinforces. This powerful
combination coincides with the descending curve of the sen-

tence: it seems to have run its course, after stating unequivocally that the most widely differing people imaginable will
agree at least in their love for cats. The *puissants-doux* opposition now symbolizes the cat's ambivalence, which explains
why two antithetical types of men can both love the cat with
equal love: each type in its own way has the same combination of power and serenity; the cat mirrors them in the animal
world—here, no doubt, one of the correspondences between
mankind and the rest of Nature.

The implicit similitude (implicit because it is our own deduction, we have reasoned it from the love of cats) is now
made explicit in line 4: the repetition of *comme eux*, with *eux*
encompassing both lovers and scholars, knocks out any interpretation that might try to assign the adjectives separately to
the two groups (Jakobson and Lévi-Strauss, [p. 15] see a
paronomasia—to my mind very far-fetched—linking *fervent*
and *frileux:* lovers and scholars are equally shivery *and*
sedentary); hence the inescapable conclusion that they are
identical, since they not only love equally, but equally resemble the cats, their *tertium comparationis.* The initial apparent
opposition discloses a deeper identity. Line 4 is a departure
from the context: I have shown earlier how strong is the unity
of the line and how it brings out the adjectives, especially
sédentaires; this line is structured so differently from the first
three that the coincidence between this contrast and the pattern
at the end of the stanza results in a veritable rhythmic clau-
sula. The parallel relative clauses constitute an addition to the
aiment clause: the momentum of the sound sequence, carried
in one breath to the caesura in line 3 and then continued despite the pause, is now all spent; the intonational curve thus
also helps make the first stanza a natural unit, not just a conventional one fused in a sestet, as Jakobson and Lévi-Strauss
would have it.

At this point, however, the importance of *frileux* and
sédentaires gives by flashback a new orientation to our sense
of the quatrain. The repeated identification *comme eux . . .
comme eux* clinches the demonstration of identity between
cats and their human counterparts. In this culminating phrase
we might have expected adjectives in keeping with those that
preceded, all laudatory; we might even have expected a cli-

maxing allusion to certain glorious qualities common to both
parties. Instead we get the mediocrity of *frileux* and *sédentaires*—a comic letdown; all the more galling because these are
every bit as true as the preceding adjectives, though they ruin
the image that has been built up. *Frileux* is fussy and oldmaid-
ish; Baudelaire used it effectively in a parodic self-portrait,
the satirical "Spleen I": *d'un fantôme frileux*. *Sédentaire*
conjures up the image of the constipated stay-at-home, epitome
of the unwholesome bourgeois. The reader takes in this surprise but has in mind the whole quatrain, so that *orgueil de
la maison* still sounds complimentary, with perhaps a touch
of parody in the *maison*, which narrowly limits the sphere of
the fame, the scope of the glory: even thus does La Fontaine's
fox cut his blandishments to the measure of the crow when
he crowns him *phénix de ces bois*—but keeps the eyrie of the
immortal bird in the neighborhood. Similarly, *mûre saison*, a
conventional poetic substitute for *l'âge mûr*, may now be felt
as a bit too elegiac, whereas without the twist in line 4 it would
simply be the expected ornamental phrase needed to beautify
everyday reality. Scholars, in the context and on the level of
amoureux, are in danger of losing their dignity: their austere
mien no longer impresses us, now that we see them as chilly
homebodies. *Amoureux* is not, like *amants*, confined to serious or tragic contexts: the shock wave from line 4 destroys
the synonymity with *amants* and actualizes the depreciatory
or condescending connotations: nineteenth-century dictionaries
rank *amoureux* below *amants*; *amoureux*, not *amants*, is the
core of many mocking phrases like *amoureux transi;* and
Baudelaire uses it elsewhere only to deride lovers (in the burlesque "La Lune offensée" their silly irresponsibility *sur leurs
grabats prospères;* in "Hymne à la Beauté" where the irony is
all his, as a comparison with the source makes clear their un-
gainly bed gymnastics: *L'amoureux pantelant incliné sur sa
belle;* whereas his *amants* are never equivocal, always
poetic).

Quatrain II: The formal singularity of line 5 clearly marks
the beginning of a new stanza, just as the character of line
4, more than its mere final position, makes it the ending of
the first quatrain. The element of unexpectedness is provided
by the apposition, which gives *Amis* a commanding post,

while *science* and *volupté* are each in turn spotlighted by the contrast with the comparatively empty *de la* (whose repetition performs the same unifying, characterizing function, for line 5, as did *comme eux* for line 4). Whereas [3]*orgueil*, also an apposition, followed explicit mention of its referent, *Les chats*, here the apposition precedes its referent, [6]*Ils*. Hence a momentary suspension while the reader's mind hesitates over whether to interpret *amis* as cats or as their admirers or as all of them together. Shortlived it may be, but the ambiguity is enough to emphasize the line, and when line 6 brings the solution, line 5 is sensed as homologous to lines 1-3 and in contrast to them, reversing them, so to say (this becomes more apparent if we rewrite 1-3: **la volupté et la science sont amies des chats*). The contrast between line 5 and the context of 1 is confirmed by the homologous relations of the two other elements in the spotlight: *amoureux-savants, science-volupté*.

The equivalence twice verified from people to cat to people, indicates plainly that their metonymic relationship is so close as to make them interchangeable: it becomes metaphoric, the cats symbolize something common to love and science.

The focus upon *Amis de la science et de la volupté* isolates it—and this isolation is intensified by its typographical concentration, which makes it quite visibly the shortest line of the sonnet. It is so isolated, in fact, that we are made aware of the cliché: the phrase is like *les amis des lettres* for "intelligentsia," or *les amis de la vérité*, generally for "the opposition" (it seems that Cicero coined it), or *ami de la bouteille*, "drunkard." With the added salt of personification, it has become the poetic stereotype for any habitual contiguity or affinity, the relation between "things that seem to have a sympathy for one another," as the dictionary of the Academy puts it in the 1835 edition, citing *Le vin est ami du coeur, il y a des odeurs qui sont amies du cerveau*, etc. Baudelaire follows suit with *le soir charmant, ami du criminel* ("Le Crépuscule du soir").

It is in the whole second quatrain, that irony is amplified. Jakobson and Lévi-Strauss are blinded by irrelevant parallelisms and do not see this. Other critics reject it because the poet's infatuation with cats makes irony less than likely. Informants, not so well versed in literary biography, *always perceive it*. Martin Turnell is the rare critic who does catch it, but he explains it away as we do an irony in real life: for him it is an "ironical" situation for scholars and lovers, who are supposed to hunt their prey, to be instead engaged in sedentary occupation (significantly, Turnell sees no irony in *frileux*, since it fits in with his exaggerated translation of *mûre saison* as "elderly"); again, for him the second quatrain is in "mock heroic style" because of the discrepancy between the cats' ludicrous ordinariness and high-sounding verse (*Baudelaire: A Study of His Poetry,* p. 262, 241). His argument is not to the point: a lover of cats would find no discrepancy—Gautier, for one, does not. Irony in literature must be a verbal structure, lest it vary with different readers' opinions as to what is exaggerated or "not really meant." The text must contain some signal that what is being said is not intended to be taken seriously, or that there is some double meaning. The first such structure is the contrast between a pattern of laudative adjectives and the *comparatively* unfavorable connotations of *frileux* and *sédentaires* (without the praise pattern, *frileux* at least looks "serious" or even poetic: Lebrun-Pindare speaks of *la frileuse hirondelle*). With this first structure as its context, a second structure is now built up in reverse: against the connotative pattern of line 4, the elevated tone of line 5, which would be appropriate to glorify the Medici, actually creates a *verbal* discrepancy which is inescapable, no matter what the reader's personal views on cats may be.

Informants unanimously ignore [6]*Ils cherchent le silence.* Undoubtedly *cherchent* is the poetic or high-tone substitute for *rechercher* or *aimer,* but this is no more than the normal transformation of prose into verse: the device marks genre, as do verse and stanza, setting the context apart from everyday contexts. It is expected and not surprising. [6]*Horreur des ténèbres,* on the contrary, draws the attention of every reader: this, of course, is because it contrasts with the first hemistich —a leap from factual-poetic to affective-poetic, and a semantic contrast between a desire and its undesirable object, as in Racine's *chercher la malédiction;* it is also because its inner structure, independent of context, brings out the powerful meaning of the group's components, thanks to an analytical subordination that separates *horreur* from its cause, thereby emphasizing twice over the concept of darkness. Moreover, *horreur des ténèbres* is a cliché: a reader of the 1850s would remember it from Racine or Delille as well. The cliché is objectionable only from the esthetic viewpoint that makes novelty the sole criterion of beauty. It may well be hackneyed, but its stereotyped form keeps it from wearing out: the inclusion of this particular cliché as an example in the *Larousse du XIXème siècle* must testify to its continued effectiveness.[5] Now if your reader is uncultivated, the cliché will strike him because of its intrinsic expressiveness; if he is well read, he will recognize it as a literary allusion, at any rate a literary form. Hence a deepening of darkness: here is no mere absence of light but an asylum for the secret life, a privileged abode for meditation, a sanctuary.

The distich (if we follow the division made by Jakobson and Lévi-Strauss) is the apex of both irony and emphasis on darkness. The attention-forcing features are, first, *L'Erèbe*, because it is a mythological allusion, because of its form (the only word in /rɛb/, aside from one name for ornithologists alone), and because it is a personification. Then *coursiers funèbres*, because it completes the mythological picture of a divine charioteer: but what may be conventional in the image is compensated for by [7]*funèbres*, which is effective both because of its meaning and because it repeats its homologue [6]*ténèbres*, first as a stereotyped rhyme and then as a moral transposition of the concept of darkness. And then [8]*servage* and [8]*fierté*, because these are concretized abstractions, as in line 5, and because the line contains a word order inversion within a clause (*au servage*, stressed in its aberrant position by the caesura). Naturally, the discrepancy we felt between [5]*Amis de la science . . .* and the preceding line is now even wider: Baudelaire invokes Erebus, son of Chaos, potent brother and husband of Night herself, father of Styx and of the Parcae and of Sleep—and states that tomcats like it in the dark. This is like La Fontaine calling a gardener a priest of Flora and Pomona; clearly this climaxes the second irony structure. But it also gives most effective expression to the es-

---

[5] *Horreur* attracts *ténèbres* so powerfully that it once caused Hugo to write *horreur ténébreuse*, without any connection with what he meant (*Dieu, L'Océan d'en haut*, v. 2465).

sential theme: *Erèbe* is the most evocative word of three connected by their sounds (*Erèbe, ténèbres, funèbres*) it summarizes them phonetically. Semantically too, since Erebus means "darkness." (Nodier goes so far as to use it as a common noun in that sense.) We may now say that the concept of darkness has been expressed, in turn, by the appropriate noun, literal but picked from the top of the ladder of expressivity, whose bottom rung might be *obscurité;* and by a metonymy (*horreur*), a metaphor (*funèbre*), a proper noun that is both metonymic as a person and metaphoric as the symbolic value of that person. Thus a paradigm of four synonyms has been transposed on to the axis of combination. These several variables (let us add the phonetic one that links three key words) represent the invariant "darkness." This, in turn, is part of a system that embraces the cats and science and love: since cats symbolize something common to love and science, this symbol tells us that love and science thrive in darkness.

So that the last two lines of the quatrain are not a separate unit: their many formal differences simply flow from the complexity of a hyperbolic image, and are needed to cap the demonstration. The dramatic temptation imagined by Jakobson and Lévi-Strauss is quite exaggerated. All we have, of course, is a statement that cats and darkness are closely associated, and then the mock hypothesis; in common parlance, I fancy it might go something like this: "They sure love the dark. Gee!—they could be the black horses of Hell, except that, etc. . . ."

Upon this note end the two quatrains and the irony—the reason being that irony has fulfilled its purpose. Intertwined with "serious" statements, irony lends them support. This is not an irony of content, that destroys; it is an irony of style, a way of saying things with tongue in cheek that attracts attention to what is being said. Irony as style is commonly used in the nineteenth century, in monographs or books of vulgarization as a way of establishing contact with the reader. I find it in Toussenel's *L'Esprit des Bêtes* (1848), the first volume of his *Zoologie passionnelle,* inspired by Fourier (we know that Baudelaire read at least the second volume), where the cat is described as the "lover of Night," or in a paper published by the same Toussenel in *l'Ecole normale,* where he celebrates the cat as the chemist, physicist, physician, etc. of the animal kingdom—in short, a friend of science. Irony and theme are the same in E. T. A. Hoffmann's *Chat Murr.*

Where Baudelaire utilizes the techniques of conventional poetry, as here, to embellish a lowly subject, his irony warns the reader, at the same time, that this is just a game, indeed, a mere convention, whose limitations he well knows. The praise of cats enables them to embody human qualities and makes their night something more than a time for backfence yowling. This "poetization" of the metaphoric vehicle allows for an ironic contrast, which in turn permits yet higher praise; and this finally prepares the way for a magnification of the cats into sphinxes through the comparison with mythical horses. Irony, by making such grandeur more acceptable to the sceptic and by underscoring it, further aids a shift in emphasis from superficial similarities (*frileux*) to an esoteric sympathy. It is now clear that the polarity of lovers and scholars defined the extreme examples of the class of men who seek the silence and the dark: these are necessary to the success of their respective strivings, so like each other—toward a life fully lived through *volupté,* toward a universe fully explored through science.

First Tercet: The domestic cat's mythologization becomes more specific and to the point. First of all, it is a new sublimation of the cat, this one based upon traditional association, perhaps because cats had their niche in the Pantheon of Egypt and surely because cats are enigmatic. This image is conveyed less by the hardly noticeable [10]*grands* than by the cliché [9]*nobles attitudes* (the fact that the *Larousse du XIXème siècle* quotes the line under *attitude* is sufficient proof of its effectiveness). It is vague, since *attitude* offers us nothing to *see* and is hardly more than a prop on which to hang some adjective like "noble," "great," "grave" that may be needed to give a description its moral meaning. On the one hand, *attitudes* reduces the plastic or visual evocation to a pose—especially for Baudelaire's contemporaries, who still regarded it as a painter's word—but a meaningful pose; for instance, in "Incompatibilité," *attitude* describes the attentive posture of mountains listening to some mysterious message; in "La

Beauté" the word lends a monumental majesty to Beauty, who *trône dans l'azur comme un sphinx incompris;* it is motion-lessness wherever that symbolizes contemplation. On the other hand, *attitudes* also functions as a screen that filters the com-plex reality of the cat, eliminates his daintiness, his nimble gait, anything that smacks of *volupté;* what is retained is the immobility, and the watchful gaze from under sleepy lids: in short, whatever makes the cat a domestic sphinx. In turn, the image of the original Sphinx is altered: there is no hint here of the details—breasts, claws, etc.—found in the sphinxes of Empire architecture and furniture, in Gautier's "Sphinx" or in the mean catwoman in Gustave Moreau's *Oedipe*—these are all too tangible. [10]*Allongés* is not exact enough to elimi-nate vagueness, nor is it incompatible with nobility, as is the pose of another of Gautier's sphinxes, *accroupi dans les sables brûlants* ("Le Lion du cirque"). The sphinx is like the "stone ghost," the statue that commands passersby to think upon the things *qui ne sont pas de la terre* (*Salon de 1859*, IX, ed. Pléiade, p. 1086).

Thus [9]*nobles attitudes,* stereotype though it is, sums up a meaning in Baudelaire's own symbolic code—"meditation upon things metaphysical"—which is stated again in common language: *songeant, rêve sans fin*—an elevation to eternity.

Sphinx adds to the mimesis of "contemplation" its arche-typal esoterism. A context of ordinary words sets in relief the foreignness of *sphinx;* the name alone suffices to evoke, like Flaubert's sphinx, contemplativeness: *mon regard, que rien ne peut dévier, demeure tendu à travers les choses sur un horizon inaccessible* (*La Tentation de Saint Antoine*, VII, ed., R. Dumesnil, p. 199).

[10]*Solitudes* keeps the reader from substituting the OEdi-pean sphinx for this brooder: reinforced by *au fond* and again by the plural, it makes clear that desert has been chosen not for the sake of its connotations of barrenness but for what it means to man as a privileged place of meditation: the poet makes a revealing joke about the working of his imagi-nation being founded upon *la Thébaïde que mon cerveau s'est faite* (*Salon de 1859*, VII, p. 1071). The interpretation given by Jakobson and Lévi-Strauss is based on the semantic field of "desert:" "the fear of cold, which brings chilly cats and

hot lovers close to one another . . . finds a suitable climate in
the solitude (as austere as the scholars themselves) of the
desert (as hot as the lovers) that surrounds the sphinxes"
(p. 15). The procedure is obvious: in accordance with the
principle of equivalence, *solitudes* is transformed into *désert*
as defined by the dictionary; equivalences are then deduced:
from "desert" as a limitless expanse, they draw the opposition
maison—solitudes; from "desert" as opposed to "oasis," the
equation with *austères;* from "desert" as "burning sands," the
opposition to *frileux* and the equation with *fervents.* Unfortunately, this system is not actualized in the poem and therefore cannot be applied. And that for the simple reason that
the text says not *désert* but *solitudes;* which is in reality
synonymous with *silence* and *ténèbres,* since, like them, it
makes contemplation possible (the three are interchangeable:
in "Le Gouffre" they describe the universe contemplated by
the poet. It may be argued that *sphinx* identifies *solitudes*
with white-hot Egypt: but the sonnet does not actualize in
words any such image. Even where a poem does contain a
precise geographical description of a desert, this is not enough
to impose upon the reader associations not verbally actualized
as well. In "Spleen II," for instance, the desert is a geographical reality: it is named, and there are allusions to the pyramids
and to the Sphinx. Yet the associative system organized
around *désert* in the language is supplanted by the symbolic
function of the word in the text (that wasteland is boredom),
and only where reality is relevant to that symbol do "natural"
associations operate (e.g. the pyramid symbolizes dead mem-
ories); but the physical climate of the desert yields in the
face of meteorological similes whose sole justification is that
they express "spleen:" *les lourds flocons des neigeuses années,*
and the symbolic mist that shrouds the sphinx *Assoupi dans
le fond d'un Saharah brumeux.* "Contemplative life, ataraxy"
—the inscape of *solitudes* has no need to conjure up, and in
fact excludes an arid African landscape.[6]

Second Tercet: The two tercets are more than convention-

---

[6] Cf. Wm. Y. Tindall, *The Literary Symbol* (1955), pp. 130-3.—The
whole tercet is quite frequently quoted in its entirety, and by critics of
all feathers; this effectiveness is probably attributable to the archetypes
as much as to the form.

ally separated by the difference in clause construction between lines 11 and 12: the abundance of nasals, twice as many as in any other line coinciding with their position, emphasizes their role as stanza boundaries (12, with a sequence of /ɛ/, contrasts with the /ã/ pattern of 11).

So long as the cats' "spiritualization" had not been achieved, no physical detail was given that might drag them back down to reality (except in line 4, and this, paradoxically, was just a way of elevating them by comparison). Now that they are a symbol, the poet refers to their physical realities. But each realistic detail is but a springboard to unreality, for an adjective transposes it and makes it a signpost towards surreality. Every one of these adjectives could apply to the sphinx: thus the creature constitutes a transition from mythic to mystic, and because it stands for esoterism, it is the key to the code the adjectives set up.

"Reality" is imposed upon the reader by [12]*Leurs reins féconds:* the group is striking at every level. The harsh juncture (/r + r/) signalizes it as a beginning and sharpens the rupture with the first tercet. Since that pattern was simplification, abstraction, its rupture must be concrete detail: hence a shift from pronouns that only allude to real subjects (*ils, qui*) to descriptive nouns that invite sensory perception. The context indicates that *reins* is a metonymy for "back;" but *féconds* suggest that it is a metaphor, "loins," for sexual potency. Then the ambiguity contaminates *étincelles.* On the one hand, *étincelles* describes the sparks (from this viewpoint, *magiques* is hyperbolic); on the other hand, it symbolizes vital parts (*magiques* then being the literal expression of the mystery of life-giving). *Pleins* belongs to colloquial style (compare *terre . . . pleine d'escargots* in "Le Mort joyeux," *ventre plein d'exhalaisons* in "Une Charogne," etc.), and therein it contrasts with the conventional style of *reins féconds.* But at the metaphoric level, it makes *reins* still more concrete. In either case it provides an animal ground that brightens the contrast of *étincelles,* a word we associate with the archetypes of fire and light. These archetypes exerted more power over the imagination in an era when electricity was still untamed and Mesmer still far from forgotten, as attested by the frequency of metaphors based upon galvanism. [12]*Magiques,* however,

is the ingredient that keeps the archetype alive forever in the
text, even for the rationalistic reader: it exteriorizes a response that the reader made wise by science now represses in
his subconscious, the immemorial surprise at a fire that does
not burn (poetic themes like the salamander and the lightning
bug obviously took their origin from some such feeling).
Perhaps this tips the scales in favor of an interpretation of
reins as a sexual image, since fire and semen, sparks and life,
are often metaphorically associated.[7] Most important, the
group *étincelles magiques* declares the existence of a second
level of reality beneath appearances. Even if there were no
archetypes behind it, the group would still suggest them: *étincelles* and *magiques* do not simply add their poetic potentiali-
ties to say something like "the sparks have a magical effect;"
in a context now dominated by *sphinx* and previously by
ténèbres and *science, magiques* must be interpreted as a substitute for an actual esoteric reference; the sparks are fire but
also meaning. The symbolism of the text has moved from
darkness and dream to light in darkness.

The last two lines owe their effectiveness to their structure
as a suspense narrative (the enjambement, and the severance
of the verb *étoilent* from its subject). The description stresses
a physical beauty whose significance is withheld until the
reader discovers, at the same time, that all this is about the
eyes of the cat, and that those eyes are supernatural.

At the outset, a vision of gold is summoned up, at once
to exploit its archetypal symbolism and to transform it into a
symbol of light. [13]*Parcelles d'or* is the agent of this alchemy:
significantly, *Larousse du XIXème siècle* quotes this whole
tercet under *parcelles*. In a "gold" context, *parcelles* actualizes
the highly poetic antithesis of infinite value in infinitesimal
room. In other words, a hyperbolic rendering of the cats'
yellow-flecked eyes: this stylistic sublimation of the color is
carried on by the second hemistich, where even the conjunction has been touched by Midas: *ainsi que* is to *comme* what
or is to *jaune. Sable,* semantically related to *parcelles* by metonymy is now its metaphoric substitute, as if all the sand in

---

[7] Line 12 exemplifies Bachelard's Novalis complex (*Psychanalyse du
feu*, pp. 47 ss, 87 ss).

the placer had turned to gold dust. *Fin* in a "sand" context lays emphasis upon what makes sand more pleasing to the eye and to the naked foot, but in the parallel structure of the line, *fin* is also in a "gold" context and its suggestiveness is therefore oriented by the jeweler's technical phrase *or fin*. Furthermore, *parcelles d'or* irresistibly calls forth the compound *paillettes d'or* frequently used in descriptions of eyes —*deux yeux de chats, phosphorescents, pailletés d'or*.[8] Their semantic equivalence and their quasi-homophony make *parcelles d'or* expressive as a modification of the more common compound—the same stylistic mechanism as in the renewal of a cliché, the adaptation of a quotation or the distortion of a word. Coming immediately after *étincelles, parcelles* works as a variation on the motif of sparkling light—a golden fire. At the peak of the rhythmic build-up of two lines unified by one sentence [14]*étoilent* all alone would have grandeur. The verb itself, with archetype for a root, and normally in the past participle, is as conventional as "star-spangled" in English. But its use in any other mode explodes the stereotype, renews the rapport with the semantic field of *étoile,* and stresses the image of light in darkness; for instance, this line of Hugo: *Nul regard n'étoilait la noirceur de leurs yeux* (*Les Quatre Vents de l'esprit,* 4.3.3). Not much is needed for such a verb to take on a suggestiveness of the unknown. This is precisely the effect attained by *vaguement:* the adverb seems to annul exactly what differentiates *étoiler* from other verbs of light—its scintillation. Literally taken, the group would be meaningless, but *vaguement* is more like a blanket negation of reality: it gives it the appearance of the unreal. The adverb functions as a device to orient the reader towards a mystical interpretation. Without *vaguement,* a smile *Entrevu vaguement au bord des autres cieux* is only the dream of an exotic idyl with some "Malabaraise." The adverb transmutes it into a yearning for eternity ("Lesbos"). As a matter of fact, this function of *vaguement* dovetails so perfectly with the esoteric connotations of *étoiler* that their grouping became a feature of Hugo's metaphysical or fantastic style: in a picture of dawn, for instance

---

[8] Zola, *Nana,* I (éd. Mitterand, 2, p. 1120). Tears cannot dampen their fire: *Votre prunelle, ou brille une humide paillette,* writes Gautier (*Poésie diverses* 1833-1838, "A deux beaux yeux").

—l'âpre obscurité . . . s'étoilait au loin de vagues auréoles—
they give the reader warning that this light in darkness is not
of the day but of God, a sign to the *voyant.*[9]

In the tercet the group exercises a final dominion over the
reader's imagination by gathering up the sparks in the eyes,
where they must have significance, and transposing that significance on to an esoteric level. Thus we escape any temptation to downgrade *mystiques* to "mysterious." The full sense
of the adjective was borrowed by Baudelaire from theology,
"allegorical of a spiritual truth"—which explains why the nouns
it modifies must be concrete: e.g. *le grenier mystique* ("La
Mort des Pauvres"), that is, Death, the Barn where the poor
will find stored for their afterlife the rewards that misery
harvests for them. Without such a contrast, *mystiques* would
be tautological. The contrast here is provided by the precise
prunelles. This conventional metonymy ceases to be a mere
ornament: it emphasizes the gaze, symbol of a questing mind.
Both Gautier's and Laforgue's reaction testify to the effect of
these two words together: they both tried to emulate it. The
rhythmic structure of the tercet shows clearly that the poem is
ending. Their meaning and the space occupied by the last two
lines develop line 12, and this relation is underscored by [13]*Et.*
The *ets* of the quatrain bound together phrases of equal
length and comparable value, all of them parts of a clause
(1, 2, 3, 5) or of a sentence (4): [13]*Et* standing out against
a pattern of six lines without similar coordination, links two
sentences, the second twice as long as the first. The tercet
seems to fan out in a final image: *et* launches the ascending
portion of the sentence, the first one in the sonnet that takes a
whole last line to descend uninterrupted. Such an ample intonational curve provides the poem with a rhythm unequivocally terminal, and yet its resounding amplitude echoes the
meaning of *mystiques.*

The poem as a whole: Obviously should be read as both a
blason, an encomiastic description, a *laus cattorum,* and as a
symbolic poem—the cats are at once cats and the hieroglyph

---

[9] *Dieu,* "L'Esprit humain", v. 235. In *Contemplations,* "A celle qui
est restée en France", 352-4, the group appears significantly in a passage
that seems to list the key words of the Hugolian contemplation.

of something else. The concluding word, *mystiques,* which is in effect a metalinguistic comment on the image of the cat, implies two meanings and invites us to a new examination of his image in that light. When the reading is over, a global, summative apprehension of the text through rereading and remembering is certainly part of the literary act of communication. Then, the total of all data and knowledge of the ending surges back to modify what we perceived at the beginning (such an effect was observable in the irony of the quatrains). Several different images can be seen as the variants of a single semantic structure—as symbols.

The fact that attentive critics are not aware of any symbolism and see in "Les Chats" a pre-Parnassian work whose "precise" imagery reflects an esthetics of the picturesque[10] may be laid to the title ("poème animalier") and to the absence of the kind of obvious explanatory statement found in most allegorical poems (*Les Hiboux,* with a similar title, *are* explained as allegory); perhaps, as well, to the necessity for finding in Baudelaire examples that support the favored idea of his development: something Parnassian was needed.

In each instance where the cats are equivalent to something else (men, mythological figures, and a surreal or supernatural image of themselves), they resemble not the appearance of these equivalents but what the latter stand for. The relationship between cats as pets and men as their masters is but an image of the cats' love for science itself and *volupté.* This link between Science and Pleasure is the symbol of the *raison d'être* that Faust and Don Juan have in common—an unending search of the absolute. Baudelaire is unequivocal: his "Femmes damnées" are *chercheuses d'infini;* poetry, art are *la soif insatiable de tout ce qui est au delà* (*Nouvelles histoires extraordinaires,* Conrad, pp. xx-xxi). Now there are two roads to the absolute: there is the quest for the Grail, *le voyage;* and there is the quest within, that is, meditation. *Mûre saison, doux, maison, frileux, sédentaire* repeat insistently that adventure is forsaken: the cats' meditativeness represents the chosen way.

[10] M. A. Ruff, *L'Esprit du mal et l'esthétique baudelairienne* (1955), pp. 245, 304; R. B. Chérix, *Commentaire des Fleurs du Mal* (1949), p. 247.

That such is their meaning is confirmed by their relationship to Erebus, an image of their love for silence and the
dark; and their relationship to the Sphinx, an image of im-
mobile mystic contemplation.

The sonnet structure can thus be described as a sequence
of synonymous images, all of them variations on the symbolism of the cat as representative of the contemplative life. The
Sphinx simile duplicates the equivalence by making the cat a
symbol of this symbol of mystic contemplation. The last
stanza reduplicates this by making him a symbol also of the
object of contemplation: he merges in himself the gaze of the
contemplator and the light in darkness that reveals just enough
of the hidden treasure to encourage the *chercheur d'absolu*—
a combination of enticement and denial common to many
symbols of esoterism (cf. the frequent image of light behind a
veil). Thus, beneath this repetitive continuity lies an antithesis
that opposes the natural cat, symbol of contemplation, to the
supernatural cat, symbol of the contemplated, of the occult
truth.

The foregoing interpretation, it seems to me, covers every
aspect of the text without contradiction. The antithesis just
outlined has the advantage over the exegesis of Jakobson and
Lévi-Strauss that it explains the transfiguration of the cats.
The poem gives not a "reason" in the world why we should see
this transfiguration as a "cosmic" one. The range of their
metamorphosis is not that wide: at most, they become like
Cheshire-Cats with only their phosphorescence left. And this,
we can explain if we take them to symbolize the contemplative
mind and to represent its poles in turn, being first the eye as
gaze and then the eye as mirror. A description of the familiar
feline postures suffices to make them acceptable as symbols of
the contemplators; but if we are to be made to see the cat as
a being related to the supernatural, a parti-pris is required
to inform his physical features with a significance; the transfiguration is then the consequence of a stylistic shift of the
description from an animal vocabulary with limited connotations (*frileux, sédentaires,* etc.) to a metaphysical one
(*magiques, mystiques*) with a boundless power of suggestion.

COMPARATIVE STRUCTURALISM

Any lingering doubt as to the symbolism of the sonnet will vanish once we find other texts, unquestionably symbolic, which are variants of the structure our sonnet actualizes.

Jakobson and Lévi-Strauss conduct such a comparative study in an effort to relate "Les Chats" to the other *Flowers* and to the poet's psychology. Here again their procedure raises the question of pertinence to the literary phenomenon at hand. In my opinion comparative structuralism as they practise it requires a radical readjustment. Their entire commentary emphasized the cats' identification with the cosmos. Another interpretation, a sexual one, was limited to their affinity with *amoureux*. Now, as a sort of afterthought, sexuality takes the spotlight: we are told that in Baudelaire's mind the image of the cat is the image of a woman and that our sonnet has a female-male ambiguity. Hence the bold conclusion: the cat's image symbolizes the poet. The sublimation of the cat symbolizes love cleansed of feminine impurity and knowledge freed of its coldness. The poet is thus ready for a mystic communion with the universe. Now I am not sure I have this quite straight,[11] but I am sure that a chasm has opened up between an almost pedestrian process of analysis and these philosophical fireworks.

These assertions are put forward as proof: 1) the use of feminine words for masculine rhymes suggests androgyny: in my discussion of metalanguage I tried to show that this could not be; 2) the words [3]*puissants et doux* amount to a description of cats as women: the sole evidence for this is a line of Brizeux where women are celebrated as *êtres puissants et doux*. Which is not convincing because, as I said before, this is a cliché (a stereotype structure linking *doux* and any adjective incompatible with "sweetness" or "softness"). The cliché

---

[11] p. 21, "De la constellation initiale du poème, formée par les amoureux et les savants, les chats permettent par leur médiation d'éliminer la femme, laissant face à face—sinon même confondus—le "poète des Chats", libéré de l'amour . . . , et l'univers, délivré de l'austérité du savant."

corresponds, I believe, to the archetype of the hero strong enough to be kind, from Homer's Hector to Rimbaud's Héraklès whose brow is *terrible et doux* ("Soleil et Chair"). The cliché is in no way used for amazons only. The only time I found it with female connotations, it described not womanhood, but motherhood,[12] which does not apply to *these* cats. 3) Androgyny is again implied by certain ambiguities in the description of the cats; and the cats in "Les Chats," being the same as those in the two poems entitled "Le Chat," must therefore represent Woman. These last two contentions can be best answered by the comparative method.

The principle of comparative structural analysis is quite simple: given several sets of data, no comparison may be drawn between empirical data pertinent to those sets, but solely between the systems within which they occur. Just because they do have common components, one system cannot be used to explain another: they must be isomorphic.

If we now compare texts, we find no correspondences enabling us to see "Les Chats" as equivalent to a "female" structure. There are, to be sure, homologies between the descriptive structures here and those in "Le Chat" (*Fleurs*, LI): the animal is, at the same time, *fort et doux;* his domain is a house too (*C'est l'esprit familier du lieu*), although the house is located in the poet's inner universe (*Dans ma cervelle*); the creature's gaze has a sphinx-like fixity, and his nature is mystic (*chat mystérieux, chat séraphique, chat étrange*); finally, the relationship between the cat and the poet is much the same as that between our cats and their composite counterpart in "Les Chats." The magic motif is here, but treated differently: stroked, the fur emits a magic fragrance instead of sparks. One feature prominent here is not mentioned in our sonnet, the meow—but this is actually another device to suggest the supernatural (the mewing is compared to poetry, to a philter, and so forth), and a variant of the darkness motif (*sa voix, qui parle . . . Dans mon fonds le plus ténébreux*). I trust I have made the parallelism as convincing as our exegetes could wish. Now for my retort: there is nothing in *Le*

---

[12] A. France, *L'Anneau d'améthyste,* III (p. 126). Abbé Guitrel calls his affection for a young man "maternelle, pour mieux exprimer ce qu'elle contient à la fois de force et de douceur".

Chat that imposes upon the reader the image of a woman. The descriptive details claimed for femininity apply as aptly to felinity; all the passages that might be alluding to love can be taken just as satisfactorily as mystical (in fact, some of these ambiguities have verbal or content homologues in "La Beauté" and "Hymne à la Beauté"). I am well aware that critics nearly always assume this cat is a girl—one line is even read as pandering to the reader's prurience. Yet all such conclusions lean upon biographical data which is by no means certainly applicable here. And even if the poet *was* inspired by some love affair, the point is that such content is *concealed* by the form or else translated to a distinctly spiritual level; *volupté* is not described in terms of Woman but is interiorized in a reverie about a symbolic cat.

As for "Le Chat" (*Fleurs*, XXXIV), it does conjure up a woman, though only by simile, and it should be noted that the description of the cat in itself does not bring to mind a woman so long as the comparison is not made formal and explicit (*Je vois ma femme en esprit*). But then the structure is entirely different from that of *Les Chats* except for the eyes and the sparks; and these are here given unrelated functions: the sparks are purely descriptive, without spiritual connotation; the eyes do not invite entry into their secret world, they are instead turned outwards, directed against the observer. So are the claws and even the *dangereux parfum*.

Lastly, in a prose poem that Jakobson and Lévi-Strauss do not mention, "L'Horloge," Baudelaire compares a mistress with a cat; he seeks eternity in her eyes. Thus cat and woman are identified, and there is some of the spiritual atmosphere of "Les Chats." But form and emphasis are completely different: in fact, the structure of our sonnet seems to be pointedly avoided. Spiritual connotations are dissociated from the "natural" cat-woman likeness: an ironic comment by the poet dismisses them as the far-fetched metaphor of a madrigal in the Gongora (or Samuel Cramer) vein; the mystic élan is negated, as it were, by the "realistic," prosaic style of the traveler telling tales of Chinese superstition. It is the woman who resembles the cat, rather than the other way around, and even that link is broken as soon as it is formed. As space and eternity are visioned in the woman's eyes, they vanish from the cat's lightless eyeballs (*le blanc des yeux*); as felinity invades the woman (*la belle Féline, la si bien nommée*), it deserts the cat (*un fort gros chat*).

Of course Baudelaire is perfectly capable of perceiving the cat in the woman, the woman in the cat. He occasionally uses the one as a metaphor of the other. But not always. Whatever the role of the cat in his private erotic imagery, it was not such as to make him write *chat* instinctively when he meant *femme*: whenever he does, we have seen that he feels obliged to provide the reader with an explanation. If *chat* means something besides the little beast, its dual value entails a selection among the descriptive features of the cat's image, the only traits retained being those common to both the animal and what he represents. This selection, in any given instance, must be our reference for interpreting that instance.

Once we have got rid of our false rapprochements, nothing in "Les Chats" calls up Woman. I am not ready to agree that [12]*reins féconds* is ambiguous: like *aine*, it is a euphemism reserved to the male procreative power, whereas *ventre* or *sein* would be used for female fertility. *Chats* and *sphinx* may be androgynous for lexicographers: but in context the masculine gender of *chats* is repeatedly underlined by *ils* and *eux*, by *coursiers* and *amis*. The mythological sphinx was indeed half or one-third female, but French, significantly, shifted from *la* to *le sphinx* during the eighteenth century; Romantic travelers to the Orient and writers of esoteric bent virtually abandoned the Greek female-bosomed monster in favor of the *grand sphinx* of the Pyramids. *Volupté* is not one way or the other (note, however, that the *chat voluptueux* of "La Géante" is definitely a tomcat), but a context containing *savants, science, silence, horreur des ténèbres* and *funèbres* rather flatly excludes any female presence. The analysts' misreading is due, I believe, to the choice of data exterior to the poems. Since *chats* is the key word, and since Baudelaire's love for cats is well attested, it was logical for our authors to assume that this is a case of obsession, which triggers the word's recurrence. This causal relationship does not, however, extend to any structure: there is no evidence that a stylistic structure corresponds to the psychological one. All that can be said with certainty is that a psychological structure may well "activate" or "sensitize" a word, and that this word will then come easy to the poet, will play a role in a number of structures that have nothing to do with its source within his mind. *Solitudes* and *chats* demonstrate that the semantic structure, the virtual system of representations centered around a word, does not remain present behind every actualization of that word.

Comparative structuralism, if consistently adhered to, should at least rid literary criticism of one great plague: the proclivity to assume that a key word or verbal obsession must always have the same meaning for the author once the obsession has set in. Semantic permanence *is* to be observed among the variants of one structure; but a verbal obsession may serve several structures. Let us give the name *code* to the lexical components that actualize a variant of a structure. We can say that in "Les Chats" three symbolic structures (semantic, but in actual texts only, not in language) representing mystery and two modes of contemplation have been implemented with a *cat-code* (*sphinx* is only a specialization of *chat*, a subcode). If the structures determined from the data of the sonnet are correct, there should be other codes actualizing them.

The contemplative-life structure subcoded in *sphinx* can be readily verified: I find it in "La Chambre double," where *Les meubles ont des formes allongées, prostrées, alanguies. Les meubles ont l'air de rêver; on les dirait doués d'une vie somnambulique.* The relational elements are the same: *allongés rêve,* wakefulness under the appearance of sleep; the bed is occupied, but hardly by a woman—like the cats, the "queen of dreams" has been virtually reduced to eyes, instrument of contemplation. Her eyes have the same ambiguity as the eyes of cats: they watch, they demand to be watched; they too are like stars, and these *étoiles noires,* in a symbolic synthesis, explicitly achieve the simultaneity of darkness and light; and so does everything else in the room: *ici, tout a la suffisante clarté et la délicieuse obscurité de l'harmonie.* To cast out any possible doubt, the "translation" is given: this room looks like a dream (it *is* a dream), its true nature is *véritablement spirituelle.* The code is made up of the stock of images evoked by "bedroom," but the fundamental theme is still the same beatitude represented by the

cats, the sphinxes and their human counterparts: contem
plation abolishes time and plunges you into blissful eternity

Another variant of the structure provides a regular com
mentary on the second tercet: in "Les Yeux de Berthe,"
there are dark eyes the description of which is synonymou
with our sonnet:

> arcanes adorés,
> Vous ressemblez beaucoup à ces grottes *magiques*
> Où, derrière l'amas des ombres léthargiques
> *Scintillent vaguement* des trésors ignorés

Arcanes and *trésors ignorés* develop [14]*mystiques:* these eye
are like the eyes of the Queen of Sheba in Flaubert's *Tentatio*
—*de grands yeux noirs, plus sombres que les caverne
mystiques*[13]—at the very moment she proclaims that she i
no woman but a universe, a "succession of mysteries." Th
motif of treasure shining in the dark is repeated in the mysti
antithesis of night as a font of light:

> des yeux obscurs, profonds et vastes,
> Comme toi, Nuit immense, éclairés comme toi!

and then the translation is given:

> Leurs feux sont ces pensers d'Amour, mêlés de Foi,
> Qui pétillent au fond, voluptueux ou chastes.

Thus is the symbolism of the eyes demonstrated: they ar
certainly not the eyes of Baudelaire's mulatto paramour a
most critics choose to think. The poet gazes into these eye
and for him they are like intercessors in his contemplation.

This act of intercession by eyes, we find again in "Le Chat
(*Fleurs*, LI), whose genuinely symbolic character I hav
hinted at before; at the end of the poem the eyes move t
where the Church Fathers and the mystics after them set th
oculi animae. When the poet looks within himself, he finds th
eyes interiorized, looking at him from out of the depths of hi
soul. These eyes of the spirit mirroring the eyes of the bod
are a definite allusion to the language of esoterism, wherei
reciprocity is a metaphor for secret "correspondences." Baude

---

[13] Ch. II, ed. Dumesnil, p. 42. The passage was published in *L'Artist*
of Dec. 21, 1856, and reviewed by Baudelaire one year later.

laire himself refers to this in the prose version of "L'Invitation
au Voyage:" he invites an allegorical flower to *se mirer, pour
parler comme les mystiques, dans sa propre correspondance.*
Finally, the parallelism between *Amour* and *amoureux*, and
between *Foi* and *savants* demonstrates the metaphysical nature
of their symbolism.

Our comparisons supply us with a tool for evaluating the
components of Baudelaire's imagery and their role: "eyes,"
for instance, are not part of a code; they appear invariably
and are therefore essential to a structure symbolic of infinity
—whose invariant is a relation *fascinating light + darkness.*
In fact, Baudelaire might almost be giving us a demonstrative
outline when he describes how make-up transforms a face into
the mysterious mask of a priestess, how that mask represents
supernatural life, how mascara, *ce cadre noir, rend le regard
plus profond . . . donne à l'œil une apparence . . . de
fenêtre ouverte sur l'infini.*[14] Certain texts in which we find
the eyes, such as "A une Passante," may seem very different
at first sight, but we can now classify them as permutation
groups of the "fascinating light" variants. In that sonnet a
glance from a woman encountered by chance on the street—
lightning, then night—sets off a mystic dream: the difference,
a shift from a gaze-code to a glance-code, is in the frustrating
briefness of this illumination. The prose poem "Le Désir de
peindre," usually associated by critics with "A une Passante"
because of the lightning in the eyes of the female character,
belongs, on the contrary, in the main group: among other
parallelisms it offers *deux antres où scintille vaguement le
mystère*—note the adverb—a variant of the "fascinating light"
structure, complete with translation. This comparative approach also explains why "Les Chats" are inseparable from
"Les Hiboux." Both cats and owls stare into darkness, their
eyes are phosphorescent, they are philosophic and come to the
same moral conclusion as the unmoving sphinx: happiness
is in sedentariness. The two poems are variants of the same
structure, and they differ only in style—"Les Hiboux" are
like a fable or an apologue.

[14] *Le peintre de la vie moderne,* XI, "Eloge du maquillage" (Pléiade,
. 1185).

A description of *Les Fleurs du Mal* based on this method should be an improvement upon the usual enumerations of images arranged by vehicles, that is, according to the codes, to the interchangeable words—these cannot lead anywhere, nor can they account for the variations of meaning in the symbolism of such words—and perhaps there is some justification for this approach to be found in Baudelaire's structuralist definition of the symbol: *la forme moulée sur l'idée.*

Towards an anthropology of literature

Victoria L. Rippere

Once upon a time the Martians decided to found an Institute for Terrestrian Studies. Inexperienced at studying the way of man, they began by hijacking an expert—an anthropologist. He instructed them in methods to the best of his ability, but alas, he was a specialist and could tell them only of the activities of certain *peoples* and was at a loss for words when it came to *people*. His last advice to the Martians before they sent him back to earth was that they capture a Harlequin, who would know a little of everything rather than everything about a little. And so they did.

"Well," said the Harlequin upon being taken to their leader, "what can I do for you?"

"We are Martians," replied the leader, "and everything human is strange to us. We come to the science of man, as you say, *tabula rasa*, except for the various artifacts of earthly life we've collected, including you. You, as a native informant, will please explain to us what all these things are about."

"Well," returned the Harlequin, "I'll try my best."

On the seventh day, the Martians convened with the Harlequin for the scheduled session: "What is Literature?" O

the speaker's table were five books: a dictionary, a concordance, a telephone book, a novel, and a book of poems.

"What is literature?" began the Harlequin rhetorically.

"Books!" came a voice from the back of the auditorium.

"Tabula rasa, indeed!" snorted the Harlequin. "In our lecture on dogs, you will recall, we said that 'all hounds are dogs
but not all dogs are hounds.' A dog is a dog. But with literature we have to say that all books are not literature and not
all literature is to be found in books. What I shall try to do
today is establish a common denominator which everything
we might call literature will share. Is that agreeable?"

"You're the informant," replied the leader of the Martians.

"This is a telephone book," said the Harlequin, holding up
the telephone book. "What do you suppose it is?"

"A book about telephones?" asked a Martian.

"No. It's a book for the convenient *use* of telephones. And
here is our first distinction between what is and isn't literature. Literature isn't practically useful."

"Does that mean it's useless?" asked the Martian.

"No. It shares in the 'otherness' proper to art as distinct
from reality. You remember what I told you about disinter-
estedness and the bird and the painting of the bowl of cherries? Birds don't know about art; all the bird sees is the cherries, not the picture at all. For him there is no 'otherness:'
cherries are cherries to eat. Now, if I were to define literature,
I would say: 'Literature is that form of art whose medium
is language.' "

"Could you elaborate?"

"As a form, literature participates in certain conventions
which are said to be formal, like genre, diction, style. As language, it possesses certain indigenous characteristics such as
the sounds and meanings of the words in the order and combinations in which they have been arranged. This is all fairly
obvious, but we have to begin at the beginning. Now, who can
tell me . . . ?"

"In the beginning was the word," called out a bright young
Martian.

"Yes and no. And here we get to the next distinction," continued the Harlequin. "Although a discrete non-literary utter-

ance may consist of a single word, such as 'yes,' 'no,'
'maybe' . . ."

"Continue!" called the leader of the Martians.

"Exactly! . . . the shortest discrete linguistic utterance
which we may properly call literature must consist of at least
two words. It is a certain relationship between the words
which enables language to become the medium for a form
of art. I shall call this relationship 'context.' "

"Context?" demanded a Martian, "I thought context was
who says what to whom when where and how. You
said . . ."

"Patience," cautioned the Harlequin. "It's that, too, but
let's see where the word is from before jumping to hasty conclusions. 'Context' is from the past participle of the Latin
contexere, 'to weave, join together.' By it I mean most basically the nexus of the woven and the weave . . ."

"I cannot tell the dancer from the dance;" quoth a Martian, "will you please say what you mean?"

". . . the relationship by which the quantitative fact of
these two words is raised to a higher, qualitative power: fiction. By 'higher' I mean no value judgment. Fact is just de-
scriptively different from fiction. Because of this potentiation
a literary utterance exists on more than just the literal level
of meaning; it means more than it says. The kind and number of different levels of meaning depend on the particular
work, its genre, its intention, and I won't try to go into them
here. I can't be exhaustive and don't want to be exhausting.
I'm just trying to point out a lowest common denominator.
Even these levels of meaning don't make an absolute, in-
fallible criterion—in real life people use irony and understate-
ment to mean more than they say. But I digress. Context is
the difference between a work and its concordance. The words
are all there, but their relationship is different. In the work
the whole is greater than the sum of its parts on every level
from the words on up. The concordance is a tool, like the telephone book. It functions in a context of reality. The literary
work creates its own contexts. Besides levels of meaning,
literature has other levels, which I suggest we call 'dynamic
contexts.' This is your 'who whom what when where how.'
They shift and change within the work. For instance, when

we discover that the 'hero' is really a scoundrel in disguise, we see his words in a different light than we did when we thought he was a good guy."

"Could you give us a literary utterance as an example?" asked a Martian.

"Sure," said the Harlequin,

" 'Luth
Zut!' "

"Hell's bells," commented a Martian.

"Not bad," replied the Harlequin, "but how about 'lyre, hell-fire' instead. It's not the words that matter but their relationship. Their relationship is that of question and answer. They need no support, linguistic or otherwise, to stand as a complete, discrete statement. They create their own context."

"What about 'Hell's bells?' " asked the Martian.

"Well, there's your irony-in-real-life. You see, that exists in a context of reality. It's a comment made by an actual Martian on the lecture of an equally actual Harlequin."

"What do you *mean* by reality?" demanded the Martian.

"What do *you* mean by reality?" returned the Harlequin. 'Reality, or what for lack of a better term we call 'reality' is just a convention by which we communicate with one another. Without it, neither of us would be here. Now to return to the poem. It, too, participates in certain conventions. Notice that each line has the same number of syllables and that they end in the same sound. We have here, in an admittedly rudimentary state, the poetic conventions metre and rhyme. Although not all literature shows metre and rhyme, it all shares the combination of novelty and familiarity."

"How so?" inquired a Martian.

"Familiarity in that it refers to life, novelty in that it shows us things we might never have seen by ourselves or, which, if we saw them, we'd let pass. It shows us relationships."

"What about the poem? What does it show?" asked a Martian.

"Here we have the relationship between a poet and a tradition of poetry," began the Harlequin.

"Where?" asked the Martian.

"In the poem. Let me explain. I said the poem gave us words in a question and answer relationship. To the 'luth,' which is literary shorthand for the lute of romantic poets who felt themselves inspired by muses, who were themselves connected with the Apollo of the classical tradition—the god of song and music, and who played a lyre—anyway, to all this tradition the poet opposes a less than reverent reply: 'zut. We have a contrast in tone between the proposition and the reply."

"Tone? They both sound the same to me," retorted the Martian.

"Don't get me wrong, now, please," said the Harlequin "Tone refers to the attitude of the author to what he's saying and is inferred from the context. Until we get to the second word there is no context. 'Luth' by itself is neutral. It connotes the neoclassical tradition, but besides that just sits there, aloof and elevated. Then the poet contrasts it to a very colloquial mildly risqué expression which connotes scorn, disgust, displeasure or rejection. Here something tricky happens. Though with the establishment of context neutrality becomes engagement, on the level of meaning the poet's 'engagement' is his rejection—or disengagement."

"Okay, but what is the poem about? We're only Martian."

"I'll have to introduce another distinction," said the Harlequin.

"That's what you're here for," said the leader of the Martians.

"Good. 'Manifest content' is what an utterance is about and 'content' is what the utterance says about it. For example the manifest content of the two sentences: 'It is raining' and 'It isn't raining' is the rain, or, more generally, the weather. But the content of each is the whether-or-not. The content of our poem is the poet's rejection of the neoclassical tradition. Its manifest content is literature."

"Literature about literature?" exclaimed a Martian. "How perfectly incestuous. I thought you said literature is about reality."

"Literature is reality. It can be about anything. Shall recite you 'Jabberwocky' again?" returned the Harlequin.

"Please don't," replied the Martian, "but tell us, if that all there is to it, why do people bother with literature?"

"Why do Martians bother with literature?" replied the Harlequin.

"To find out what life on earth is all about," replied the leader of the Martians.

"Well, then, why do you suppose people bother with it?" came the reply. "And they have even more reason to be interested in it."

"I never thought about it that way," confessed the Martian.

"See," chided the Harlequin, "literature *is* good for something, after all. Q.E.D. You have just undergone an apprenticeship in geometry."

"I thought we were talking about literature," said the Martian.

"We are. I was just getting back to the poem. The poet damns neoclassicism because he knows that art may refer to life without having to imitate it. On a different occasion, he pointed out that when man wanted to imitate walking, he invented the wheel, which doesn't resemble a leg at all. But it does essentially the same thing: move. You remember Aristotle and the catharsis? Well, literature still offers a sort of catharsis but it's no longer an apprenticeship in stoicism. Rather, it's now an apprenticeship in geometry, in following a tentative hypothesis from the given to the Q.E.D. Literature is still to be a paradigm for experience, but by analogy rather than by direct imitation. In the poem, the contrast in tone and diction is an analogue of meaning."

"I'll take your word for it," said the Martian, "but now that we know what *good* is literature, how can we tell what *is* good literature?"

"That's hard. We don't want to start with any *a prioris,* but unless we start somewhere, we can't start anywhere. If we don't know what we're looking for, we often don't see anything. In my example, I started by looking for the relationship of the words. Not that that's exactly a critical superstructure imposed arbitrarily, but you see I did start with an idea of what to look for. Most generally, we look for relationships."

"What you're saying, then, is that we have to be resolutely wishy-washy?" suggested a Martian.

"In principle, yes," replied the Harlequin. "We only see in the work what we've looked for in it, but as long as we recognize this, we can hope to avoid some of the extremes to which literary scholarship is capable of going." He picked up the novel and the telephone book and held them up for his audience to see.

"Suppose we came to our task with the notion that literature was an 'arrangement of content according to a harmonious pattern.' We couldn't tell the difference between the novel and the telephone book, and if we had to judge them, we'd probably favor the phone book. But as long as we recognize the fact of the artifact, all's well that ends well. Roland Barthes has spoken of the 'fatal duplicity of the author, who questions under guise of affirming' and the corresponding duplicity of the critic, who 'affirms under guise of questioning.' Both author and critic are performing an act of faith. And the fact that the critic recognizes the 'rôleness' of his rôle brings about what we might call a teleological suspension of wishy-washyness. You remember the story I told you about Abraham?"

"Uhuh, but get to the criteria for judging, the relationships we're supposed to look for," said the leader of the Martians.

"Is there a blackboard among your earthly artifacts?" asked the Harlequin. "I'd like to make a list."

As the blackboard, hijacked from an Eastern university for inclusion in the Museum of the Martian Institute for Terrestrian Studies, was wheeled into the room, some of the Martians in the back of the auditorium climbed up on their neighbors' shoulders in order to see better. The Harlequin noticed that the pieces of chalk and the eraser, as well as the chalk tray itself, were duly labeled. On the board, the Harlequin wrote a list:

Criteria people use in evaluating literature

1. Mimetic plausibility (work has an adequate vision of life or a surface veracity)
2. Thematic plausibility (proportionateness of theme to its embodiment)
3. Symbolic plausibility (interpretation of work accords with patterns of life)
4. Affective (work appeals to the emotions, praise of intensity)

  5. Moral acceptability
  6. Generic (work accords with the conditions imposed by its genre)
  7. Traditional (work accords with its tradition)
  8. Intentional (work fulfills author's expressed intention)
  9. Multifariousness (work is susceptible to a number of complementary interpretations)
  10. Formal (work fulfills its function as an esthetic object, has coherence)
  11. Rhetorical (work succeeds in using all its devices to enhance meaning)

"Remember," said the Harlequin, "these are criteria that people actually use. I'm being descriptive. Are there any questions?"

"What about when somebody is looking for something else in a work and says so and then judges the work by it?" asked a Martian.

"We could call that element 12 and name it 'citation of criteria.' I think that takes care of just about all the possibilities."

"Now, Harlequin," said the leader of the Martians, "can you give us a demonstration of evaluation, using the little poem you used as an example?"

"Gladly," replied the Harlequin. "And now, beneath this patchwork surface of mine, I show my true colors. I'm a formalist. The question I ask first is: 'Does it cohere?' Yes, it coheres. And the next question is rhetorical: 'Do its devices enhance its meaning?' By all means. Therefore I think it is a good poem."

"Aren't you leaving the question of *value* out of *evaluation,* though?" asked the leader of the Martians.

"No, just the question of taste. One ought to be able to evaluate a poem without necessarily liking it, just as one has every right to like poems he knows are not really terribly great."

"Granted," said the Martian, "but is it a good poem *because* it coheres?"

"I think rather it coheres because it's a good poem. It could still cohere and be a terrible poem, if, for example, it lacked thematic plausibility. But I dare you to find a good poem that doesn't cohere."

"Someday I'll take you up on that," replied the Martian. "One last question: why did you choose that particular poem to use as an example?"

"Because it's exemplary," replied the Harlequin. "It's literature at its most basic, the world in the grain of sand, with nothing superfluous to get in the way of our seeing the relationship of the words to each other. Remember: 'Literature is context, context literature' is all I know and all you need to know. It's the difference between all these books and all other books. I can't begin to tell you . . ."

"Well," cut in the leader of the Martians, this has been a most instructive session of our anthropological seminar, but now we must adjourn to lunch. We will reconvene in two hours to discuss the next topic on our busy agenda, which is: "What is Lycanthropy?"

"And all the rest is literature," murmured the Harlequin.

The Apollinaire poem "Luth/Zut!" is from *Le Poete assassiné* (Paris, 1947, p. 49). The Roland Barthes quotation is from his *Sur Racine* (Paris, 1963, p. 11). The "criteria people use in evaluating literature" is derived from Alan C. Purves' "Elements of Criticism and Interpretation," in *Horace Mann-Lincoln Institute Interim Reports* (Teachers College, Columbia University, New York, 1965, p. 5).

BIBLIOGRAPHIES

Linguistics

Elizabeth Barber

I. Linguistic Structure

Modern structural descriptive linguistics may be said to have begun with de Saussure, in Geneva. His influence, direct and indirect, on what followed has been immense. In Europe, the Prague school—led by Trubetzkoy—developed in one direction, the Copenhagen school in another. In America, Bloomfield (with considerable heritage from the American descriptivist Franz Boas, and with Sapir as pacer) developed a separate school. World War II disrupted the free communication of ideas, and the various schools emerged from isolation in the late 1940's to find they had diverged enormously. For perhaps a decade they maintained their individualities, exploring each other's advantages and disadvantages. Then attempts at synthesis began. Jakobson worked out a synthesis of the Prague and American views; later Chomsky incorporated much of Jakobson's approach into his own branch of post-Bloomfieldian linguistics; and recently Lamb has begun combining the Hjelmslevian theories with the American.

1. Bloomfield, Leonard. *Language*. New York, 1933.
   A general introduction to linguistics; the portions on linguistic structure *per se* provide a clear account of the principles basic to the American "Bloomfieldian" school.
2. Chomsky, Noam. *Aspects of the Theory of Syntax*. Cambridge, 1965.
   The most up to date form of the theory of generative grammar. See 3, 21.
3. Chomsky, Noam. *Syntactic Structures*. The Hague, 1957.
   The most important early statement of a radically new approach to syntax in particular; an attempt to counteract the restricting influence of the procedural orientation of Bloomfieldian structuralism. The theory described is now commonly known as "transformational" or (somewhat misleadingly) "generative" grammar. See 2, 12, 22.

4. de Saussure, Ferdinand. *Cours de linguistique générale.* Paris, 1916. Transl. W. Baskin, *Course in General Linguistics* (New York, 1959).

A posthumous compilation (from the lecture notes of his students) of the linguistic views of a great pioneer in linguistic structuralism.

5. Gleason, H. A., Jr. "The Organization of Language: A Stratificational View," *Monograph Series on Languages and Linguistics* 17 (April, 1964), 75-95.

A basic discussion of "stratificational theory" as developed by Lamb and Gleason; another attempt to get away from the procedural orientation of Bloomfieldian linguistics. See 8, 11, 23.

6. Halliday, M. A. K. "Categories of the Theory of Grammar," *Word* 17 (1961) 241-292.

Recent views of a leading British linguist; in the general path set by Firth (himself heavily influenced by Hjelmslev: see 8).

7. Harris, Zellig. *Structural Linguistics.* Chicago, 1951.

A detailed statement of an extreme form of Bloomfieldian-School structuralism; treats both phonology and morphology.

8. Hjelmslev, Louis. *Omkring sprogteoriens grundloeggelse.* Copenhagen, 1943. Transl. F. Whitfield, *Prolegomena to a Theory of Language;* two editions: a) *Memoir 7, Indiana Publications in Anthropology and Linguistics* (Baltimore, 1953); and b) Madison, 1961.

The major formulation of the Copenhagen school's attempt to build a theory of linguistic structure by deduction rather than induction; an extremely influential work.

9. Jakobson, Roman, Gunnar Fant, and Morris Halle. *Preliminaries to Speech Analysis, the Distinctive Features and their Correlates.* Cambridge, 1952.

Phonological structure treated by a combination of Prague school (see 17, 18) and Bloomfieldian linguistics; quite influential on recent work (e.g. on Chomsky, 2).

10. Joos, Martin, ed. *Readings in Linguistics.* 2nd ed., New York, 1958.

An anthology of important papers published in America, 1925-1956: mostly on Bloomfieldian structuralism, a few on historical subjects (applying Bloomfieldian principles), and one collating and restating the principles of de Saussure (4) from the perspective of the Bloomfieldian school of 1947.

11. Lamb, Sydney M. "Kinship Terminology and Linguistic Structure," *American Anthropologist* 67 (1965), 37-64.

Recent trends in "stratificational grammar" (see 5); based heavily on Hjelmslevian theories (8) as point of departure. See also 23.

12. Lees, R. B. Review of Chomsky, *Syntactic Structures* (3), *Language* 33 (1957), 375-408.

An enlightening comparison of generative grammar with Bloomfieldian methods, and a discussion of some vital problems facing the Bloomfieldian linguists of the late 1950's—problems which Chomsky was trying specifically to remedy.

13. Martinet, A. *Phonology as Functional Phonetics*. Oxford, 1949.

A short, very clear, illustrated statement of the view of phonologic structure developed by the Geneva and early Prague schools. See 17, 18.

14. Nida, Eugene A. *Morphology*. 2nd ed., Ann Arbor, 1949.

Morphological analysis, both in principle and in practice, as evolved during and just after the war by the Bloomfieldian school.

15. Pike, Kenneth L. "Dimensions of Grammatical Constructions," *Language* 38 (1962), 221-245.

A discovery-oriented method of handling grammatical structures in matrices; the latest fruit of the branch of Bloomfieldian linguistics known as "tagmemics."

16. Sapir, Edward. *Language: An Introduction to the Study of Speech*. New York, 1921.

An early nontechnical (but not easy) formulation of linguistic structure and its relation to the other behavioral sciences.

17. Trubetzkoy, N. S. *Grundzüge der Phonologie* (*Travaux du Cercle Linguistique de Prague* 7). Prague, 1939. Transl. J. Cantineau, *Principes de Phonologie* (Paris, 1949).

Phonological analysis, in principle and in detail, according to the prewar Prague school. See 9, 13, 18.

18. Vachek, Josef, ed. *A Prague School Reader in Linguistics*. Bloomington, 1964.

A short anthology of important Prague school papers, 1911-1963, with emphasis on the period of 1928-1948. (Note also the bibliographical discussion by Vachek in his preface.) See 9, 17.

II. Peripheral Structures

The fields of phonetics and semantics have generally been considered to lie outside the central focus of descriptive linguistics—but only just so. It should be noted, however, that the Prague school has never divided off phonetics so sharply as de Saussure and the Bloomfieldians, while recently Chomsky has done away with the separation of semantics (and to some extent phonetics) from the core of his grammar.

Phonetics:

19. Joos, Martin. *Acoustic Phonetics.* Supplement to *Language,* Monograph 23 (1948).

    The basic publication on the recent science of acoustic phonetics and on the sound spectrograph; particularly valuable for the analysis of resonants and vowels.

20. Pike, Kenneth L. *Phonetics.* Ann Arbor, 1943.

    A detailed structuralized account of traditional articulatory phonetics; especially valuable concerning stops.

Semantics:

21. Greimas, A. J. *Semantique structurale.* Paris, 1966.

    A synthesis of the ideas of Jakobson, Hjelmslev, Brøndal, Bloomfield, and Propp to form a unified general theory of semantics applicable to a range of problems extending from individual word meanings to the semantic structure of a whole literary work (Bernanos).

22. Katz, Jerrold J. and Jerry A. Fodor. "The Structure of a Semantic Theory," *Language* 39 (1963), 170-210.

    The latest methods for handling semantics structurally within generative grammar. See also 2.

23. Lamb, Sydney M. "The Sememic Approach to Structural Semantics," *American Anthropologist* 66 (1964), 57-78.

    The stratificational approach to semantics. See 5, 11.

24. Ullmann, Stephen. *The Principles of Semantics.* 2nd ed., Glasgow, 1959.

    A basic textbook representing approximately the state of semantic analysis before the recent surge of new approaches to the subject.

25. Wells, Rulon S. "Is a Structural Treatment of Meaning Possible?", in *Proceedings of the Eighth International Congress of Linguists.* Oslo, 1958.

    A de Saussurian discussion (by a basically Bloomfieldian scholar) of the problems of a semantic system tied to a formal structure.

III. Diachronic (Historical) Linguistics

In the nineteenth century, scholars who concerned themselves scientifically with languages were interested primarily in the history of languages rather than in the sheer description of them. Gradually they came to realize, however, that an adequate description was a prerequisite for accurate historical work. As the quality of description improved, they developed careful methods of historical analysis.

26. de Saussure, Ferdinand. *Mémoire sur le système primitif des voyelles dans les langues indo-européennes.* Leipzig, 1879.
     The first major example of the use of the principle of linguistic structure as an argument in a (historical) linguistic problem: a classic work, for both historical and structural linguistics.

27. Hoenigswald, Henry M. *Language Change and Linguistic Reconstruction.* Chicago, 1960.
     A detailed structuralized account of the chief modern methods of historical analysis: comparative and internal reconstruction.

28. Meillet, Antoine. *La méthode comparative en linguistique historique.* Oslo, 1925 (reprint Paris, 1954).
     A brief, simple, well-illustrated description of the basic principles of historical linguistics.

29. Pedersen, Holger. *Sprogvidenskaben i det Nittende Aarhundrede: Metoder og Resultater.* Copenhagen, 1924. Transl. John W. Spargo, *Linguistics in the Nineteenth Century* (Cambridge, 1931); reprinted as *The Discovery of Language* (Bloomington, 1962).
     A short history of the development of historical—and (incidentally) structural—linguistics in the last century.

IV. Journals

The three most important American outlets for modern structural linguistics:

30. *International Journal of American Linguistics.* Auspices of Linguistic Society of America, American Anthropological Association, Conference on American Indian Languages; 1935-. C. F. Voegelin, ed.

31. *Language.* Auspices of Linguistics Society of America; 1924-. W. Bright, ed.

32. *Word.* Auspices of Linguistic Circle of New York; 1945-. R. Austerlitz, W. Diver, L. G. Heller, A. Martinet eds. The European journals of importance to structural linguistics include two older ones (published somewhat irregularly) and several brand new ones:

33. *Acta Linguistica.* Auspices of Cercles Linguistique de Copenhague and de Prague; 1939-. Louis Hjelmslev, ed.

34. *Journal of Linguistics.* Auspices of the Linguistic Association of Great Britain; 1965-. J. Lyons, ed.

35. *Lingua: International Review of General Linguistics.* Published in Amsterdam; 1937-. A. J. B. Reichling, E. M. Uhlenbeck, W. Sidney Allen, eds.

36. *Linguistics: An International Review.* Published in The Hague; 1964-. (No editor given.)

37. *La Linguistique.* Published in Paris; 1965-. A. Martinet, ed.

Anthropology

Allen R. Maxwell

The "structuralist" approach in contemporary anthropology stems from a number of sources which have affected each other in varying degrees since their inceptions. Some of these precursors of modern structuralism have exercised greater intellectual weight than others, however. The following, while not telling the complete story, do account for the major twentieth century origins of the structuralist approach in current anthropological practice:

1. The line Émile Durkheim—Marcel Mauss—Claude Lévi-Strauss) stemming from the French sociological school of the early 1900's. (For discussion and references see C. Lévi-Strauss, "French Sociology," p. 503-537 in G. Gurvitch and W. E. Moore, eds., *Twentieth Century Sociology*, New York, 1945.)

2. The Dutch anthropologists, including J. P. B. de Josselin de Jong, F. D. E. van Ossenbruggen, W. H. Rassers, F. A. E. van Wouden, *et al,* working especially during the first half of the twentieth century in the Indonesian area.

3. The British "structural-functional(-ist)" approach dating from the early work of Bronislaw Malinowski and A. R. Radcliffe-Brown in the first two decades of this century, and followed by that of E. E. Evans-Pritchard and others. (A standard work for this approach is *Structure and Function in Primitive Society,* Essays and Addresses by A. R. Radcliffe-Brown, Glencoe, Ill., 1952.)

4. The early work in Amerindian linguistics, commencing with that of Franz Boas around the turn of the century, and followed by that of Edward Sapir, Benjamin Lee Whorf, and many others.

At least one other style of thought, outside these four, deserves mention (especially in connection with Claude Lévi-Strauss): the linguistic group known as the Ecole de Prague and in particular one of its most distinguished members, Roman Jakobson. (For statements on this group and bibliography, see Vachek, 1966 and the linguistics bibliography in this issue.)

The anthropological literature dealing with the different usages of "structuralism" is large and growing rapidly. This short list of items could be multiplied several times over, with no diminution in overall quality. This selection is unavoidably slanted toward certain interests; others would probably choose to emphasize other aspects of "structural anthropology."

Items especially rich in bibliographical references are marked with an *

L'Arc, Revue trimestrielle, no. 26 (Aix-en-Provence).
*1965. Claude Lévi-Strauss.
    Including articles by Bernard Pingaud, Luc de Heusch, Claude Lévi-Strauss, Gérard Genette, Célestin Deliège, and Jean Pouillin; notes by Jean Guiart, J.-C. Gardin, Célestin Deliège, and Pierre Clastres; with bibliographies of writings on and by Lévi-Strauss.

Banton, Michael, general editor.
1965. *The Relevance of Models for Social Anthropology,* A(ssociation of) S(ocial) A(nthropologists of the Commonwealth) Monographs 1. Frederick A. Praeger, New York; Tavistock Publications, London.
    See particularly: D. M. Schneider, "Some muddles in the models; or, how the system really works;" B. E. Ward, "Varieties of the conscious model: the fisherman of South China;" M. D. Sahlins, "On the sociology of primitive exchange." All three articles are concerned with "models" in anthropology, the former two make reference to Lévi-Strauss' work.

Beidelman, T. O.
1964. "Pig- (guluwe); an essay on Ngulu sexual symbolism and ceremony." *Southwestern Journal of Anthropology* (Albuquerque) 20.4:359-392.
    An essay on symbolism and ceremonial conceptualization among an East African people.

Burling, Robbins.
*1964. "Cognition and componential analysis: God's truth or hocus-pocus?" *American Anthropologist* 66.1:20-28.

A discussion of some of the issues currently being debated within the framework of "componential analysis." Note also comments by D. H. Hymes and C. O. Frake, and Burling's rejoinder, p. 116-122, in the same issue.

Conklin, Harold C.
*1962. "Lexicographical treatment of folk taxonomies," p. 119-141, *in* F. W. Householder and S. Saporta, eds., *Problems in Lexicography*. Indiana University Research Center in Anthropology, Folklore, and Linguistics, Publication No. 21. (International Journal of American Linguistics 28.2.4.)

An important paper discussing some of the issues and techniques involved in the "ethno-scientific" approach to ethnography.

Cunningham, Clark E.
1964. "Order in the Atoni house." Bijdragen tot da Taal,- Land- en Volkenkunde (s'-Gravenhage) 120.1:34-68.

An examination of the relations between the conceptions of and the functions of houses and their constituent parts in an East Indonesian (Timor) society.

1965. "Order and change in an Atoni diarchy." *Southwestern Journal of Anthropology* 21.4:359-382.

Cosmology, politics and the social order in an East Indonesian (Timor) society.

Durkheim, Émile, and Marcel Mauss.
1963. "De quelques formes primitives de classification: contribution à l'étude des représentations collectives." *L'Année Sociologique* (Paris) 6:1-72, 1901-1902. Translated as *Primitive Classification,* and edited with an introduction, by Rodney Needham. Cohen & West, London, 1963.

One of the first works to deal with symbolic classification and antecedent to much of the current work in this area.

Esprit, Nouvelle Série no. 11, novembre, 1963 (Paris).
1963. *"La pensée sauvage et le structuralisme."*

Including articles by Jean Cuisenier, Nicolas Ruwet, Marc Gaboriau, Paul Ricoeur, and "Discussion avec Claude Lévi-Strauss."

Frake, Charles O.
*1962. "The ethnographic study of cognitive systems." p. 72-84, *in* T. Gladwin and W. C. Sturtevant, eds., *Anthropology and Human Behavior*. The Anthropological Society of Washington, Washington, D. C.

A lucid exposition of some of the aims and concerns of the "ethnoscientific" approach to ethnography. See also the Comment by H. C. Conklin, p. 86-93.

Griaule, Marcel, and Germaine Dieterlen.
1954. "The Dogon." p. 83-110, *in* Daryll Forde, ed., *African Worlds, Studies in the Cosmological and Social Values of African Peoples.* Published for the International African Institute by the Oxford University Press, London, New York, Toronto.

An essay describing the very intricate views of a West African people on their social life.

Goodenough, Ward H., ed.
*1964. *Explorations in Cultural Anthropology,* Essays in Honor of George Peter Murdock. McGraw-Hill Book Company, New York, San Francisco, Toronto, London.

This work includes a number of essays utilizing a "structuralist" approach (see, e.g., the articles by H. C. Conklin, C. O. Frake, P. Friedrich, W. H. Goodenough, F. G. Lounsbury, L. Pospisil, *et al*).

Hammel, E. A., ed.
*1965. "Formal Semantic Analysis." *American Anthropologist* (67.5.2) Special Publication.

A collection of 14 papers plus introduction dealing especially with componential analysis and some of its applications.

Hertz, Robert.
1907. "Contribution à une étude sur la représentation collective de la mort. *L'Année Sociologique* 10:48-137, 1905-1906.
1909. "La prééminence de la main droite: étude sur la polarité religieuse." *Revue Philosophique de la France et de l'Étranger* (Paris) 68:553-580. Both essays translated as *Death and the Right Hand* by Rodney and Claudia Needham, with an introduction by E. E. Evans-Pritchard, Cohen & West, London, 1960.

Two pioneering studies of symbolism; however for strong, but constructive, criticism of the former essay, see Tom Harrisson, "Borneo Death," Bijdragen tot de Taal-, Land- en Volkenkunde 118.1:1-41:1962; and esp., p. 28-41.

Homans, George Caspar, and David M. Schneider.
1955. *Marriage, Authority and Final Causes: A Study of Unilateral Cross-cousin Marriage.* The Free Press, Glencoe, Illinois. Also, p. 202-256, *in Sentiments & Activities,* Essays in Social Science, by George Caspar Homans. The Free Press of Glencoe, 1962.

An early criticism of Lévi-Strauss' work of 1949.

L'Homme, revue française d'anthropologie.
1961. Publiée par l'École Pratique des Hautes Études—Sorbonne. Sixième Section: Sciences économiques et sociales. Mouton & Co, éditeurs, Paris—La Haye.

A journal, begun in 1961 by Émile Benveniste, Pierre Gourou and Claude Lévi-Strauss, containing many articles of interest utilizing a structural approach.

Hubert, Henri, and Marcel Mauss.

1899. "Essai sur la nature et la fonction du sacrifice." *L'Année Sociologique* 2:29-138, 1897-1898. Translated as *Sacrifice: Its Nature and Function* by W. D. Wallis, with a foreword by E. E. Evans-Pritchard. University of Chicago Press, 1964.

Hymes, Dell H., ed.

*1964. *Language in Culture and Society, A Reader in Linguistics and Anthropology*. Harper & Row, New York, Evanston, and London.

An important collection of 69 papers, reviews and essays, with valuable commentary and bibliography.

de Josselin de Jong, J. P. B.

1952. "Lévi-Strauss's Theory on Kinship and Marriage." Mededelingen van het Rijksmuseum voor Volkenkunde, Leiden, No. 10. E. J. Brill, Leiden.

An exposition and criticism of *Les structures élémentaires de la parenté,* by C. Lévi-Strauss.

de Josselin de Jong, P. E.

1965. "An interpretation of agricultural rites in Southeast Asia, with a demonstration of use of data from both continental and insular areas." *The Journal of Asian Studies* 24.2:283-291. The Association for Asian Studies.

An exchange (comments, by George Condominas and Hildred Geertz, reply by de Josselin de Jong) illustrating some of the issues at stake in the use of the structural approach as used by some of the Dutch workers.

Leach, E. R.

1954. *Political Systems of Highland Burma, A Study of Kachin Social Structure*. With a foreword by Raymond Firth. Harvard University Press for The London School of Economics and Political Science. (Republished with a new introductory note by the author as Beacon Paperback 192, Beacon Press, Boston, 1965.)

One of the more important publications in anthropology in the last two decades, challenging some of the previously held ideas on "social equilibrium," and particularly relevant to the problem of "synchronic change."

1958. "Concerning Trobriand clans and the kinship category *tabu*." P. 120-145, *in* J. Goody, ed., *The Developmental Cycle in Domestic Groups*. Cambridge Papers in Social Anthropology, No. 1. The University Press, Cambridge.

An exposition of the "social category" theory of kinship terms; criticized by Lounsbury, 1965.

1961. *Rethinking Anthropology.* London School of Economics Monographs on Social Anthropology No. 22. The Athlone Press, University of London.

A collection of Leach's essays printed elsewhere, excepting the title essay which was written for the volume. Leach usually is concerned with anthropological data and is either stimulating or grating, depending on one's point of view, but always rewarding. His writings are quite technical, but bear profitable results.

1961a. "Lévi-Strauss in the Garden of Eden: an examination of some recent developments in the analysis of myth." *Transactions* of the New York Academy of Sciences, Ser. II, Vol. 23, No. 4, p. 386-396.

An illuminating discussion of the study of myth, with an example taken from Genesis.

1965. "Claude Lévi-Strauss—Anthropologist and Philosopher." New Left Review, No. 34, p. 12-27.

A statement and evaluation of Lévi-Strauss' work by a British anthropologist.

Lévi-Strauss, Claude.

1949. *Les structures élémentaires de la parenté.* Presses Universitaires de France, Paris. (English translation forthcoming.)

A work of major theoretical importance, dealing mainly with cross-cousin marriage systems and the valuation of women and goods in the exchanges.

1958. *Anthropologie structurale.* Librairie Plon, Paris. *Structural Anthropology,* translated by C. Jacobson and B. G. Schoepf. Basic Books, New York, London, 1963.

A collection of 17 essays on language, art, methods, and social organization; see particularly "The Structural Study of Myth" for basic insight into structural analysis.

1960. "Four Winnebago myths: a structural sketch." P. 351-362, *in* S. Diamond, ed., *Culture in History,* Essays in Honor of Paul Radin. Published for Brandeis University by Columbia University Press.

An illuminating application of structural analysis to some North American data.

1960a. "On manipulated sociological models." Bijdragen tot de Taal-, Land- en Volkenkunde 116.1:45-54.

Lévi-Strauss' reply to the criticism of his "Les organisations dualistes existent-elles?" by Maybury-Lewis (see Maybury-Lewis, 1960).

*1962. *La pensée sauvage*. Librairie Plon, Paris. (English translation forthcoming.)

A work concerned with conceptualization, classification and social organization; with a final chapter dealing with some of Sartre's assertions in *Critique de la raison dialectique*. (see *Esprit,* 1963.)

1964. *Le Cru et le cuit, Mythologiques*. Librairie Plon, Paris.

An imposing work, refining the approach used in earlier studies, making use of musical notation in the analysis of myths. Deals with societies of the Americas, primarily South.

Livingstone, Frank B.

1959. "A formal analysis of prescriptive marriage systems among the Australian aborigines." *Southwestern Journal of Anthropology* 15.4:361-372.

A lucid discussion of the formal relations, and the logic of operation, of prescriptive marriage systems and some of their structural implications.

Lounsbury, Floyd G.

1964. "The structural analysis of kinship semantics." p. 1073-1093, *in* H. G. Lunt, ed., *Proceedings* of the Ninth International Congress of Linguists. Mouton & Co., The Hague.

A very good introduction, technical but very clear, to "componential" analysis, which has developed in the last decade from a blending of techniques by linguists and anthropologists.

1965. "Another view of the Trobriand kinship categories." P. 142-185, *in* Hammel, ed., 1965.

An exposition of the "extensionist" theory of kinship terms, and an argument against the "social category" theory of the meaning of kinship terms espoused by Leach, 1958.

The issues involved in these two approaches, and their resolutions (here, to the semantics of kinship terms), should have significant implications for further work in semantic analysis and the scientific study of vocabulary, topics which have received increased interest in recent years.

Mauss, Marcel.

1950. "Essai sur le don. Forme et raison de l'échange dans les sociétés archaiques." P. 145-279, *in Sociologie et Anthropologie,* par M. Mauss, précédé d'une "Introduction à l'oeuvre de Marcel Mauss" par Claude Lévi-Strauss. Presses Universitaires de France, Paris. Translated as *The Gift, Forms and Functions of Exchange in Archaic Societies* by Ian Cunnison, with an introduction by E. E. Evans-Pritchard. The Free Press, Glencoe, Illinois, 1954.

An essay on economic exchange which has been widely received in contemporary anthropology.

Maybury-Lewis, David.

1960. "The analysis of dual organizations: a methodological critique." Bijdragen tot de Taal-, Land- en Volkenkunde 116.1:17-44.

A criticism of Lévi-Strauss' "Les organisations dualistes existent-elles?" (included in *Anthropologie structurale*); see also Lévi-Strauss' reply, 1960a.

Needham, Rodney.

*1962. *Structure and Sentiment, A Test case in Social Anthropology*. The University of Chicago Press.

An extended argument against the criticisms put by Homans and Schneider, 1955, to Lévi-Strauss' 1949 work. See, however, the review of Needham by F. G. Lounsbury, *American Anthropologist* 64.6:1302-1310.

Ortigues, Edmond.

1963. "Nature et culture dans l'oeuvre de Claude Lévi-Strauss." *Critique* (Paris) 19.189:142-157.

A review of *Anthropologie structurale*, *Le totémisme aujourd'hui*, and *La pensée sauvage* by Lévi-Strauss.

Rassers, W. H.

1959. *Panji, the Culture Hero; A Structural Study of Religion in Java*. With an introduction, "W. H. Rassers and the anthropological study of religion," by J. P. B. de Josselin de Jong. Koninklijk Instituut voor Taal-, Land- en Volkenkunde, Translation Series 3. Martinus Nijoff, The Hague.

Four essays, originally published between 1925 and 1940, of general interest, on the structural analysis of Javanese mythology, religion, art, drama, and social organization.

Romney, A. K., and P. J. Epling.

1958. "A simplified model of Kariera kinship." *American Anthropologist* 60.1.1:59-74.

A lucid discussion of the relationships involved in kinship terminology, the partition of individuals into social groups, and territoriality in an Australian society.

Romney, A. K., and R. G. D'Andrade, eds.

*1964. *Transcultural Studies in Cognition*. American Anthropologist (66.3.2) Special Publication.

A collection of 9 papers, plus introduction, summary and discussion, from a conference dealing with linguistic, anthropological and psychological approaches to cognition.

Sebag, Lucien.

1965. "Le mythe: code et message." *Les Temps Modernes* 20.226: 1607-1623.

   A philosophical discussion of the underpinnings of myth, its analysis and function.

Sturtevant, William C.

*1964. Studies in ethnoscience. P. 99-131, *in Romney and D'Andrade,* 1964.

   A good summary and synthesis of some of the recent developments in anthropology.

Vachek, Josef.

*1966. *The Linguistic School of Prague.* Indiana University Studies on the History and Theory of Linguistics. Indiana University Press, Bloomington & London.

   A discussion of the basic principles and theses of this group, with a short biographical dictionary, two papers newly translated from Czech, and a bibliography.

Verstraeten, Pierre.

1963. "Lévi-Strauss ou la tentation du néant." 2 parts. *Les Temps Modernes* 19.206:66-109; 19.207-208:507-552.

White, Harrison C.

1963. *An Anatomy of Kinship, Mathematical Models for Structures of Cumulated Roles.* Prentice-Hall Series in Mathematical Analysis of Social Behavior. Prentice-Hall, Englewood Cliffs, New Jersey.

   A structural approach to anthropological material which is mathematical, but not statistical.

Wallace, Anthony F. C.

*1962. "Culture and cognition." *Science* 135:351-357.

   A good introduction to the subject of componential analysis. The method is applied to data from American-English kinship.

van Wouden, F. A. E.

1935. *Sociale Structuurtypen in de Groote Oost.* J. Ginsberg, Leiden.

   A very important work for the theory of social structures; it has especially influenced later Dutch anthropologists working in the Indonesian area.

Jacques Lacan: A partial bibliography

Anthony G. Wilden

The main published writings of Lacan between 1945 and 1964 are listed below in chronological order of publication, followed by a list of related articles. Dates following in parentheses refer to the date of composition or delivery of the item.

Section A.

Lacan, Jacques.

1. "Le temps logique et l'assertion de certitude anticipée: un nouveau sophisme," *Cahiers d'Art* (1945), p. 32-42.

> Lacan uses a well-known sophism to illustrate the insufficiency of static logic to account for dialectical temporalisation in intersubjective relations and draws from the development of his thesis the methodological concepts of the *temps pour comprendre* and the *moment de conclure* employed by him in the practice of analysis.

2. "Le Stade du Miroir comme formateur de la fonction du Je, telle qu'elle nous est révélée dans l'expérience psychanalytique," *Revue française de psychanalyse,* XIII (1949), p. 449-455. (Delivered at Zürich, 17 July, 1949. The original paper on the *stade du miroir* was delivered at Marienbad, 16 June, 1936, but never published in its original form.)

> The concept of the *stade du miroir* as revealing the "fundamental ontological structure of the human world" is of crucial importance for Lacan's viewpoint. In spite of its basis in psychological research, elaborated more fully in item 3, it appears to have been ignored in Anglo-Saxon psychoanalytical literature. This article also contains a brief but revealing critique of "the contemporary philosophy of being and nothingness."

3. "Propos sur la causalité psychique," *Evolution psychiatrique* (1947), No. 1, p. 123-165. Reprinted in: *Le problème de la psychogénèse des névroses et des psychoses* (ed. Henri Ey), Bibliothèque neuro-psychiatrique de langue française, 1950, p. 23-54. (Lecture given 28 September, 1946)

> This is probably the best introduction to the thought of Lacan, since it is a full elaboration of his early positions and yet not written in the dense and hermetic style of much of his later

work. Linking his thought with the Hegel of the *Phenomenology*, he probes the meaning of madness for man and its relation to "normality." Literary critics will find particularly absorbing his brilliant analysis of Molière's Alceste. The article also elucidates the concept of the *stade du miroir* and provides it with biological parallels.

4. "Some Reflections on the Ego," *International Journal of Psycho-Analysis*, XXXIV (1953), p. 11-17. (Address to the British Psychoanalytical Society, 2 May, 1951.)

This item is listed mainly because it was published in English. It is a brief statement in appropriate technical terms summarizing and developing items 2 and 3. Whether because of the language, the translation, or the audience, it does not come over with the verve and thought-provoking virtuosity one expects from Lacan.

5. "Le Mythe individuel du névrosé ou 'Poésie et vérité' dans la névrose," Centre de la documentation universitaire, Paris, 1953.

In many respects this typescript report of Lacan's seminar is an essential preliminary to item 6, part of that item being a condensation of what is more clearly and fully elaborated here. The "Poésie et vérité" is the "Dichtung und Wahreit" of Goethe, all the more interesting because of Goethe's great influence on Freud.

6. "Fonction et champ de la parole et du langage en psychanalyse," *La Psychanalyse*, I (1956), p. 81-166. (26-27 September, 1953)

Dense, often hermetic, this is the "Rapport de Rome," probably the best-known of Lacan's writings. One of his most extended presentations, it contains the germ of all the later development of his thought, branching into psychology, anthropology, linguistics, and eastern and western philosophy making evident the influence of Hegel, Heidegger, Saussure and Lévi-Strauss in particular. From the *stade du miroir* to the death-instinct, it extends far beyond the limits of its title It is in ruthlessly criticizing accepted notions of analytical technique as well as those current in certain areas of psychology, especially in the United States, that Lacan initiates his profound questioning of the nature of interhuman relation and his first full-bloom theoretical statement of the structure of intersubjectivity and its grounding in Language. A translation of the *Rapport*, which will include a complete bibliography, is presently being undertaken, to be published in early 1967 by the Johns Hopkins Press.

7. "Discours de Jacques Lacan (26 September, 1953)," *Actes du Congrès de Rome, La Psychanalyse,* I (1956), p. 202-255.

This is the résumé, mainly verbatim, of the spoken communication by Lacan which followed distribution of printed copies of the *Rapport* (item 6). It includes interventions by other members of the new *Société française de psychanalyse.* In view of the difficulty of the text of the *Rapport,* this less formal statement constitutes a helpful elucidation of and commentary on its main theses.

8. "Introduction au commentaire de Jean Hyppolite sur la *Verneinung,*" *La Psychanalyse,* I (1956), p. 17-28. (Seminar of 10 February, 1954)

This article, with items 9 and 26, constitute a commentary, of paramount philosophical and psychological importance, on the 1925 article by Freud (title translated into English as "Negation"), expanding it into an examination of the genesis of thought itself, of the Symbolic order and its relation to the Real, and of the relation of the symbol of negation to the concrete attitude of *dénégation (Verneinung),* the one presocial the other, social.

9. "Réponse au commentaire de Jean Hyppolite sur la *Verneinung de* Freud," *La Psychanalyse,* I (1956), p. 41-58. (Seminar of 10 February, 1954)

10. "Le Séminaire sur 'La lettre volée'," *La Psychanalyse,* II (1956), p. 1-44. (Given 26 April, 1955)

Apart from the obvious interest of this commentary on the *Purloined Letter,* the introduction is of profound theoretical importance. Besides bringing out the unity of the evolution of Freud's thought in relation to the concepts of repetition and automatism, continuing the elaboration of the function of the signifier begun in items 8 and 9, and developing mathematically the implications of the *Fort/Da,* it contains the clearest elaboration of what Lacan means by the four-way structure of intersubjectivity and the relation of the other to the other, without which many of his other remarks on the subject remain incomprehensible.

11. "La chose freudienne ou Sens du retour à Freud en psychanalyse," *Evolution psychiatrique* (1956), p. 225-252. (Amplification of lecture at Vienna, 7 November, 1955.)

This is probably the most poetical in nature of all Lacan's writings and defies summary. Beginning from a comparison of Hegel and Freud on the *moi,* Lacan continues the elucidation of the *je-moi* distinction and deals with the sense in which he views the *moi,* elaborating the function of the discourse of the Other as he ranges over the whole field of analysis and beyond.

12. "Situation de la psychanalyse et formation du psychanalyste en 1956," *Etudes philosophiques* (1956), no. 4, p. 567-584.

A more general statement of Lacan's theses, partly echoing item 6.

13. "La psychanalyse et son enseignement," *Bulletin de la Société française de Philosophie,* LI, no. 2 (1957), p. 65-101. (Session of 23 February, 1957.)

This verbal communication and discussion is of extraordinary value, since the nature of his audience (including Hyppolite, Berger, Alquié, and Merleau-Ponty) seems to have drawn Lacan into more elaborate explication than is often the case. Since his remarks center around much of the extremely complex item 15, which develops the notion of the "fonction du père" and its relation to the signifier, this is a text of prime importance.

14. "L'instance de la lettre dans l'inconscient ou la raison depuis Freud," *La Psychanalyse,* III (1957), p. 47-81. (14-26 May, 1957)

Since this is the one text where Lacan goes into the linguistic orientation of his theory in detail, dealing with the function of metaphor and metonymy, the signifier and the signified, as well with the cogito and the Other, it is one of the most important theoretical articles. It is not concerned with "linguistic interpretation," however, for, as he has put it, "la linguistique, c'est l'interprétation." This is the first published text to mention the important concept of the "points de capiton" developed in his seminar. It is translated in this issue.

15. "D'une question préliminaire à tout traitement possible de la psychose," *La Psychanalyse,* IV (1958), p. 1-50. (December 1957-January, 1958)

This complex theoretical article deals in detail with the Lacanian concepts of the signifier, of the *béance primordiale* of foreclusion, of the name of the father, rejoining his remarks on madness and mankind written ten years earlier (item 3). These concepts have had a profound influence in France; for their application in a brilliant study, see item 28. See also the Leclaire articles (items 31 and 32 in particular).

16. "Jeunesse de Gide ou la lettre et le désir," *Critique,* no. 131 (April, 1958), p. 291-315.

A further example of the profound contribution the psychoanalytic viewpoint has made to the understanding of literature

17. "A la mémoire d'E. Jones: Sur sa théorie du symbolisme," *La Psychanalyse,* V (1959), p. 1-20. (January-March, 1959)

> As the title suggests, this article is of basic importance to understanding what Lacan means by *le symbolique.*

18. "La direction de la cure et les principes de son pouvoir," *La Psychanalyse,* VI (1961), p. 149-206.

> In spite of its apparent technical orientation, this article continues Lacan's interrogation of Language. He further brings out the difference between the other and the Other, and, what is particularly important, analyses the nature of man's desire, first examined in item 3. With the relation of desire to need and to demand, the unity of the whole development becomes clearly visible. Leclaire's clinical study of desire (item 32) provides a helpful elucidation.

19. "Maurice Merleau-Ponty," *Temps Modernes,* nos. 184-185 (1961), p. 245-254.

> This includes a brief critique and evaluation of the Sartrean and Merleau-Pontian positions and shows fairly conclusively the sense in which they need to be methodically expanded to deal with all the data of experience.

20. "Kant avec Sade," *Critique,* no. 191 (1963), p. 291-313. (September, 1962)

> The comprehension of this article requires in particular an understanding of the diagrammatic terminology employed by Lacan in his structural demonstrations—see the summaries of his seminars by J.-B. Pontalis.

Section B.

> Since the bulk of Lacan's work over the last decade is that of his unpublished seminars, the summaries listed below are of particular importance. They represent the only access to fundamental developments of Lacan's thought and cannot be found elsewhere at present.

Pontalis, J.-B.

> *Compte-rendus* of Lacan's seminars 1956-1959. These are published in the *Bulletin de Psychologie* as follows:

21. "La relation d'objet et les structures freudiennes" (five articles), *BP,* X/7 (April, 1957), p. 426-430; X/10 (April, 1957), p. 602-605; X/12 (May, 1957), p. 742-743; X/15 (June, 1957), p. 851-854; XI/1 (Sept., 1957), p. 31-34.

22. "Les formations de l'inconscient" (two articles), *BP,* XII/2-3 (Nov., 1958), p. 182-192; XII/4 (Dec., 1958), p. 250-256.

23. "Le désir et son interprétation" (two articles), *BP*, XIII/5 (Jan., 1960), p. 263-272; XIII/6 (Jan., 1960), p. 329-335.

Section C.

Although there is no easy access to the thought of Lacan, nor any substitute for reading his original works, the following items, particularly the three articles by Leclaire, will provide clarification on specific points as well as examples of Lacan-oriented analysis and criticism. The Leclaire-Laplanche article is the fullest published development of Lacanian-inspired analysis in reference to a specific case. Rosolato's article on semantics is valuable for its examination of various semantic and linguistic theories in considering the problem of *sens* from a Lacanian point of view, and his brief article on *le symbolique* provides a very necessary clarification of the linguistic vocabulary employed by Lacan as well as some reflections on etymology without which the reader might well miss the full import of much of Lacan's writing. Tort's article brings out some of the prevailing misconceptions concerning Freud. There is a lengthy intervention by Lacan on item 34 (Lévi-Strauss) which picks up again his remarks on the structural study of myth in item 6.

Green, A.

24. "La psychanalyse devant l'opposition de l'histoire et de la structure," *Critique,* XIX (1963), p. 649-662.

Heidegger, M.

25. "Logos," trans. J. Lacan, *La Psychanalyse,* I (1956), p. 59-79.

Hyppolite, J.

26. "Commentaire parlé sur la *Verneinung,* de Freud," *La Psychanalyse,* I (1956), p. 29-39.

27. "Phénoménologie de Hegel et psychanalyse," *La Psychanalyse,* III (1957), p. 17-32.

Laplanche, J.

28. *Hölderlin et la question du père,* Bibliothèque de psychanalyse et de psychologie clinique, Paris, 1961.

Laplanche, J. and Leclaire, S.

29. "L'inconscient," *Temps Modernes,* no. 183 (July, 1961), p. 81-129.

Leclaire, C.

30. "A propos de la "Cure-Type en Psychanalyse" de M. Bouvet," *Evolution psychiatrique* (1956), p. 515-540. (First of three articles: I, critical.)

31. "A la recherche des principes d'une psychothérapie des psychoses" *Evolution psychiatrique* (1958), p. 377-411. (II, theoretical.)

32. "L'obsessionel et son désir," *Evolution psychiatrique* (1959), p. 324-409. (III, clinical.)

33. "Point de vue économique en psychanalyse," *Evolution psychiatrique* (1965), p. 189-213. (Translation in summary by D. Plain: "The Economic Standpoint: Recent Views," *International Journal of Psycho-Analysis,* XLV (1965), p. 324-330.)

Leclaire, S.

34. "Sur les rapports entre la mythologie et le rituel," *Bulletin de la Société française de Philosophie,* L, no. 2 (July-Sept., 1956). (Session of May 26, 1956 in which, amongst others, Lacan, Goldmann, Jean Wahl, and Merleau-Ponty took part.)

Pontalis, J.-B.

35. "Freud aujourd'hui," *Temps Modernes,* nos. 124, 125, 126 (May-July, 1956), p. 1666-1680; 1890-1902; 174-186.

Reboul, J.

36. "Jacques Lacan et les fondements de la psychanalyse," *Critique,* XVIII (1962), p. 1056-1067.

Rosolato, G.

37. "Sémantique et altérations du langage," *Evolution psychiatrique* (1956), p. 865-899.

38. "Le Symbolique," *La Pychanalyse,* V (1959), p. 225-233.

Tort, M.

39. "De l'interprétation ou la machine herméneutique," *Temps Modernes,* no. 237 (February, 1966), p. 1461-1493.

Conclusion.

Many other references could be added in order to assist the reader in recognizing the echoes (usually identified only once, and then used without reference) within Lacan's writings. For example: Roman Jakobson on binary opposition and aphasia, on metaphor and metonymy (the relation of similarity and the relation of contiguity); Wittgenstein's *Philosophical Investigations;*

Peirce's theory of the linguistic sign; Maurice Leenhardt on the *parole* of the Melanesian; the theory of information. Lacan's influence ranges from Roland Barthes on semiology to Louis Althusser on Marx. Many key definitions in Lafon's *Vocabulaire de Psychopédagogie et de psychiatrie de l'enfant,* published in 1963, will be found to come directly from Lacan. The reader who has become familiar with Lacan's structural representations will find the article on the unconscious by Leclaire and Laplanche (critical, theoretical, and clinical) of compelling importance because it brings together the Lacanian and Freudian terminology.

But, naturally, the one writer without whom it can be categorically stated that Lacan cannot be properly understood is Freud himself, who discovered structuralism before "structuralism" discovered him. Apart from the central works and the five great psychoanalyses (and as long as the reader watches for Freud's use of *Vorstellung* and *Repräsentanz*), the article on narcissism and the *Ich-Ideal* (*stade du miroir*), those on the unconscious, on repression, on the metapsychology of dreams, or fetishism, on the psychotherapy of hysteria (1895), and perhaps most especially the analysis of the repression of *"Signorelli"* in the *Psychopathology of Everyday Life,* will be found to be particularly important for Lacan's dictum that the unconscious is the discourse of the Other. But the interested reader is left to discover on his own, by the painful process of "working-through," where and how Freud said it himself—and where and how Lacan provides an integration of the philosophical, psychological, and methodological currents of the mid-twentieth century within his structural framework.

For the reader who may be somewhat discouraged to find that a large number of Lacan's articles have been allowed to go out of print, I can report that a collected edition (some 800 pages) is due to appear at *Le Seuil,* probably in 1967. It will include an introduction by the author.

Structuralism and literary criticism

T. Todorov

This bibliography is limited to theoretical works based especially on the methods of structural linguistics.

Barthes, R. *Essais critiques,* Paris, 1964. A number of these essays treat structural analysis in literature.

Erlich, V. *Russian Formalism, History-Doctrine,* 's-Gravenhage,

1955. At the present time this is the best study of the formalists.

Garvin, P., ed. *A Prague School Reader on Esthetics, Literary Structure, and Style,* Washington, D.C., 1964. Texts by Mukarovsky, B. Havránek, F. Vodicka, V. Procházka.

Genette, G. "Structuralism et critique littéraire," in *L'Arc,* 26 (Lévi-Strauss), 1965. A theoretical study.

Levin, S. R. "Deviation—Statistical and Determinate—in Poetic Language," in *Lingua* 12 (1963), 3. An application of the notion of grammaticality to poetic language.

Lévi-Strauss, C. "La Structure et la forme," in *Cahiers de l'institute de Sciences économiques appliquées,* 99, 1960. A discussion of some fundamental notions beginning with the work of V. Propp.

Lévi-Strauss, C., and Jakobson, R. *"Les Chats* de Baudelaire," in *L'Homme,* II (1962), No. 1: 5-21. Example of the structural analysis of a sonnet.

Lotman, JU.M. *Lekcii po structural'noj poetike vyp.* I (Trudy po znakovym sistemam, I), Transactions of the Tartu State University, Tartu, 1964. In the tradition of Russian formalism.

Mukarovsky, J. "Strukturalismus v estetice a ve vede o literature," in *Kapitoly z ceské poetiky* dil I: Obecné veci básnictví. 20, Nakladatelstvi Svododa, Praha, 1948. One of the founders of the Prague Linguistic Circle writes about structuralism and literary analysis.

Poetics. Poetyka. Poetika. PWN-Mouton, Varsovie—'s-Gravenhage, 1961. Acts of a Congress on poetics; several of the papers are concerned with the structural study of literature.

Propp, V. *Morphology of the Folktale,* Bloomington, Ind., 1958. A structural study of the fantastic tale; the Russian original appeared in 1928.

Readings in Russian Poetics, Michigan Slavic Materials, 2, Ann Arbor, 1962. A reprint, in Russian, of the most valuable texts of the Russian formalists. Included are: M. M. Batin, B. M. Ejenbaum, R. Jakobson, Ju. Tynjanov, V. V. Vinogradov, V. N. Volosinov.

Revzin, I. I. "O celjax strukturnogo izucenija xudozestvennogo tvorcestva," *Voprosy literatury,* 6, 1965. A theoretical study.

Rossi, A. "Structuralismo e analisi letteraria," *Paragone,* 1, 180, 1964. An overall view which includes a bibliography.

Ruwet, N. "L'analyse structurale de la poésie," *Linguistics* 2, 1963. Discussion and concrete analysis of S. R. Levin's *Linguistic Structures in Poetry* (1962).

L

Sebeok, Th. A., ed. *Style in Language,* Cambridge, Mass., 1960. Acts of an interdisciplinary conference.

Simpozium po strukturnomu izuceniju znakovyx sistem. Tezisy dokladov. Moscow, 1962. Some of the papers are devoted to the structural study of literature.

Souriau, E. *Les deux cent mille situations dramatiques,* Paris, 1950. An important precursor of structural analysis in literature.

Stender-Petersen, A. "Esquisse d'une théorie structurale de la littérature," *Recherches Structurales,* TCLC, 5, Copenhagen, 1949. A theory of literature derived from glossematics.

Théorie de la littérature. Textes des formalistes russes, Paris, 1966. A selection of the most important texts of the Russian formalists.

Todorov, T. "L'Heritage méthodologique du formalisme," *L'Homme,* 1, 1965. Sets Russian formalism off against the present state of structural linguistics.

Wellek, R., Warren, A. *Theory of Literature,* 3rd ed., New York, 1963. A classic and indispensable handbook.

Selected General Bibliography

The Editor

Bastide, Roger, ed., *Sens et usage du terme structure dans les sciences humaines et sociales,* LaHaye, Mouton & Co., 1962.

Communications, revue du centre d'études des communications de masse. (Special issues devoted to "Recherches sémiologiques" can be consulted with great profit. See No. 4, which includes a critical bibliography; No. 8 on "Le vraisemblable"; No. 11 on "L'analyse structurale du récit.")

Derrida, Jacques, De la grammatologie, Editions de Minuit, 1967. (Unquestionably the most important and far-reaching individual work on the philosophical implications of structuralism and semiotics, in these last years and the years to come. See also, by the same author: "La structure, le signe et le jeu," in *L'écriture et la différence,* Le Seuil, 1967.)

Ducrot, Oswald, T. Todorov, D. Sperber, M. Safouan, F. Wahl, *Qu'est-ce que le structuralisme?,* Le Seuil, 1968. (Five specialists of the second generation are testing the structural methods in their respective fields—linguistics, poetics, anthro-

pology, psychoanalysis and philosophy. Each essay is followed
by a bibliography.)

Gandillac, Maurice de, Lucien Goldmann, Jean Piaget, eds., *En-
tretiens sur les notions de génèse et de structure,* LaHaye,
Mouton & Co., 1965.

Hoijer, Harry, ed., *Language in Culture,* Proceedings of a Con-
ference on the Interrelations of Language and the Other
Aspects of Culture held in Chicago, University of Chicago
Press, 1963.

Lepschy, G. C., *La linguistique structurale,* Payot, 1968. (Translated from the Italian. Thorough and well documented. Good
bibliography.)

Nutini, Hugo G., *Essays in structural analysis,* Appleton-Century-
Crofts, 1969. (An American anthropologist comments on
Lévi-Strauss' methods.)

Ortigues, Edmond, *Le discours et le symbole,* ed. Montaigne,
1962.

Piaget, Jean, *Le structuralisme,* Que sais-je?, P.U.F., 1968. (A
very clear and straightforward introduction to structuralism,
by the famous psychologist.)

Revue internationale de philosophie, special issue on "La notion
de structure," No. 73-74, 1965, fasc. 3-4.

Schefer, Jean Louis. *Scénographie d'un tableau,* Le Seuil, 1969.
(An important semiotic analysis of a painting.)

Sebag, Lucien, *Marxisme et structuralisme,* Paris, Payot, 1964.

Simpozium po strukturnomo izucheni ju zuakovyh sistem, Academy
of Science of the USSR, Moscow, 1962. (Symposium on the
structural study of systems of signs.)

Verstraeten, Pierre, *Esquisse pour une critique de la raison struc-
turaliste,* doctoral dissertation, University of Bruxelles, 1964.

Yale French Studies, No. 41, 1968, "Game, play, literature." (The
structural implications of "play.")

Contributors

Elizabeth Barber, who studied Archeology and Greek at Bryn
Mawr, is a Ph.D. candidate in the Linguistics Department at Yale.
Her particular field of interest is archeological linguistics.

Geoffrey Hartman, Professor of Comparative Literature in Cor-
nell, is on sabbatical leave this year. He is the author of *Words-
worth's poetry.*

Jacques Lacan's career is traced in Mr. Miel's article and his writings are listed in Mr. Wilden's bibliography.

Claude Lévi-Strauss holds the Chair of Social Anthropology in the Collège de France. During World War II, he was associated with the Smithsonian Institution.

Philip E. Lewis, a graduate student in French literature at Yale, is a Danforth Fellow and a Woodrow Wilson Fellow. He contributed to the YFS issue on Proust.

André Martinet, who was Professor of Linguistics at Columbia from 1947 to 1955, is now Director of the Institute of Linguistics in the University of Paris, Professor at the Sorbonne, and Research Director at the Ecole Pratique des Hautes Etudes.

Allen R. Maxwell, Jr., who holds degrees in Anthropology and Linguistics from the University of Michigan, is currently a graduate student in Yale. He will do ethnographic field research in Southeast Asia next year.

Jan Miel teaches in the College of Letters program at Wesleyan (Conn.) University. He is finishing a book on Pascal's theology.

Sheldon Nodelman, a member of the History of Art Department in Yale, has taught at Bryn Mawr and Princeton. His special interests are Roman art, modern art, and problems of structural analysis in the plastic arts.

Michael Riffaterre is Professor of French in Columbia. He is preparing a book on styles of poetry.

Victoria L. Rippere is a research assistant in the German Department of University College in London.

Harold Scheffler teaches Anthropology in Yale. He has done field work in the Solomon Islands and is the author of *Choiseul Island Social Structure.*

T. Todorov, who holds a *licence* from the University of Sofia and a doctorate from the University of Paris, is writing a structural analysis of literature. He has published articles in *Communications, L'Homme,* and *Langages.*

A. G. Wilden, a graduate student at Johns Hopkins, has translated some of Jacques Lacan's works. He will publish an analysis of Montaigne from the Lacanian viewpoint.